Records of Streets and Alleys in Shaocheng

少城街巷志

（汉英对照）

袁庭栋　著

朱　华　[美] 莫莉·戈西奇　陈星君　王　聪　陈凤译

Written by Yuan Tingdong

Translated by Zhu Hua, Mollie Gossage, Chen Xingjun, Wang Cong, Chen Feng

四川文艺出版社

图书在版编目（CIP）数据

少城街巷志：汉英对照/袁庭栋著；朱华等译
. —成都：四川文艺出版社，2023.1
ISBN 978-7-5411-6360-9

Ⅰ．①少… Ⅱ．①袁… ②朱… Ⅲ．①城市道路－介
绍－成都 Ⅳ．①K927.11

中国版本图书馆 CIP 数据核字（2022）第 075328 号

本书的译著由四川师范大学外国语学院、四川师范大学 MTI 翻译研究中心资助

SHAOCHENG JIEXIANG ZHI（HAN YING DUIZHAO）

少城街巷志（汉英对照）

袁庭栋 著

朱 华 ［美］莫莉·戈西奇 陈星君 王 聪 陈 凤 译

出 品 人 张庆宁
策划组稿 袁 沙
责任编辑 李国亮 邓艾黎
封面设计 叶 茂
内文设计 叶 茂
责任校对 段 敏
责任印制 桑 蓉

出版发行 四川文艺出版社（成都市锦江区三色路 238 号）
网 址 www.scwys.com
电 话 028-86361802（发行部） 028-86361781（编辑部）

邮购地址 成都市锦江区三色路 238 号四川文艺出版社邮购部 610023
排 版 四川胜翔数码印务设计有限公司
印 刷 成都勤德印务有限公司
成品尺寸 168mm×238mm 开 本 16 开
印 张 23 字 数 360 千
版 次 2023 年 1 月第一版 印 次 2023 年 1 月第一次印刷
书 号 ISBN 978-7-5411-6360-9
定 价 168.00 元

本书的出版承蒙我所居住的成都市青羊区各社区和广大居民朋友的大力支持，特此鸣谢！

Thanks for the great support of the communities and residents in Qingyang District, Chengdu, where I live, for the publication of this book!

前　言

　　城市中的一条又一条街巷构成了一个城市的总体印象，反映着一个城市的基本特征。每一条街巷的名称都是历史发展的产物，是语言的、地理的、历史的多侧面的综合。每一条街巷都是人们的家园，都是社会和时代的一种标志，是后人了解与研究这个城市的一面又一面镜子，是后人阅读与研究城市这本大书的一页又一页篇章。

　　成都是我国著名的历史文化名城，她有过古蜀文明时期的辉煌，神奇的三星堆文化和金沙文化一直为全世界文化学者与旅游者所瞩目；她有过两汉时期经济文化的高度繁荣，当时所获得的"天府之国"的桂冠和"文章冠天下"的美誉，至今仍在人们的口中流传；她有过唐宋时期全面的盛世，"扬一益二"的富足和"天下第一名镇"的风情，使她不仅成了世界第一张纸币的产地，而且吸引了全国几乎所有知名文士来此生活与创作，故有"天下词人皆入蜀"的佳话。如果从准确的历史记载来考察，成都最早建城是在战国后期的公元前311年，主持建城的是当时的秦国蜀郡郡守张若。从那时起，成都城的位置从来就没有迁移，名字也未改变，而这种两千多年城址不迁、城名不改的历史文化名城，在我国就只有成都一个。

　　本书是我的《成都街巷志》这部大书中有关成都少城的一部分。

　　今天所称的成都少城，是成都城区的一个片区，它就是清代成都的满城，位于成都城区的西部，在清代是八旗的军营，民国时期是达官贵人和文化名人的居住区，中华人民共和国成立之后是很多党政机关的办公区和宿舍区，改革开放之后是著名的旅游文化区。今天，本地人无不到少城休闲娱乐，外地人无不到少城观光游览。为什么？因为少城是成都城区文化旅游资源的富集区，是体验成都历史文化、风土民情的首选区。很多人都说，少城是成都的精华，游成都却没有游过少城就有如没有游过成都。正是因为如此，在成都市青羊区大力支持下，特地编辑出版了这本《少城街巷志》。

需要说明的一点是，成都的城市建设一日千里，街巷面貌日新月异，本书的修改速度实在赶不上成都的变化速度，书中对今天成都少城的某些描述极有可能已经成为过去，这就只能请读者鉴谅了。

袁庭栋
2020 年 12 月

Foreword

A city is made up of streets. One after another, they construct the overall feel of a city, presenting its fundamental character. Their names are the products of a developmental process, syntheses of language, geography and history. Each street has been called "home" by someone at some points in time. Each street is a sign, and a mirror revealing something about a society, about an era. The streets are the pages that future generations flip for research of the city of Chengdu—such a big book in China.

Whether for history or culture, Chengdu is one of China's most renowned cities. She has witnessed the glorious ancient Shu civilization as well as the mysterious Sanxingdui and Jinsha cultures that have long attracted scholars and tourists from all over the world. Brought to new heights of the economic prosperity in the Han Dynasty (202 BC ~ 220 AD), she earned such honors as the "Land of Aboundance" (*Tianfu*) and "literary crown of the world" —epithets that still circulate in present day speech. She flourished again through the Tang-Song period (second only to Yangzhou in economic status at the time), making it "the number-one town in the world". Chengdu was even the first place in the world to make and circulate paper money. It is not only a place for business, but also for the arts. Famous literati from all over the country have come to reside and create their masterpieces here—hence the saying "All the poets go to *Shu*." According to written records, Chengdu was established in 311 BC during the late Warring States period under the direction of Zhang Ruo, the governor of Shu in the State of Qin. From that time forward, for over two thousand years, neither the location nor the name of the city has ever changed, making it unique among all the cities of China.

This book is an account about Shaocheng (also known as the Small City) in Chengdu and an excerpt from my greater work, *Records of Streets and Alleys in Chengdu*.

Today, the so-called Shaocheng is a district located west of the city center. But in the Qing Dynasty (1636 ~ 1921 AD) it was called "Manchu City" where the Eight Banners garrison was stationed. During the Republic of China (1912 ~ 1949 AD), it was home to many important cultural figures and hosted many famous dignitaries. After the founding of the People's Republic of China in 1949, it became an office and dormitory area for various government and party institutions. Since the Reform and Opening-up in 1978, it has become a famous cultural site and a tourist destination. Today, Chengdu locals are still pursuing the Shaocheng lifestyle of leisure, while Chengdu visitors are invariably drawn to Shaocheng's various sites. And why? Because Shaocheng is a concentration of rich cultural and tourism resources as well as the choice district for experiencing local Chengdu customs of the past and present. Many say that Shaocheng manifests the essence of the entire city, so no visit to Chengdu would be complete without a visit to Shaocheng. With the great support of Qingyang District, Chengdu, *Streets and Alleys of Shaocheng* is specially edited and published to introduce this wonderful part of the city to friends from all corners of the world.

One point warrants clarification. Urban construction is progressing at such a tremendous pace that revisions to this book can hardly keep up. Therefore, some of the accounts of "today's" city may already be describing the place of the recent past. In these cases I can only beg the readers' forgiveness.

Yuan Tingdong
December 2020

目 录

Contents

清城与满城

唐代以后的成都城墙，基本上沿袭罗城的格局。五代后蜀时期，曾经在罗城的西部和北部修建了一道很大的用于防御的羊马城，作为罗城的外郭，周长有21公里。可是由于完全是夯土所筑，没有砖砌，所以在北宋时期就完全毁去了。宋代对成都城墙有过五次维修，但是在宋末元初的战火中罗城大部被毁，其中的子城全部被毁。明代在罗城的基础上重修了大城，当时称之为府城，在子城的基础上新建了蜀王府，即一般所称的皇城。与过去最大的不同是大城仍然保留了原来的不方不正、不南不北的格局，但是蜀王府却是按正南正北向规划建筑的一座方方正正的新城。新城虽然不是很大，但是环有护城河，外面还有一道不小的外墙，称为萧墙。这道萧墙的范围大致是：东至今天的顺城街，南至今天的东御街、西御街，西至今天的东城根街，北至今天的羊市街、西玉龙街。

1644年，明朝亡，张献忠农民军攻占成都，接着占据了大半个四川盆地，就以成都为西京，建立了大西政权，自称大西皇帝，他的皇宫就设在原来的蜀王府里。1646年，张献忠率军北上抗清，包括蜀王府在内的整个成都城在战火中全部被毁。

清朝的军队在清顺治四年（1647）占领成都的时候，成都已经成为一片荒草荆榛、麋鹿纵横的废墟，既无居民，也无房舍，清政府只好把四川省治暂设在今天的阆中。直到清顺治十七年（1660），四川省治才迁回成都，并先从官署开始，一步步着手成都的恢复。康熙四年（1665），开始重修城墙。康熙五十七年（1718），清政府动员全川各府州县分段承包，加快进度修建成都的城墙与街道。第二年，新的成都城基本建成。雍正五年（1727）进行过一次补修。乾隆四十八年（1783），在四川总督福康安主持下，集全川之力，全部用砖石进行了一次彻底的重修，这也是成都城最后最重要的一次重修。工程由各州县分别负责，按统一规格施工，两年半之后全部完工（这期间福康安离任，由继任总督李世杰接替完成）。所以，准确地说，当代还能见到的成都古城墙是在乾隆五十年（1785）最后建成的。从此以后，成都城的城墙、大街、大桥与城内各主要建筑的格局基本上一直保持到了现代。

清代成都城的格局与过去是有同也有不同。相同的是在城池的格局上完全沿袭自秦代龟城以来的不南不北、不方不正的形状。四道城门的位置不是在正东、正南、正西、正北方向，而是在东南方、西南方、西北方、东北方。而这不方不正的城区的四角，反而是大致在东、南、西、北四个方向。为什么老成都人在问路、指路时爱说倒左手、倒右手（"倒左手""倒右手"这种说法很有可能是在"湖广填四川"大潮中从湖南方言中传入的），而不是说向东、向西，其基本原因就在于成都的城池与街道不南不北的格局。

清代修建的成都大城的形状和规模与明代大致相同，但是范围稍有一点扩大。按文献记载城墙周长 22 里 8 分，这是当年的尺寸，中华人民共和国成立以后经过实测，应当是今天的 12 公里稍多一点；城墙高 3 丈，相当于今天的

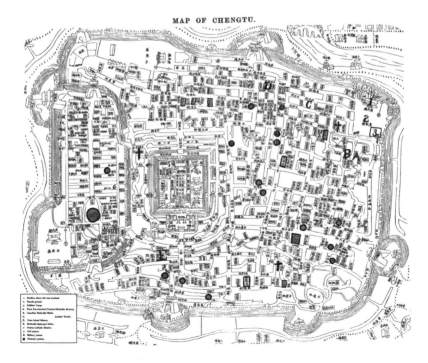

1895 年外国传教士印制的成都地图　杨显峰提供

10 米左右。清代的城墙虽然今天已经拆去，但是因为城外的护城河仍然是唐代就已经形成的两河抱城的府河与南河，所以清代成都城的形状，基本上就是今天沿府河、南河、西郊河的内环线的形状（西边无内环线，大体上就是今天的同仁路与西郊河一线）。

在老成都人的口中，经常可以听到这样一句话："成都穿城九里三。"因为嘉庆《四川通志·城池》中就有"东西相距九里三分，南北相距七里七分"的记载。但是经过中华人民共和国成立初期的实测，东西相距是 4.6 公里，南北相距是 3.85 公里。所以"九里三分"这种记载和民间说法，只是一个约数。

按照古代建城的一般比例，清代的成都城墙的底宽大约与城高相当，都是 3 丈，也就是 10 米左右。顶部的宽度是 1 丈 8 尺，相当于今天的 6 米，相当于一条当时的街道的宽度（这是初建时的尺寸，在两次重建中都有所扩大）。每逢初春的正月十六，成都人有全家上城"游百病"的习俗，认为这天登城一游，全年都可以免生疾病。这一习俗自明清以来，全国各地多有，或称为"走百病""溜百病""散百病"，或登城，或过桥，或郊游，官府也允许老百姓自由登城（平时是不行的）。清人的《竹枝词》曾经这样写道："说游百病免生疮，带崽拖娃更着忙。过了大年刚十六，大家邀约上城墙。"

清代后期，制度废弛，原本是用于防卫的城墙无人管理，在比较宽阔的城墙之上逐渐有人修建房屋，一段一段的棚屋有如后世的棚户区，甚至有的官方机构也在城墙上建房。例如位于南城墙内拱背桥的四川机器局开办了一个专门用来培养技术工人的工业学堂，招生 50 余人，这个学堂就完全修建在南城墙上。成都城墙上的这些房屋建筑一直保持到 1958 年城墙被拆除之时。直到今天，其最后的遗迹在下莲池街 4 号院（即新南苑）内都还可以见到。

与明代的成都城最大的不同在于，清代在成都大城之内的西部专门修建了一个满城，用来作为满蒙八旗官兵及其家属的驻地。这样基本上又回归到了两千年前秦代成都的大城接小城的格局（原来明代蜀王府的位置，新建了规模较蜀王府要小的贡院，不再看作是原来的小城），使成都这座古老的城市走过了一条大城接小城—大城套小城—大城接小城的曲折之路。在两千多年中，既有大城又有小城的格局一直未变，这在我国的所有城市中是独一无二的。我们在文献中所能见到的最早的一首描绘成都的诗歌，是晋代张载的《登成都白菟楼》，诗中"重城结曲阿"的"重城"；诗圣杜甫到成都之后所写的第一首诗《成都府》中"曾城填华屋，季冬树木苍"的"曾城"；成都诗坛上著名的女诗人薛涛的《上川主武元衡相国》一诗中"落日重城夕雾收"的"重城"，都写的是古代成都城的这一特点。

康熙五十七年（1718），清政府专门安排了八旗官兵长驻成都，但是人数不多。三年后，又调原来驻防湖北荆州的八旗官兵3000人入川。在参加了平定准噶尔的军事活动之后，留下一支军队（其中有骑兵1600人、步兵400人、军官74人、匠役96人）永驻成都，所以当时又称为"荆州营"。清人《竹枝词》对此有如下记载："满城城在府西头，特为旗人发帑修。仿佛营规何时起？康熙五十七年秋。""湖北荆州拨火烟，成都旗众胜于前。康熙六十升平日，自楚移来在是年。"据康熙六十年（1721）的数字，驻防旗兵的眷属有3000多人。这以后，八旗兵丁陆续有所增加，至清末的光绪三十年（1904），在籍旗人5100多户，21000多人。成都八旗是满蒙混合编制，每旗分为三甲，头甲、二甲为满族，三甲为蒙古族。八旗官兵都是带家眷的，必须为他们修建永久性的兵营，加之在清初时期的民族矛盾还比较深，时任四川巡抚的年羹尧就奏请清廷在成都城中新筑一城，专门供八旗官兵居住。这座城中之城从康熙六十年动工，一直修了20多年才全部完工，这就是后来称之为"满城"或"少城"的新城。

满城的城墙周长约2.7公里，城内有八旗官街8条、兵丁驻地街巷42条、通道5条（按：关于清代满城中的街道数目，各种记载并不完全一致，此据《成都满蒙族志》）。其范围东至今天的东城根街，南至今天的君平街，东边的城墙也就是大城的城墙，北至今天的西大街。在满城的中间有一条横贯南北的主要通道，就是今天的长顺街。在长顺街的两边是一条又一条的胡同，很像一根蜈蚣虫的形状，蜈蚣虫的头部就是满城的最高官员驻防将军的衙门，所以这里至今还叫"将军衙门"。胡同这一名称是从当时北京移用过来的，有两条胡同还有"头条""二条"之别，更是典型的北京名称。民国以后，这些胡同都重新起了名字，而且按照南方的习惯改称为街、巷，不再按北京的习惯称为胡同。这些街巷名称在当年曾经被编成不同版本的顺口溜，如"黄瓦对红墙，长发对吉祥……"。

清末的少城街道　杨显峰提供

在满城之中，八旗官兵与其家眷是按八旗的上三旗、中三旗、下二旗的等级来进行布局的，每"甲"分地也是按八旗的等级递减。这里的"甲"是八旗兵丁住宅分地的标准，一名披甲士兵即可分得一"甲"地。"甲"的面积按八旗等级递减，马甲又多于步甲。最高的上三旗马甲可分地 80 平方丈左右，约合今天的 882 平方米；最少的下二旗步甲也可分地 40 平方丈左右；而将官则可以依不同等级分得份地数亩甚至数十亩。八旗驻地大体上是正黄、镶黄二旗居北，正白、镶白二旗居东，正红、镶红二旗居西，正蓝、镶蓝二旗居南。再细一点按今天的街道位置看，正黄旗驻今天的西大街至西马棚街一带，官街（即该旗驻地）是西马棚街；镶黄旗驻今天的八宝街至东马棚街一带，官街是东马棚街；正白旗驻今天的东门街至商业后街一带，官街是商业街；镶白旗驻今天的商业街至东胜街一带，官街是东胜街；正红旗驻今天的槐树街至实业街一带，官街是实业街；镶红旗驻今天的泡桐树街至西胜街一带，官街是西胜街；正蓝旗驻今天的将军街至人民公园一带，官街是仓房街（在今人民公园内）；镶蓝旗驻今天的柿子巷、金河街至包家巷街一带，官街是蜀华街。

满城在清代是相对封闭的，有着自己的四道城门，外面的汉人未经准许不能进入，里面的满人未经请假也不能外出。东面靠北是受福门，俗称小东门，在今祠堂街口；东面靠南是迎祥门，俗称大东门，在今东门街口；南面是安阜门，俗称小南门，在今小南街口；北面是延康门，在今宁夏街口。西面因为满城的城墙也就是大城的城墙，所以没有再开城门，而是与大城同用清远门，其位置在满城的西北角上，在今西大街口。最主要的城门是位于今天祠堂街与西御街交界处的小东门，城楼上曾经挂着内外两道巨匾，上面分别写着"少城旧治"与"既丽且崇"。满城中由于人口较稀（最多时也只住了两万多人），空地较多，旗人又喜欢种树种花，所以是花木扶疏，绿荫掩映。清人的《竹枝词》曾经这样写道："满洲城静不繁华，种树种花各有涯。好景一年看不尽，炎天武庙赏荷花。"直到1945年，著名文学家叶圣陶还说："少城一带的树木真繁茂，说得过分些，几乎是房子藏在树丛里，不是树木栽在各家的院子里。"

由于满城的最初功能就是一座大兵营，所以就只有住房、官府与仓库，不允许有商店、茶楼、酒肆之类的设置。满城中所需要的各种生活物资基本上都是通过大东门运入之后，集中放在几个大仓库之中，这些仓库也都设置在靠近大东门的一大片空地（即今天的人民公园）之内。偌大一个满城，绝大部分建筑都是住房，里面很幽静很舒适。除了衙门可以修成院落之外，每家每户的住房大多是一排三间式的平房，或是加上偏房的三合院，前后可以有花园，有篱笆，有矮墙，但是都不是四合院的形式。我们在今天还能见到的当年满城中的老房子，基本上都是在民国时期改造之后的建筑，也是以铺面房和只有小天井的三合院为多而少有四合院，这是满城之中建筑的一个重要特色。

按多年来成都就有大城和少城的历史特点，成都人一般都把满城称为少城。这种称呼至今不仅保留在老成都的语言习惯中，例如今天的人民公园在老成都的口中仍然被称为少城公园；同时也还保留在一些成都的地名与单位名称中，例如少城街道办事处、少城餐厅等等。改革开放以后，成都最早的一项大型街道工程是在1981年至1984年间修建了贯通东西的蜀都大道。蜀都大道共分为11段，其中从东城根街到小南街的一段被命名为少城路，基本上是在原来的永兴街、牌坊巷和祠堂街的基础之上扩建的，这一段正是在清代少城的范围之内。

1906 年少城内的文昌宫　杨显峰提供

　　辛亥革命以后，满城不再被保留，从 1912 年拆北段城墙开始逐渐被拆除，一直到 1935 年拆除了在小南街最后的一段才算被完全拆完。与此同时，大城的城墙砖、城顶面砖、女儿墙砖等也不断被有权有势者拆去用作修建私宅，但是没有出现过公开的大规模的拆毁。由于大城内城墙上的城墙砖拆得最多，所以呈现出一片片的长满各种杂草乃至小树的土坡，以至出现了几处被称为"垮城墙"的小地名。

　　1935 年，对旧的大城城墙进行了最后的一次维修，目的并不是为了维护古迹，而是为了可能有战事到来时的防御。这是因为当时的红四方面军从通、南、巴川陕革命根据地西渡嘉陵江，打下了江油等地，直逼绵阳一带。成都市官商各界害怕红四方面军进攻成都，遂成立了一个"城墙工程委员会"，对城墙进行了维修，特别是将城上的雉堞（俗称垛口、女儿墙）全部恢复，还在城上修建了若干个堡垒。这应当是成都历史上对城墙所进行的最后一次维护工程。到了抗日战争开始之后，旧城墙又被开了几处豁口，以方便城内居民"跑警报"，一些外来成都的无房难民又在城墙上修建了若干简易民房，形成了若干段棚户区。

1910 年少城内的毛竹　杨显峰提供

中华人民共和国成立以后，城墙依旧保留，在四川省人代会上曾经就成都城墙是否应当拆除进行过讨论，因为意见不一致，就一直未作决定。1958 年 3 月，中央工作会议在成都召开，毛泽东主席来成都（这是他一生中唯一一次来成都）的第二天，即 3 月 5 日，他在当时的中共四川省委副秘书长周颐陪同下，乘车浏览成都市容。他在车上就成都城墙的去留问题说了这样一段话：“为什么不能拆除？北京的城墙都拆了嘛。这城墙既不好看，又妨碍交通，群众进出城很不方便。城墙是落后的东西，拆了后方便群众交通，土可以做肥料，砖可以修房子。拆掉是先进，不拆是落后。”根据毛泽东主席的这一指示，成都市人民委员会（即当年的市政府）于 1958 年 4 月 11 日发出了如下的通告：“为了城市环境卫生和城市建设，计划将我市现有城墙分期全部拆除，城墙土作为填沟填塘和消灭蚊蝇滋生之地，城墙砖石作为城市建设之用……”根据当时的资料，城墙（含残段与基址）全长 12.33 千米，有缺口 22 处，完整的残段高 7.5 米，顶部平均宽 14.5 米，底部平均宽 18.5 米，共有条石约 5 万条，城砖约 602 万匹，积土约 132 万立方米，墙上与墙脚有棚户建筑 4 万平方米。

1958 年 6 月，成都市成立了拆除旧城墙总指挥部，按分片包干的任务安排，连城墙附近有些学校的学生都有每天挖多少砖的任务（例如十六中的学生每天的任务是 10 匹）。不到半年，出动了民兵 297160 人次。原来的清代大城基本上被拆除，城墙砖或用于市政工程建设（例如人民南路上的锦江大桥和东郊的下水道工程在修建时就用了不少城墙砖），或用于大炼钢铁时各个单位修建"小高炉",城墙土则用来填平了 365 处池塘与洼地,或用来烧制砖瓦(有一个统计材料说是共建砖窑 110 个,烧砖 760 万匹),成都城内第一个成规模的砖厂汪家拐砖瓦厂就是这样于 1958 年开办起来的(该厂 1960 年与类似的金河砖瓦厂合并,更名为成都第一砖瓦厂,城墙土用完之后几经转产,成为后来的成都市保险柜厂,厂址仍在城边街 12 号)。当然,长期以来也有一些居民自行挖取城墙砖私用。据老人回忆,上池正街一位三轮车夫的妻子就是因为挖下部的城墙砖而被垮下的城墙土掩埋而当场丢了性命。1970 年为了"准备打仗"而发动群众烧制"战备砖",又挖去了大量的残存墙土。到了今天,仅留下了几段残墙遗址。据笔者的考察,目前还保留下来的成段的残墙遗址有:

五丁桥南边、北较场西北角的老城墙,长约百米,是在原来的遗址上重建修复的,所以很完整,也很壮观。城面砖多是收集到的老城墙砖,是目前仅有的可供参观的成都老城墙。沿着这段城墙往东,在成都城墙北面的至正门两侧,也还有一段老城墙。

猛追湾西侧华星路上的锦江华庭小区内有几十米长的一段残墙,在修建新楼盘时已经加以修复,但原来的城墙形体仍清晰可见。

迎曦下街的一段残墙,原来隐没在民居的后面,因为街道改建,就暴露在人们的面前。40 多米长、结构比较完整的城墙,还有上下城墙的石梯台阶,估计是原来水东门旁的一部分,有关部门在加以维护之后保护了下来,现在是东安北路后面娇子苑楼盘内的一处景观。

2013 年锦江华庭中的城墙遗址　杨显峰摄影

在锦里西路的北面，是一排长长的民居，民居后面就是过去的西较场，今天的成都军区联勤部。在民居与联勤部大院之间，还有断断续续的1000多米老城墙残墙，有的残墙成了民居的后墙，有的残墙上面已经修了房屋。由于这段残墙正好夹在民居与联勤部大院之间，所以得以原样保存下来，而且还是目前保存下来的最长的一段清代的老城墙。

2009年锦里西路的城墙遗址　袁庭栋摄影

在新南门的两侧，20几年前都还有长达140多米的残墙，有些段落已经修起了简易的房屋，曾经以"建国东街城墙"的名称列名于成都文物保护单位。近年来在城市改造之中，这一段残墙大多被毁，但是仍然可以看到一些，今天的下莲池街4号院（即新南苑）内，还有几十米明显的残墙，几幢住宅楼就建在残墙之上。在今天的下莲池街12号院内（原教练公所街），则还有老城墙的南城墙最东一段的残迹。

在同仁路与实业街交口处原成都水表厂厂区内，还有一段长约30米、高约9米的老城墙。有趣的是，抗日战争时期的四川省防空指挥部在这段城墙内挖了一个防空洞，面积有170平方米，可容纳100人左右，当时的四川省防空指挥部就设在这个城墙内部的防空洞里。中华人民共和国成立以后，这个防空洞成为成都水表厂存放汽油的仓库，故而得以保存下来。由于成都城区是一片平地，过去的地下水位又高，挖地几尺就会见水，所以极难修建防空洞。据笔者所知，目前成都还能见到的抗日战争时期的防空洞废墟只有三处了，一处在祠堂街，一处在文庙前街，另一处就在这里。

同仁路南端的西侧，残存了一小段老城墙遗址，而且就在过去的"水西门"附近。近年来已被修复，而且雕刻有"水西门"三个大字。只因为它隐藏在一个叫"锦都"的楼盘之内，一般人很难见到。

青莲上街还有一段残墙，而且有可能是明城墙的位置，详见"青莲上街"。

满城的街道格局在民国时期变化很小，到成都解放时，原满城区域内共有街巷49条。中华人民共和国成立以后因为各种原因的变化，现存街巷47条。

金河

　　金河又称金水河，是成都城内从西到东横贯全城的小河，是唐宣宗大中七年（853），在当时的西川节度使兼成都府尹白敏中的主持下，在疏通城中小河的基础上修成的，其目的是为了给城内的大量居民提供生活用水的方便，也是为了向城外排出雨水与生活污水。因为是从西边入城，遂按古代五行学说中关于西方属金、金生水的说法，命名为金水河，简称金河。由于唐代金水河的河道位置目前已不很清楚，再加之城内的河道容易淤塞，历代都要加以疏浚，在多次的疏浚之中河道也可能有小的变化，所以当代还能看到的明清时期的金水河是不是唐时的河道已经难以确证。在考古发掘中，1984年在修建西干道时曾经在东御街西南口和祠堂街发现过旧河床遗址，河中密布木桩，极有可能就是唐代的金河故道。明清时期的金河已向南移，与唐宋时期的金河走向大致平行。当代金河的河道是明嘉靖四十五年（1566）在四川巡抚谭纶和成都知府刘侃的主持下，对金河进行了一次大规模的整治之后确定下来的，当时的河道宽约10米，深约3米。

清末的金河　　［法］杜满希提供

最初的金水河应当是从西城墙外的郫江引水入城。郫江改道之后，从城西新开的西濠（西濠是郫江改道之后为了让西边仍有一条护城河而开凿的小河，后来就演变成了今天的西郊河）引水，经过西城墙入城。清代的成都西城墙也就是满城的西城墙，为了保证满城的安全，在西城墙下的入水口建有铁窗，称为水关，由军队看守，小船出入时才能打开。与此同时，在水关处还建有闸门，以防夏天的洪水。这个入水口在老成都人的口中被称为水西门，具体位置在中华人民共和国成立以后的消防机械厂内，即近年新建的楼盘长富新城范围内。金河由西往东穿过全城，一直到今天的东门大桥以南的位置穿出城墙，汇入府河。不同的是，东边的水关是一条开敞的通道，小船可以溯流而上到达城中，老成都也把这里称为水东门。在成都东边还有一条水东门街，这条街是民国初年新开武成门（即俗称的新东门）之后建的街道，是因为有一条下水道从这里排入府河而得名，与金河是没有关系的。

水西门遗址　杨显峰摄影

金河的长度，按清同治《成都县志》卷一的记载是 1526 丈，合今 5087米。金河的水量在不同时期由于疏浚的情况不同而有所不同（清代在雍正以后，如无特殊情况，金河每年都得疏浚，经费由水利同知衙门在都江堰岁修费的余额中支出，而都江堰岁修费是由成都附近 9 个用水县按亩均摊，所以基本上是有保障的），明清时期河道中一直都可以通行小船（明末清初河道破坏，阻断通航。清雍正年间的成都知府项诚率众疏浚之后恢复了河道的通航功能）。从府河入金河的小船可以溯金河而上，将货物运入城内。明代时，蜀王府所需的物资可以通过金河运到三桥码头，清代则是将小船直接开到半边桥的满城东城墙水关外（因为无论是陆上还是水上，汉人都是不能随便进入满城的）。满城中的柴粮仓库当时都修在今天的人民公园范围之内，而这些柴粮仓库的物资基本上都是由金河中的小船运来的。根据笔者对家住金河边的老人们的访问，1950 年春政府就组织群众对金河进行了一次疏淘（同时还疏浚了御河），加宽了堤岸，修筑了保坎，一直到 1958 年以前，在金河中偶尔还有小船通行。

由于金河的河道不宽，河中的小船也与锦江中的船只不同：一是船不大，只能载重三四百斤。二是不用舵、不用桨，只用不长的竹篙。三是不分船头与船尾，故而被叫"两头望"，在河中行驶时也不准掉头，只能直来直去地上下行驶。为了城市的环境卫生，金河行船还有一种约定俗成的规矩，运送各种食物的船只都在上午和中午入城，运尿水的船只都在下午五点左右入城。

多年来，我们读过很多赞美锦江的诗文，其实过去的这条穿城而过的金河也是成都的一条既十分美丽，又造福万家的母亲河。明代嘉靖年间大修金河之后，成都知府刘侃在《重开金水河记》中说："金河之漪，洋然流贯阛阓（街市），蜀人奔走聚观，诧其神异，由是釜者汲，垢者沐，道渴者饮，纩者浣澼（指漂洗丝绵），园者灌。濯锦之官、浣花之姝，杂沓而至，欢声万喙，莫不鼓舞。"这是有关金河的一段十分详细又十分传神的重要记载。清代满城中的金河两岸仍然少有房屋，多是农田菜地，所以一直到民国初年还有文章说这里是"田连阡陌，树木丛生"。

最令人想象不到的是，金河中还曾经使用过小型的水轮机。此事发生在清末的 1880 年前后。当时丁宝桢在拱背桥一带的金河畔建四川机器局制造枪炮，他从山东带来的杰出的技师曾昭吉特地制造了小型水轮机，夏秋之时就在金河中蓄水带动发电机发电，冬春时才全部用火力发电，每天可以节省煤炭 500 多公斤，一年可以节省煤银 4000 多两。丁宝桢为此事专门向光绪皇帝有过报告。遗憾的是这个小型水电站的详细情况未能记载下来（今天看来，金河中的水电站应当是一座试验性的季节电站，成都的也是四川的第一座真正意义上的水电站是 1929 年建在中和场化龙桥的小型水电站，名叫中和民有水电股份有限公司，装机 3 千瓦，创办者是生于中和场的曾经留学法国里昂水电学校的邹昕楷，这个小型水电站一直经营到 1934 年，因为用水纠纷而关闭）。

1935 年金河边的洗衣妇女　杨显峰提供

金河也曾经被用作全城的消防蓄水池。1940 年，为了准备在日寇轰炸后救火所需的大量用水，曾经在金河上修建了四个闸门，分段蓄水，形成了几个巨大的消防蓄水池。

"文革"中的 1971 年，根据部署，为了准备打仗而必须修建防空洞。成都市决定将金河断流，将河道砌砖砌石，再在上面修建拱形的顶盖，就算是建成了一条很长的"防空洞"。笔者当时就在龙王庙正街和川大历史系师生们一起参加劳动，亲手毁了一段金河，修了一段根本不能防空的"防空洞"。记得当年的金河两岸都是垂柳，河中流水潺潺，河边的居民可以在河里洗衣，鱼虽然很少，但有不少鸭子畅游其中。

在灾难深重的"文化大革命"中，成都的城市建设中有三大蠢事：一是毁金河与御河，二是毁皇城，三是毁昭觉寺为动物园。可以设想，假如今天的成都城中还有一条垂柳拂面的金河穿城而过，有一座被御河环绕的雄伟的皇城耸立城中，还有一座规模宏大而古老的昭觉寺，将是何等气象！

不过金河还没有完全被毁。这是因为金河有一段是从人民公园中穿过的，所以就不得不把公园中的一段保留了下来，没有改为"防空洞"，这就是今天人民公园大门内拱桥下面的那几十米小河，虽然已经不再有潺潺流水了，但是总还能见到一点历史的痕迹。据老人们回忆，一直到中华人民共和国成立之初，少城公园里的金河中都还有游船出租，游客可以将船一直划到通惠门下。

今天的成都虽然没有了金河，但是还有一条金河路，还有一条金河边街，在金河路上还有一座著名的金河宾馆，一听这些名字就知道那都是当年金河流过的地方。

由于是从市中心的人口密集区穿城而过，所以清代的金河上桥梁密布，有一些桥的名字当代作为街道名称还在使用，按从西到东的方向走，就有半边桥街、古卧龙桥街、锦江桥街、青石桥街、向荣桥街、余庆桥街、拱背桥街。这几个在当代还在使用的以桥为名的街道，当年都是有桥的。除了这些桥之外，金河上原来还有好多桥今天不仅桥没有保存下来，而且连地名都没有保存下来。如还在城墙之外的清源桥（桥上还建有一座奎星阁），在今同仁路口的金花桥（这座桥的位置很可能就是汉晋时期成都很有名的市桥的位置），在今柿子巷口的红板桥，在今将军衙门南侧的节旅桥（又称节里桥，这是金河上唯一的一道没有桥栏的平板式木桥，中华人民共和国成立以后还在使用），在今小南街北口的通顺桥，在今人民公园侧门的斜板桥，在今人民公园内的拱背桥、银定桥，在今天府广场的三桥，在今染房街东口的锦江桥，在今新半边街的太平桥和一洞桥，在今红星路上的老卧龙桥，在今龙王庙正街的板板桥和景云桥，在今下莲池的金津桥，当时在出城墙处的铁板桥，在今清安街的普贤桥，在今天仙桥南路的大安桥等，一共有22座桥。清代为了河中行船的需要，金河上从半边桥开始，下游所有的桥梁原来都是拱桥。据老年人的回忆，最高的一座是古卧龙桥，要比其他的桥高出一尺多。

西门

和东门一样，成都人都把西门叫作老西门，因为在成都城的西边后来也有了一道新西门。

秦代的成都城有几道西门，由于史料不足，目前无法确知。汉代很可能有两道西门，目前只知道其中有一道门叫市桥门。唐代的情况比较清楚，西门有两道，名字就叫大西门与小西门。小西门的位置大致与秦汉时期的市桥门相当，所以又叫小市桥门。五代前蜀时把所有的城门都改了名字，大西门改为乾政门，小西门改为延秋门。宋代时恢复大西门与小西门的旧名，元代沿用宋制，没有变化。明代初年成都的城墙都还有五道城门，东、南、北各有一道，西边是两道，位置与唐代的大西门与小西门相似，靠北的叫清远门，靠南的叫延秋门（其位置应当与当代的通惠门相近）。明太祖洪武二十九年（1396），把小西门即延秋门封闭，只保留了大西门，即清远门。清代保留了明代的格局，西门只有一道清远门，位置一直如过去一样靠北，几乎已经在城的西北角了，即西月城街的位置。在清远门上也修有城楼，名为江源楼。

民国时期的成都西城墙　　［法］杜满希提供

　　清代成都城的西部是满城，大城的西城墙也就是满城的西城墙。所以成都城的西门也就是满城的西门。正由于这个原因，清代成都城的西门实际上是满城专用，汉族同胞不得随意进出。如果要去郫县、灌县等地，大多要从北门或南门绕道，这也就是为什么在民国以前成都的南门外与北门外要比西门外热闹得多的原因。

通惠门附通惠门路

　　由于清代的西门在满城之内，位置又太靠北，就使得清代的成都人（包括满城内的满蒙同胞）要从西南方向出城十分不便，特别是去青羊宫赶花会，城内的民众都得从老南门或是北门出城之后，顺着城墙绕一个大弯子。正如清同治年间一首《竹枝词》所说的："武侯祠畔路迢迢，迂道还从万里桥。转向青羊宫里去，明天花市是花朝。"民国初年，满城的城墙被拆，从城内的西南方向出城就有了可能。为了方便城内的居民出城到青羊宫赶花会，1913年的四川督军胡景伊就下令在西较场外向二仙庵、青羊宫方向的西城墙处新开了一道城门，以《左传·闵公二年》"务财训农，通商惠工"之句取名通惠门，就是寓意着流通互惠、便利工商的意思。通惠门的开通一下子大大方便了群众。正如清人在一首《竹枝词》中所写的："捷径分开通惠门，往来舆马若云屯。手车载得如花貌，碾起红尘十丈奔。"

　　生长于成都的著名文史学家唐振常先生曾经在两篇回忆家乡的文章中说过，通惠门建成之时，曾经在城楼之上高悬着在清末四川新政之中多有建树的周善培先生所写的十六个大字："既丽且崇，名曰成都。文明建设，今有古无。"这件事在笔者所见到的有关成都掌故的文章都没有记载，但却可见当年主事者的城建方略。

　　老一辈的成都人一般将通惠门称作新西门，而把原来的西门称为老西门。

　　今天的成都没有了城门，当然也就没有通惠门，但是还有一条通惠门路。当年在通惠门修成之后在通惠门内形成了一条通道，并逐渐形成了街道，就叫作通惠街。中华人民共和国成立以后，街名仍旧。1981年地名普查时改名为通惠门街，东起同仁路口，西到十二桥。蜀都大道建成之后分段命名时，命名为通惠门路。

　　通惠门路南侧就是清代的西较场，是当年的满蒙八旗进行操练的场所，民国时期也一直为军队所用，中华人民共和国成立以后长期为成都军区后勤部

（今联勤部）驻地。抗日战争时期，蒋介石的中央军逐渐进入四川，在这里设有军事委员会特务团，连同斜对门的将军衙门，共同成为国民党宪兵特务系统在成都的大本营。为了在市民面前为自己涂脂抹粉，西较场的大门上刻有仿当年广州黄埔军校大门上的一副早期名联："升官发财，请往他处；贪生怕死，勿入斯门"。成都市民对于这种挂羊头卖狗肉的行径嗤之以鼻，有人将这副对联改了几个字，改为"升官发财，请走此路；贪生怕死，快入此门"，成为当年的一席笑谈。

民国初年的通惠门外十二桥　杨显峰提供

成都解放前夕，胡宗南部下的第三军军长盛文在这里成立了"成都防卫总司令部"，颁布了镇压人民群众的"十杀令"（实际上是 12 条），在全城疯狂镇压与屠杀一切他们认为的可疑者，公开在春熙路上杀人示众，故而成都人民把当时的西较场称为"人肉案桌"（"案桌"是成都方言，即肉铺中摆放与切割猪肉的大桌子）。也就是在这个"人肉案桌"中，盛文秉承蒋介石与胡宗南的旨意，部署了两个团的兵力打算将成都全城炸毁，而且已经做出了具体的安排，只是由于中共地下党成功策反了这两个团，才使得成都免除了一场巨大的灾难。

长顺街

　　长顺街是成都市区一条很长的街道，在清代可是一条极为重要却又没有名字的街道。

　　清代在成都市区偏西部修建了满城，中间有一条中轴线式的主要通道，在它的两边再分出许多条胡同。有人把当年满城的街巷分布比作一条蜈蚣，将军衙门就像是蜈蚣的头，这条通道就像蜈蚣的条状身躯，两边的许多条胡同就像蜈蚣的很多条脚。因为满城的每条胡同都是分配给一部分满蒙兵丁及其家属的用房，所以都有名字，唯独中间的这条主要通道是公用的，故而一直没有命名。民国时期满城被拆除，原来的一条条胡同都改名为街或巷，这条主要通道也就给命名了。最初是用了一个表示长久通顺的名字叫作通顺街，可是因为在城北早已有了正通顺街与东通顺街，为了不致重复，又才改名叫长顺街，仍然包含着长久通顺的寓意。

2020 年的长顺上街　张西南摄影

长顺街很长，全长约 1700 米，所以又被从南向北分为长顺上街、长顺中街和长顺下街。这其中的长顺上街有一点很特殊，就是在最南边一分为二，成了"丫"字形东西两条街。这是因为长顺街最南端就是满城的最高军政官署将军衙门，将军衙门的东西两侧当然都有南北方向的通道，这两条通道原来都没有街名，民国初年为长顺街命名时，就把将军衙门的东西两侧的通道都叫长顺上街，而以东边的为主。两条长顺上街向北一直到支机石街口相会，这一格局就被一直保持到今天（严格来说，这种命名是不妥的），在金河路的金河宾馆两侧可以看到两个长顺上街的街口，而且都立有路牌。据笔者的调查，这种情况在成都所有街道中是唯一的一例。

可能是由于满蒙同胞喜欢吃牛肉的习俗浸润，位于满城中心的长顺街上曾经出现了两种成都最著名的牛肉名肴。中华人民共和国成立以后，这两种牛肉名肴都曾上过北京人民大会堂的国宴。

夫妻肺片创始人郭朝华、张田政夫妇

风靡全国的蜀中名菜夫妻肺片，原来是 20 世纪 30 年代郭朝华、张田政夫妇在长顺上街街边小摊所卖的麻辣肺片（有老人回忆说在摆摊前还曾经推车沿街叫卖，故而曾有"车行半边路，肉香一条街"之说），因为滋味绝佳，遂被人们称之为"夫妻肺片"，有了名声之后，才发展成为一个小店。正如《锦城旧事竹枝词》中的描绘："开店渊源卓马风，唱随举案利攸同。君试牛刀妾司味，拌和佳材莫忘葱。"中华人民共和国成立以后，夫妻肺片先在半边桥街开小店，后迁到提督街，才成为一个比较大的餐馆，更加远近闻名。

初期的夫妻肺片原来还有一个很流行的名字叫"两头望"。这是因为早期的肺片就是从钵钵牛肉演变而来的，原无定称，"肺片"本应写作"废片"，就是牛身上的下脚料牛头皮和牛肚。把这些牛身上的下脚料用五香卤水煮好以后切成大片，拌上麻辣鲜香的调料，装在大号瓦钵钵中，插上几双筷子，摆在街巷边上，供钱包不鼓的好吃客或小孩子一片一片地买来吃，按片算钱，笔者小时就曾是这样的顾客。由于站在街边吃钵钵牛肉的形象颇为不雅，而钵钵牛肉的味道又是那样地诱人，所以那些爱面子的好吃客往往是先向两头望一望，确信没有熟人瞧见后，再下筷子，所以钵钵牛肉就得了一个"两头望"的俗称，以后才有了"夫妻肺片"的雅号。对于这一蜀中名菜名字的演变，1943年出版的《新成都》的记载最能说明问题，书中的名称是"牛肉肺片"，括号中的另一名称是"盘盘牛肉"。

原在长顺街与奎星楼街交口附近的治德号由姚树成开创于1934年，主要出售红烧牛肉面与小笼蒸牛肉，而又以小笼蒸牛肉闻名全城。当年的一种主要吃法是用来夹锅盔，有如成都特色的三明治。中华人民共和国成立以后，治德号小笼蒸牛肉成了成都名小吃，总店曾经先后在人民西路、银丝街营业，现在开在三洞桥街。

成都的西城有三条南北向的主要大街，从东到西是东城根街、长顺街和同仁路。这三条大街都因为太长而被分为上、中、下三段。需要注意的是，东城根街和长顺街的上、中、下三段的次序是从南往北排的，上、中、下三字是排在街名之后的，如东城根上街和长顺下街。而同仁路的上、中、下三段的次序正好相反，不仅是从北往南排的，而且上、中、下三字是排在街名之前的，即上同仁路、中同仁路、下同仁路。这种情况是历史形成的，并没有什么理由，但是对于不熟悉街道的朋友来说，往往会把上、中、下三段的南北方位加以混淆，所以有必要在这里加以提醒。

东城根街附老东城根街 横东城根街 西城根街

"城根"的本义是城脚边,这一词汇古已有之,如唐诗中就有韦应物《酬秦征君徐少府春日见寄》的"城根山半腹,亭影水中心"。在近代将"城根"作为街道名称却是北京方言。这种称呼在成都方言中本来是没有的,是清代住在满城里面的满蒙同胞用的老北京人的称呼(北京在今天仍然还有"皇城根",不过已经改为"黄城根"了)。今天仍然还在使用的街道名称中,成都仅此一例。据笔者不很全面的考察,甚至在整个南方也仅此一例。成都的叫法与北京也有一点不同,就是北京方言中叫"城根"一定要加上儿化韵(包括距北京不远、受北京影响的保定),而成都是不加儿化韵的。"胡同""城根""牌楼""小淖坝""大坑沿儿"是成都地名中几个明显的北京方言的遗存,目前在知名街道中只还保存下来一个"东城根"。

东城根街所指的东城,就是清代满城的东城墙,是清初在完全拆除了明代蜀王府的外城即萧墙的西墙之后修建的,建筑所用的城砖有的就是蜀王府外城的城砖,其墙基就是蜀王府外城的墙基。因为清代的满族同胞把满城东城墙脚下的沿墙道路叫东城根,所以民国初年拆除满城之后在这里所形成的街道也就叫作东城根街。

东城根街是在民国初年分段陆续建成的,是成都城中在民国时期修建的第一条街道。1913年开始拆除满城城墙(革命老人、著名教育家张秀熟曾在一首题名为《东城根街回溯》的竹枝词中写道:"漫话成都城坊考,癸丑我是见证人。祠堂东门两街口,城墙拆尽路未平。"这里的"祠堂东门"指的就是祠堂街口的满城东门,"癸丑"就是1913年),1916年开始在拆除满城东城墙的基础上修建马路。1918年初步建成时,当时主管四川军政事务的四川靖国军总司令、四川辛亥革命元老熊克武曾经将其命名为靖国路(这是为了纪念当时拥护孙中山先生的四川靖国军就在此街组建），还曾经在今天的东胜街口建立了一座石碑，上面由另一位四川辛亥革命元老、靖国军的另一位负责人但懋辛手书了"靖国路"三个大字（但氏工书法，特别以榜书名世，今天的郫县望丛祠中望帝与丛帝陵墓前石碑上的大字就是但氏所书）。由于附近居民把这里称为东城根已成习惯，所以这个靖国路的街名并未流行。1924 年，担任四川督办的杨森在成都市中心几处实行扩建马路的计划，东城根街也被拓宽，并从南面的祠堂街一直拉通到北边的青龙街口，总长度超过了 1.5 公里，从南到北分为东城根南街、东城根上街、东城根中街、东城根下街四段。这种名称与分段一直保持到今天。但是今天的东城根下街并不是原来的东城根下街，而是为了将原来拐弯的东城根下街取直而新开通的街道。原来的东城根下街与东城根中街之间有一个拐弯，街道仍然保留，但是为了与新建的笔直的东城根下街有别，就命名为老东城根街。

20 世纪 80 年代的东城根下街集贸市场　杨显峰提供

在老东城根街以西、新建的东城根下街以东还有一条不长的横东城根街。这是中华人民共和国成立以后新开东城根下街时切断的原东二道街的东段，因为已经与原来的东二道街分别位于大街的东西两边，所以命名为横东城根街。

东城根街是民国时期建成的新街，商业并不繁盛，但是在老成都人的文化生活中，位于东城根街与西御街交口处有一家锦春茶社却是让人难以忘怀的。锦春茶社的出名在于当年远近闻名的"锦城三绝"或称"锦城三子"：贾瞎子演唱的竹琴、周麻子提壶掺茶的绝技、司胖子卖的花生米（民国后期，成都还有另一种著名的"锦城四绝"，是指全市最著名的曲艺艺人，即竹琴贾树三、扬琴李德才、相书曾炳昆、清音李月秋）。

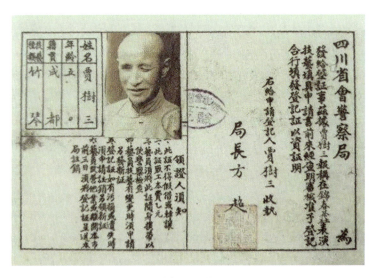

1941 年贾树三的从艺登记证

贾树三在演唱中能够熟练地运用广东、陕西、苏北等多种方言，充分地反映了成都这个移民城市的文化特色，这在清末的成都艺人中是很少见的。

贾瞎子（1894—1951）本名贾树三，回族，生于成都回族聚居的皇城坝。一岁时父母双亡，三岁时双目失明，从此人们都称他为"贾瞎子"。贫困的家世让他六岁时就沿街叫卖梨膏糖，十岁时向一位李姓的草药郎中学唱竹琴，以后先后拜马少成与蔡觉之为师，并将过去的五人坐唱（有如今天的扬琴）改为一人独唱，一人唱一台戏，一人唱多个角色。他吸收了川剧名家与扬琴名家的唱腔精华，成为闻名全川的竹琴圣手，开创了竹琴演唱中的"贾派"。从 1930 年开始，他在成都文化界知名人士、《国民公报》主笔谭创之的大力支持之下，在锦春茶楼设竹琴专场，每天晚上演唱，风雨无改（抗日战争时期为了躲避轰炸，曾短期改在老西门外茶店子），长达20年，创造了民间艺人专场演唱的一项难得的纪录，也是成都现代文化史上极光彩的一页。正如挂在台口的由谭创之撰写的名联："听罢悲欢离合，回首依然贾瞎子；拍开风花雪月，伤心谁问李龟年？"不仅是成都的各界人士喜欢他的演唱，连冯玉祥这样的生长在北方的军政领袖、胡愈之这样的走遍全国的著名记者、谢添这样的著名演员，都是他的"粉丝"。冯玉祥说："我认为北京的刘宝全（唱京韵大鼓的一代'鼓王'）和四川的贾树三可称为独唱双绝。"当代著名作家茅盾先生抗日战争时期在成都时曾经这样说过："在成都不听贾瞎子的竹琴，枉自来成都。"成都著名政坛前辈、曾任四川军政府都督的尹昌衡曾赠贾瞎子如下一联："盛时之元音已杳，今又逢师旷重来，绝技出瞽盲，最好是《楚道还姬》《李陵饯友》《浔阳送客》《子胥渡芦》，串生旦净丑而各肖神情，慷慨激昂惊四座；历年之国步多艰，只赢得长沙痛哭，幽情寄弹唱，恍如闻'渐离击筑''雍门抚琴''越石吹笳''祢衡挝鼓'，从忠孝节义以扶维教化，发扬蹈厉足千秋。"

周麻子本名失传，是成都传统茶艺的卓越代表。他在为客人服务时，总是右手提装满开水的紫铜茶壶，左手手掌上卡着6个黄铜茶船，上面放着重叠的6个白瓷茶碗加茶盖（多的时候可以拿着十几副盖碗茶茶具），走到茶桌之前，只见他左手一撒，茶船有如飞碟旋转到各位茶客面前，再听到"嚓嚓嚓"的一阵声响，一个个茶碗如鸟归巢般放进了一个个茶船之中，然后他抬起右手，铜壶中的一道道水流从茶客的耳边飞过，注入茶碗，桌面上不见一滴水珠。茶客们正在惊叹不已之时，他用左手的小指头将桌上的茶盖轻轻一挑，只听见当当声响，一个个茶盖就稳稳地盖在了茶碗之上。这种茶艺是完全从实用出发的，用最快速度为客人服务的技艺，是用多年的勤学苦练得来的真功夫。

中华人民共和国成立以后，有此技艺者愈来愈少。1989年秋，笔者还在人民公园鹤鸣茶社中看过一位吴师傅的表演，现在已经基本上失传了。改革开放之后成都出现的由廖氏兄弟开创的长嘴壶掺茶技艺，是以武术功夫为基础的表演技艺，与传统的以快速掺茶为目的短嘴茶壶的实用技艺是两种路数，未可同日而语。

　　司胖子的确是一个大胖子，是姓司还是姓司马已无从确考。他专门手提竹篮在茶馆书场叫卖用纸包装的炒花生米与南瓜子，口中不停地反复叫喊着四句话："金钩花生，五香胡豆，慢慢细吃，很有味道。"花生米都是一样大，颗颗香脆而且红衣不破，南瓜子全是"鸦雀嘴"，粒粒均匀饱满。如果发现有一颗霉烂，立即赔你两包，这在当时的成都也是一绝。

　　今天的东城根街是成都市中心南北向的重要街道，也是很多重要的党政机关与企业的所在地，交通十分繁忙。可是过去的东城根街向北止于八宝街，向南止于西御街，两端都呈丁字形，对于市中心的交通大有不便。20世纪90年代在城市改造之中，东城根街向北新建了万和路直达府河上的五丁桥，向南新建了文翁路直达南河上的南河桥，交通大为疏畅。因为这三条大街形成了成都市中心的又一条主要的南北通道，而又是以东城根街为主干，所以不少市民都把万和路称为东城根街北延线，把文翁路称为东城根街南延线。

　　东城根街上的东城根街小学是出生于成都的著名作家巴金的母校，从1991年5月15日起，巴金曾经先后9次给学校的孩子们写信或寄书，鼓励孩子们读书时认真读书，玩耍时放心玩耍，说话要说真话，做人要做好人。为了永远地纪念这位文坛巨匠，东城根街小学已经正式更名为巴金小学，塑造有巴金的铜像。

　　既然有东城根，也应当有西城根。清代满城西边城墙边的通道当时就叫西城根，也有人叫作西城根街。辛亥革命之后，把西城根正式命名为同仁路，西城根的名称也就消失了。

君平街附君平巷

在人民公园后面，有一条纪念严君平的君平街。今天还保留在成都老街名中的历史人物，以严君平为最早。

严　遵（约前80—10）字君平，本名庄遵，因为东汉避讳汉明帝刘庄的"庄"字，把"庄"改写为"严"字，庄遵就成为严遵了。严遵是西汉晚期著名的隐士式的思想家，是扬雄的老师，在当时有着极高的地位和影响。在汉代就被誉为"文章冠天下"的成都，当时就留下了生平事迹记载的著名文士只有三位——司马相如、严君平和扬雄（汉以后再加上资阳的王褒，称为"蜀四贤"或"蜀四君"）。严君平一生基本上以卖卜为生，对道家思想有很深的研究。正如李白在《咏严遵》一诗中所说："观变穷太易，探玄化群生。"虽然他只为后人留下了一部不完整的《老子道德指归》，但却是一本极为重要的道家著作。

严君平生前在成都生活的地点应当是今天的支机石街，而且严遵死后在支机石街建有严真观。清初支机石街被划入了满城，汉族群众是不能随便进入满城的，这使得要想去凭吊或祭祀严君平的汉族文士很不方便，于是就把满城南墙外的这条新建成的街道命名为君平街。当时街上有一个庄姓的大户人家遂自称为严遵的后裔，并把街上的一座祭祀文昌帝君的梓潼宫改建为严遵观。时间一长，人们就误以为这条君平街就是汉代的严遵故居了。

2009 年君平园　袁庭栋摄影

　　君平巷是君平街南边的一条小巷，原名火巷子，因为与城北万福桥的另一条火巷子（这条火巷子已在城市改造中被拆除）同名，所以重新命名为君平巷。

　　为了纪念严君平，2006 年在君平街上兴建了主题游园君平园，园内有严仙亭、指归廊、通仙井等文化景观。

　　早期的记载只说严君平是成都人，较晚的记载又明确说是邛崃人。在今天的成都郊县中，邛崃和彭州都有君平乡，郫县和邛崃都有君平墓，不过以郫县唐昌横山子的君平墓保存得最为完好，墓前过去还有严君平的祠庙。清人许儒龙有《君平墓》一诗写道："傍水沿边碧草芳，春风吹柳客登堂。从前地止疑丘垄，自此人皆仰蜀庄。遗庙有情灵爽托，著书无恙妙玄昌。千秋享祀今重现，快与行人话夕阳。"

小南街

小南街与南大街毫无关系，也不相邻。

小南街有新老之分。老的小南街北起祠堂街，南到君平街，其得名是由于清代的满城。因为它位于满城之内，而且在最南部，是进入满城南门通阜门（通阜门的位置在今天小南街与君平街交口处稍北一点的小南街上）之后的入城通道，当时把通阜门称为小南门，所以就把这条街称为小南门正街，进入民国以后，简化为小南街。近年来在城市改造之中，小南街作为长顺街的南延线而被延长，向南直到南河，成为一条很长的新的小南街。

民国初年，小南街北口临金河之处（今努力餐附近）建有一处闹市之中的竹篱茅舍，大门上写着"柴扉"二字，著名的民国女杰杜黄就住在这里。

杜　黄（1879—1929）本名黄铭训，湖北汉口人，自幼喜新学、善社交，与四川长宁人杜德舆（又名杜关，号柴扉）结婚之后，改名杜黄，并于光绪二十七年（1901）迁居北京。她在北京结识了辛亥革命时期的著名女英雄秋瑾，志趣相投，结为姐妹，并投身于民主革命与女权运动。她先在家中开办杜氏女子家塾，然后在四川营胡同创办四川女子学堂，这是北京最早的女子学校。光绪三十年（1904），经秋瑾介绍参加同盟会，是北京同盟会的第一个女会员。她奉同盟会总部的指示，在北京创办《中国妇女会报》和《国光报》（亦称国光新闻社），在天津设立同盟会京津据点，成为同盟会军事部的唯一女成员，参加了一系列反清活动。她又与已经参加同盟会的丈夫一道联络北方各省的帮会组织，在北京成立哥老会的公口"乾元公"，专门从事反清活动，为革命者筹措经费，被四川辛亥革命元老熊克武称为"女孟尝"。当年震动朝野的几次谋刺活动如炸摄政王载沣、炸袁世凯（未遂）、炸宗社党首良弼，她都参与策划并提供炸弹，成为公认的"同盟女杰"。武昌起义之后，她把在北京牺牲的同盟会四川籍的四烈士全部礼葬于万牲园（今北京动物园），并亲写挽联，如给成都的彭家珍烈士所写的挽联是："霹雳应手神珠驰，亏君戎马书生，尽抖擞神威，当十万横魔剑；子规夜啼山竹裂，怅我刀弓侍婢，认模糊战血，留千秋坠泪碑。"袁世凯窃国以后，杜关与杜黄夫妇拒不与袁合作，辞去在京一切官职，回到杜关的故乡成都，联络各方力量反袁。此时杜黄身染重病，在医治数年之后，于1921年毅然出任四川第一支女兵队伍的司令官，挥旗练兵。1923年，她与另一位蜀中女杰胡兰畦（有关介绍见"酱园公所街"）组织四川妇女联合会，这也是成都历史上第一个妇女联合会。杜关与杜黄夫妇晚年的时候更多是在草庐之中潜心书画，门前挂有"小楼流水樊川宅；老屋秋风工部家"的对联。1929年秋，夫妻二人相隔11天先后逝世，留下了一段在蜀中久久流传的佳话。

20世纪初小南街上的金河桥　［法］杜满希提供

　　1943年，成都市利用原来小南街上的成都市立第一小学的校舍开办了成都市立医院，由彭道尊担任院长。虽然规模不大，只有50张病床，却是成都市官方建立的第一所综合医院，内、外、妇、儿、五官科俱全。这所医院以后迁到了致民路，就是中华人民共和国成立以后的成都市第二工人医院和今天的成都市第七人民医院的前身。

同仁路

在长顺街西边与其相邻的是同仁路，同仁路的由来也与清代满城有关。

今天的成都人很熟悉东城根街，可是很少有人知道原来还有一条与之相对的西城根街。东城根是满城的东城墙边，西城根是满城的西城墙边。由于清代满城的西城墙也就是成都大城的西城墙，所以西城根街也就是成都大城的西城墙里面沿城的一条通道。这个西城根街就是同仁路的前身。

按照清代的制度，满蒙八旗的每个男子都编入旗籍，全民皆兵，一生下来就列入军籍，有一份俸禄，但不能从事工商产业（清末管理松弛以后才有极少数旗人离开满城到大城中从事商业或艺术事业，那就必须脱离原来的旗籍，当时叫作"离旗"。例如著名的川菜前辈厨师、"正兴园"创办人关正兴就是"离旗"的正白旗蒙古族人）。成都的普通八旗兵丁与家属除按月领取粮食之外，每月还有二两饷银，逢年节另有赏赐，各级官员当然另有官俸。清代末期满城内的旗人共有5100多户、21000多人。由于清政府的财力枯竭和官员的贪污中饱，这些旗人中只有少数仍然保留着不练武、不打仗、成天吃喝玩乐的八旗子弟的生活，多数普通旗人的生活却日渐贫苦，有的甚至靠拆房度日。到了清政权被推翻以后，绝大多数旗人一下子就没有了生路，新成立的军政府又不可能再给他们发放粮饷，而如果不解决这些旗人的生计问题则可能出现严重的社会动乱。事实上，清政权被推翻之初，满城中旗人的情绪的确十分紧张，不少旗人还在实业街上的三英小学中聚集，打算与新政权拼死一搏，多年未用的库存武器也被发放到了青壮年手中，在满城中还有三营成建制的旗兵。在这种情况下，四川保路同志会副会长兼交涉部长、军政府副都督罗纶作为军政府的代表，约同愿意和平解决事端的满族士绅代表、四川省咨议局议员赵荣安，前往将军衙门与清政府最后一任成都将军玉昆进行会谈。在玉昆主持下，决定和平解决旗人问题，尽可能弱化汉族同胞与满蒙同胞之间的矛盾冲突。为了达到此目的，罗纶偕夫人迁入满城东门街赵荣安的一位亲戚家中住下，以身家性命作为担保。这以后又经过了东较场的兵变、赵尔丰被杀等几起几伏，最终经双方代表（军政府代表是在成都教育界德高望重的、在旗人中有不少学生的师范学堂监督徐炯以及周凤翔，旗人方面的代表是文锦章、广兴廷、文钧安，另有士绅代表数人参加）在西御街的川东会馆中进行具体商谈之后决定，先是发给每个旗人三个月薪饷，以后再发三月。旗人所有房屋一律发给管业证，允许自由买卖。军政府拨出 10 万银圆，设立旗人生计筹备处，尽力解决旗人的生计困难。其中的 7 万元分配给旗人，另用 3 万元在支机石街中的关帝庙（又称支机石庙）和西城根与今天实业街交口处建立了手工作坊，收纳旗人子弟 70 余人学习技艺，生产机织线袜、毛巾等日用品，以解决部分家庭的生计问题。与此同时，将军玉昆被礼送出川，满蒙旗人交出全部武器。就这样，成都满城终于得以和平易帜，全城得以平安。为了表示由汉人组成的新政权对于旗人不再如清王朝那样搞民族歧视，而是要一视同仁、五族共和，于是就把手工作坊命名为同仁工厂（这个工厂一直经营到 1920 年，因为军阀混战、管理混乱而倒闭）。满城被拆除之后，原来的西城根街也就逐渐成了一条众人通行的道路，1923 年在经过整修（主持者为市政公所技正杨宝康）之后，形成了一条"长二千零八尺""宽一丈四尺"的马路，就把同仁工厂所在的

罗纶

这条西城根街命名为同仁路，这个街名一直用到现在。由于同仁路比较长，所以又分为上同仁路、中同仁路和下同仁路三段。

在同仁路西侧的城墙边，原有满城中的箭道，种有不少树木，面积达十余亩。1924 年曾把支机石街以北的这一地区，再加上原来的同仁工厂一部分，建为森林公园，是为成都城中最早出现的森林公园，其中有百年楠木千余棵。因为原来的支机石庙就在公园的南端，所以又被称为支机石公园。这个公园在民国前期是成都除少城公园、中山公园之外的第三大公园，还曾经是当时的群众集会的场所。例如在 1928 年春天著名的"一中事件"中（有关介绍见"西胜街"），成都各学校学生代表数百人举行的声援一中同学的集会就是在这里

举行的。抗日战争时期，森林公园被空军层板厂占用，楠木林也被砍伐，公园遂不复存在。

2022 年的同仁路罗城遗址标志　董青青摄影

由于同仁路的位置就是老成都的西城墙边，所以近年间在位于上同仁路的原成都纸箱厂和位于下同仁路的成都制药一厂，先后发现了唐代成都城墙（即罗城）遗址，从而可以知道，从唐代到清代，成都城墙的西面位置基本上没有移动。在今天的上同仁路与二道桥街的交口处，用条石与古砖垒着一圈似墙非墙、似堡非堡的建筑，上面还栽有大叶榕，那个位置就是前些年发掘出来的罗城遗址的位置。附近的楼盘聚星城的开发商是一个有心的知识分子，在修建聚星城时，他就把收集到的条石与古砖在那个位置修建了一个那样的建筑，用以作为罗城遗址位置的地理标志，可以算是今天凭吊唐代成都的一个去处。在罗城遗址位置的一家茶馆也改名叫唐城，并在门前挂着由成都收藏家江功举撰写的对联："古址遗残墙杜陵觅句曾来此；少城留雅座时彦谈茶正在斯。"

1988 年的上同仁路　张西南摄影

在同仁路与支机石街相接处，也就是在过去的支机石庙的地方，有一个十分完整而精致的三进四合院，这就是在 1980 年成立的成都画院。成都画院初建时是在青羊宫侧的二仙庵中临时办公。1984 年，在当时的成都市市长米建书的大力支持下，成都市房管局先是把原来鼓楼街上需要拆除的静安旅馆的两个清代四合院整体搬迁到这里来进行重建，四年后又把红星路上需要拆除的叶家祠堂的一个清代四合院整体搬迁到这里来，与原来的两个四合院有机地结合在一起进行重建，才形成了今天的前、中、后三进的大院落。2004 年，同仁路改建扩建工程的原方案对成都画院这个大院落的前部有所影响，在成都市政府的坚持之下，决定保护成都画院的完整，对同仁路的工程方案作了调整（今天看到的扩建后的同仁路在支机石街这一段不是笔直的而是弯的，就是为了保护成都画院而将同仁路街道走向作了调整的结果），这才保存了今天在成都城区还能见到的最完整、最有代表性的清代后期风格的成都四合院，这也是成都市唯一的一处四川省级文物保护单位的四合院。在它门前有两株树龄近千年的古银杏，就是原来的严真观、后来的支机石庙前的古银杏，就连银杏树下花坛上的用砖也全部都是古砖。1987 至 1989 年，成都画院进行了一次全面的维修。2007 年又进行了一次工程量更大的内部改造，按"修旧如旧、保持原貌、完善功能、合理利用"的原则，将原来的几个院落以通透式展厅为主重新进行安排，不仅成为一处很漂亮、很有特色的具有川西民居风格的美术馆，而且也是全国唯一的老建筑四合院美术馆。

在原来的同仁路 48 号，曾经有一个幽静的小院，因堂前有两株楠木古树，而名为双楠堂。在这个小院之中，发生过一件成都当代文化史上的憾事——古琴大师裴铁侠夫妇碎琴自尽。

裴铁侠（1884—1950） 成都人。1904 年留学日本，早期同盟会会员。1912 年回国，曾任四川司法司司长、川东道道尹、《西成报》总编辑。1915 年赴京任内务部顾问。因见政局混乱、国事日非，遂退出政界，回到成都，潜心古琴技艺，收藏海内名琴，成为一代著名的古琴大师。1937 年成立"律和琴社"，1947 年又成立"岷明琴社"，都由他自任社长。他收藏了一张我国古琴制作史上的巅峰作品——唐代四川制琴大师雷威制作的"雷琴"（唐代四川雷氏为我国历史上最著名的制琴世家，传名于后世者就有 9 人之多，他们所制作的古琴均可以称为"雷琴"，其中又以峨眉雷威为其顶峰。唐代著名文学家与书法家欧阳询为雷威琴的题词是"合雅大乐，成文正音，徽弦一泛，山水俱深"。目前传世的唐代古琴共有 18 张，题名"九霄环珮"的雷琴只有 4 张。2008 年刚故世的成都古琴名家王华德先生珍藏有一张古琴，琴身右侧刻有"大唐咸通二年雷威制"字样，是北宋制作的仿雷琴），以及另一张唐琴"古龙吟"。他在以琴会友之中迎娶的夫人沈梦英又从娘家（其父为成都治印名家沈靖卿）带来又一位雷氏名家雷宵制作的另一张"雷琴"，于是他家拥有了号称"大雷"与"小雷"的令同行美慕不已的"双雷"，以及宋、元、明、清各种名琴 20 多张（他所藏的宋琴"龙嗷"至今收藏于四川大学博物馆）。抗日战争中为躲避日本侵略者的轰炸，他迁居西郊外沙堰山庄，在此撰写并用木版刻印了著名的《沙堰琴编》《沙堰琴余》。《沙堰琴编》辑琴曲 14 首，均有记有注，有的还有词。《沙堰琴余》分为琴律、琴音、琴腔、琴品、琴辩，是多年来研习古琴的心得体会。由于他长期沉湎琴艺而深居简出，不问世事，除琴友外几乎不与人交往，中华人民共和国成立以后对人民政府的政策法令懵懂无知，对新旧社会的巨大变革不能理解与适应，加之性格孤傲自负、子女生计困难，遂决定与"双雷"一道"玉碎"以求解脱。1950 年 6 月（一说在 1951 年上半年）一天夜里，他夫妇二人将"大雷"

"小雷"两张雷琴一起砸碎，然后双双服毒自尽，人琴俱亡，只留下了"本来空寂，何有于物，去物从心，立地成佛"16个大字与一行小字："大小雷琴同登仙界，金徽留作葬费，余物焚毁。铁叟笔。"其实就在这时，国内音乐界的朋友正在为他安排最适合的工作。中国音乐家协会副主席、中央音乐学院民乐系主任查阜西专门发函邀请他携"双雷"赴京从事古琴研究工作。可惜函件到时，人琴俱亡，遂成为成都文化史上的一大憾事。著名诗人、四川大学教授曾缄以此为题，写了著名的长诗《双雷引》，其中有"支机石畔深深院，铜漏丁丁催晓箭"等句，至今还在诗歌爱好者之中流传。

1937 年裴铁侠与琴友合影 （前排右二为裴铁侠， 右三为古琴大师查阜西）

八宝街

　　八宝街东起青龙街，西接西大街，成都人多把它看作西大街的一段。八宝街在清代是满城中的顺城胡同，到了清末民初，这里已经成了贫民的聚居区，多以成都人所称的篾笆（用竹片编成的厚竹席）为墙壁，所以被人们称为笆笆巷。由于笆笆巷的名称太不雅，后来就以"笆笆"的谐音改名为寓意吉祥的"八宝街"。

　　"八宝"是在我国民间长期流行的多种吉祥物的总称，各地所指不尽相同，有如今天还在使用的八宝箱、八宝粥一样，基本上是一种表示其多的泛称。不过在民间工艺美术中一般都以宝珠、方胜、玉磬、犀角、古钱、珊瑚、银锭、如意为八宝。

西大街

　　成都的西大街只有很短的一段，不与城中心相连，偏处于城区的西北角，这种情况在清代就已形成。清代的成都城的西部是满城，满城北城墙的位置就在今天西大街的北边，今天的西大街是满城中最北的一条胡同，因为正对清远门（也就是成都的老西门）所以名叫清远胡同。清远胡同在长顺街之西，与之相对的还有东边的一条胡同，因为顺着满城的城墙，所以叫顺城胡同。民国时期拆除满城之后，因为清远胡同是出老西门的必经之路，所以就改名为西大街，顺城胡同则改名为八宝街。八宝街以东是原来在满城之外的青龙街，西大街的西边则是紧邻城门的西月城街。这样，成都人从骡马市拐弯向西走出老西门就要经过青龙街、八宝街、西大街、西月城街这四条街。严格来说，这四条街实际上是一条街的四段，有如东大街分为几段一样，所以不少成都人干脆将其统称为西大街。

1970 年的西大街　冯水木摄影

 1995 年被国内贸易部认定为"中华老字号"的成都著名小吃"谭豆花"的创始人叫谭玉成，于抗日战争以后开业于西顺城街上的安乐寺，当时是摆摊经营，其所经营的麻辣鲜香、价廉物美的豆花面受到人们的喜爱。中华人民共和国成立以后迁到盐市口经营，正式以"谭豆花"为店名，仍然主营豆花面。改革开放之后，盐市口地区进行城市改造，"谭豆花"被拆除，餐馆一度歇业。近年来，谭氏后人予以恢复，以"小谭豆花"的店名开业于西大街，经营以豆花面为主的多种川味小吃，保持了价廉物美的优良传统，颇受消费者的好评。

西大街上的 "小谭豆花" 20 世纪 90 年代 成都市建设信息中心提供

 四川省歌舞团自 1953 年成立以来（1984 年改制为四川省歌舞剧院）一直就在本街的北侧，至今未迁。

将军衙门

今天的金河宾馆一带，成都人都称之为将军衙门，在旁边还有一条将军街。在这些地名之中的"将军"，并不是一般意义上对高级军官的尊称，而是一种专门而又特别的官称。

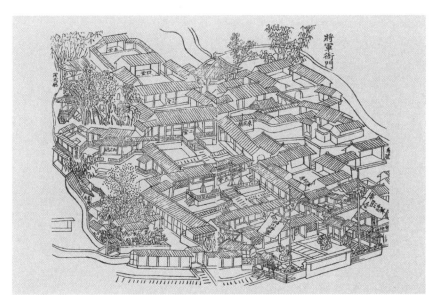

将军衙门图　原载同治《成都县志》

清王朝初期在全国的军事要地都驻有八旗重兵，以驻防将军为最高统帅。以成都为例，其官衔的全称是"镇守四川成都等地方将军、统辖松建文武、提调汉土官兵、管八旗事"，一般都简称为成都将军。将军只能由满蒙贵族担任（清代中叶以后，在特殊情况下汉族总督可以短期代理将军的职务，但不能叫兼任，只能叫兼署。在古代官制中，"署"就是代理的意思。例如成都人相当熟悉的同治时期汉族四川总督吴棠就兼署过成都将军），除了负责当地的军事防务之外，还是当地满蒙八旗事务的总管，其实质是朝廷或满蒙贵族派在当地的最高代表，是皇帝的耳目。在当时各省的官职序列之中，除了少数以御前大臣、大学士的官衔出任总督者外，将军的地位都在总督之前，居于首位，表面上不具体管理地方政务，但对所有的地方官员都有监视之责，可以将地方的一切情况独自密报清廷，而地方上的最高官员总督与巡抚给清廷的重要奏章上报时都得有将军的副署，否则就不得上奏，不能起任何作用。例如清末的四川总督、人称赵屠户的赵尔丰在逮捕保路同志会的领袖蒲殿俊、罗纶等人之后，一心要把他们处死。可是在上奏朝廷之时，将军玉昆不同意，不副署，赵尔丰就无法上奏，当然也就杀不了他们。

1910 年将军衙门内的印月亭　杨显峰提供

四川在清代初期满蒙八旗的最高官员只设副都统，第一任副都统是法喇，统率有八旗兵丁与家属共 5000 余人。乾隆四十一年（1776）始设将军，首任将军为明亮，今天的金河宾馆所在的地方，就是清代的成都驻防将军的衙门。清代前期的将军衙门因为在名义上是驻军的指挥所在，所以建筑并不宏伟。清同治七年（1868），在当时的驻防将军崇实的主持下（崇实在成都任职多年，又爱好书法，现在成都的武侯祠等地还可以见到他所题写的匾额楹联），对其进行了大规模的扩建与改建，成为一座中轴二门五进、两旁多院并有花园的大型建筑，大门上的两道匾额上写着"望重西南"和"控驭岩疆"，表明了将军衙门的权威与职责。

清政权被推翻之后拆除满城时，将军衙门只是把大门拆掉了，多数建筑继续使用，一直是民国时期军事部门的办公场所，北洋系的陈宧，滇军的罗佩金，川军的熊克武、刘成勋、杨森、刘文辉、刘湘等将领都曾经在这里办公。刘文辉的二十四军司令部曾经长期设在这里。抗日战争初期，蒋介石的军事力量逐步进入成都，于1935年11月5日在这里正式成立了重庆行营驻蓉办事处，1939年2月13日正式成立了国民政府军事委员会委员长成都行辕，故而一直是蒋介石集团在成都最主要的据点之一。从1940年到成都解放，这里又是四川全省最大的特务机构四川省特种工作委员会（由在川的军统、中统、宪兵、三青团系统合组，1946年曾经改名为四川省党政军干部联席会议，但是仍然按习惯简称为"特委会"）的所在地，设有关押政治犯的特别监狱，曾经关押过大量的中共党员和革命志士。1949年12月7日深夜，在成都发生的对革命志士的疯狂大屠杀所以会发生在十二桥，就是因为这些革命志士中的大部分都是从关押在将军衙门的特别监狱中押出去杀害的，十二桥就在将军衙门的西侧。

国民党四川省特委会设在将军衙门中的监狱　杨显峰提供

将军衙门在中华人民共和国成立以后长期是成都军区的第三招待所，改革开放以后就在原来招待所的旧址修建了金河宾馆，但是仍然还是成都军区的第三招待所。

半边桥北街附半边桥南街

在人民公园的东南边有一条半边桥街，以原来的半边桥而得名。清代这里是大城与满城的交界处，金河从此流过。金河上的一座桥下面就是分隔大城与满城的水栅，上面还有棚栅式的建筑，并有兵丁把守。桥面的西半边属于满城的范围，桥面的东半边属于大城的范围。清人的《竹枝词》曾对此有过颇有微词的形容："右半边桥作妾观，左半边桥当郎看。筑城桥上水流下，同一桥身见面难。"当时人们就把这座桥称为半边桥（其实半边桥的正式名字应当是灵寿桥，过去还曾经有一位名叫刘彝铭的文士在桥上题写过桥名）。北起祠堂街、南到陕西街的街道就叫半边桥街，也被简称为半边街。过去的半边桥街还曾经以在今人民公园侧门附近的半边桥为界，分为半边桥北街和半边桥南街。在近年的城市改造中，半边桥北街和半边桥南街都已被拆除，原来的位置变成了绿化带与市场。

清代为了保卫满城的安全，在半边桥下的金河中设有水栅，从府河中进入金河的船只最远就只能航行到半边桥为止，半边桥也就成了过去能够通航的金河水运的终点码头。当年满城中所需的各种生活物资基本上是从满城东门受福门进入，有专门的满城官员在那里检查验收，而受福门就在半边桥的北边，满城中最重要的粮食与物资仓库诸如永济仓、大粮仓、柴薪仓、草料仓等也都设在半边桥以西的今天人民公园范围之内。所以，成都市中心地区当年从半边桥到三桥这一段金河两岸就曾经是一个十分热闹的小型水码头贸易区，故而《锦城旧事竹枝词》这样写道："半是少城半大城，铁栅跨河满汉分。流向三桥输炭米，蜿蜒直到水东门。"

20 世纪 90 年代的半边桥南街　严永聪摄影

　　1925 年，在前清状元骆成骧的大力提倡之下，以继承和发扬传统武术为宗旨的四川省国术馆成立于少城公园内的半边桥街侧门内（具体位置在今半边桥南街 35 号省文化局宿舍区），骆成骧亲任馆长，武术名家刘崇俊任副馆长，对推动四川的武术发展起过不小作用。著名的青羊宫花会上打擂比武的"打金章"就是由四川省国术馆组织的。四川军政要员刘文辉、杨森、刘湘、王缵绪等都曾经兼任过馆长。

　　民国时期的半边桥街上的主要商店是前店后坊的皮鞋店，有老成都最著名的"前进"皮鞋店，还有名号为"光荣""大胜""可行""一新"的多家皮鞋店。抗日战争时期，著名影星白杨等人专门到此选购皮鞋，曾经引起大量路人围观，成为报纸上的重要新闻。

　　半边桥街上过去有几家在成都颇有名气的餐馆。由郭朝华夫妇创建的蜀中名菜"夫妻肺片"早期曾在少城公园侧门右边拐角处开店，只有一间铺面。由廖永通创建的著名小吃"痣胡子龙眼包子"就开在半边桥北街西侧（近年来在太升南路开店），也只有一间小铺面。清真食品店"王胖鸭"最初开在西御街东端，"文革"中因为修建金河与御河的人防工程而迁至半边桥街。"王胖鸭"是采用填饲成都麻鸭与挂炉烤鸭技术加灌卤汁的成都风味烤鸭，是从清朝宫廷烤乳猪的技术移植的，不是后来大量出售的、加工技术相对简单的卤制白油桶鸭。在老成都人心中印象特别深的，是一家名字很古怪但又引人注意的甜食店"口叩品"，其主要食品是煮红苕。"口叩品"中的那个"叩"字早在汉代的《说文》中就有收录，从二口会意，其义为"众人并呼"，就是喧哗的"喧"字的异体。由于"叩"字的写法在古籍中基本不用，绝大多数人都不认识，加上绝大多数成都人都按成都方言把亲嘴称为"打啵"，于是人们就把这个二口会意为"众人并呼"的"叩"字的本义误认为就是二口亲嘴，读为成都方言中的"啵"，即波字的儿化音，这样"口叩品"的名字就被喊了几十年。当年九眼桥边还有一家川菜馆叫"大埜春"，店招中也有一个绝大多数人不认识的罕见字。于是"东有大埜春，西有口叩品"就成为多年来成都的一桩趣谈。中华人民共和国成立以后，"口叩品"曾经在西御街开店，但是其主打产品不再是煮红苕，而是各种凉粉。

当年的金河从水西门入城之后，因为从闹市中穿过，所以桥的分布很密，在半边桥的上游原来还有好几座桥，都在原来的满城内，现在已经没有相关的地名留下来。半边桥是当年金河上若干座桥之中在今天还在街道名称中留下桥名的最上游的一座桥。

包家巷附后包家巷

包家巷原来是清代满城中的永明胡同，又名聚元胡同，胡同内最有名的住户是蒙古族的巴尔特氏。巴尔特氏后人多改姓"包"，附近居民多称为"包家"，所以这条胡同在民国时期就改称为包家巷。

1920 年，原来在陕西街的四川最早的西医学校四川陆军军医学校迁入包家巷，还附设一个陆军医院，停办于 1926 年，一共办了 8 期，毕业学生 400 多人，组织有军医学校毕业同学会。1926 年，以军医学校毕业同学会的力量为基础，又在军医学校原址开办了官办的四川医学专门学校，学制 7 年（预科 2 年，本科 5 年），并附设医院。四川医学专门学校只办了 7 期，于 1936 年停办，由四川善后督办公署接管，改为善后督办公署军医研究班。1938 年，刘湘病故，其部属就将其更名为甫澄纪念医院（刘湘字甫澄）。由于这所纪念医院既非官办，又非私立，所以只能是昙花一现，办得有气无力，不久就被官方收回，改办医士职业学校，并且以培养助产士为其办学特色，其附属医院也成为妇产科专科医院。这是成都第一家以妇产科为特色的专门学校与专科医院。中华人民共和国成立以后，就在这里开办了成都市第一妇产医院，成都人一般称为包家巷产院。成都市第一妇产医院在 2000 年与成都市第九人民医院合并，既称成都市第九人民医院，也称成都市妇产科医院。2008 年 11 月 28 日，成都市妇产科医院庆祝了 70 周年生日。70 年中，共有 40 万成都人在这家医院里出生。所以很多成都人都说："成都市 40 岁以上的本地人有一半是在包家巷出生的。"2010 年 12 月 23 日，这所医院迁往城西新光华片区日月大道的新址，与原来的成都市妇幼保健院、成都市儿童医院合并为新建的成都市妇女儿童医学中心。2011 年 7 月，又挂牌成为重庆医科大学附属成都妇女儿童中心医院。

1936 年，一代名医叶心清在包家巷开设了自己的诊所。

叶心清（1908—1967）大邑人。1913 年去汉口投靠叔父谋生，得遇名医魏庭兰，遂从师 12 年，尽得"绝命三针"的金针疗疾真传（"金针"是以九成赤金加一成紫铜铸制），成为我国独树一帜的金针高手（魏氏金针疗法共传三人，另二人一个弃医从政，一人死于火灾）。1933 年，他在重庆开设国粹医馆，1936 年回成都行医，名震蜀中，一时要人如于右任、蒋鼎文、胡宗南、宋希濂、刘文辉等都邀请为其治病。中华人民共和国成立之后，他被辛亥革命元老但懋辛和著名实业家卢作孚邀至重庆行医，曾经以 8 次针疗治好了贺龙元帅久治不愈的右臂难举的痼疾。1956 年中国中医研究院成立，卫生部从全国礼聘 30 位全国名医进京，叶心清为其中之一（成都名医入京者还有蒲辅周、杜自明，重庆名医入京者还有任应秋、沈仲圭、冉雪峰）。在北京时，他主要为中央领导人与外宾治病，治疗的病员包括刘少奇、朱德、宋庆龄、董必武、邓小平、陈毅、罗荣桓、叶剑英、李富春、谭震林等党和国家领导人 20 多人。何香凝送过他手绘梅花，沈钧儒送过他书法，吴玉章赠诗有"今日华佗又复生"之誉。他为江青治好了严重的神经官能症之后，毛泽东主席亲笔书写了《娄山关》词相赠。他还出国为越南的胡志明主席、柬埔寨的西哈努克亲王等十几个国家元首治病。1957 年经苏联外交部门出面邀请，他在我国驻阿联大使陈家康率领下去也门为王室治病（当时我国还未与也门建交），治好了也门国王在很多国家无法治愈的剧烈头痛，治好了也门太子周身溃烂流黄水的恶疮，被也门称为"东方神仙"，为此他不得不在也门为王室成员治病三个月方能回国。叶心清是成都杏林在全世界影响最大的一位名医。

1913 年 4 月，四川劝业道周善培在包家巷开办了四川历史上第一个职业技术学校——四川职业学校，同年 8 月改名为四川省立第一甲种工业学校（甲种工业学校是当时各省根据民国政府在 1913 年颁布的新学制设立的职业学校，一般简称为"甲工"，学历相当于中学，而相当于高小的职业学校则称为乙种学校，所以有的资料把"甲种"写为"甲等"是错误的。成都只设立了这一个"甲工"，原来位置在今天的包家巷 82 号附 1 号院，当年的一幢教学楼作为成都中药材公司的宿舍至今仍存），下设机械、染织、应用化学三科。陈毅元帅曾经于 1916—1917 年在这里就读染织专科。这所学校于 1937 年迁往学道街，并入四川省立成都高级工业职业学校，就是中华人民共和国成立以后的成都电子高专的前身。甲种工业学校在包家巷办学时，在曾经留学日本的校长郭玉珊的策划下，将学生的生产实习安排为生产仿日本式人力车（即黄包车）。成都在民国时期的市内主要交通工具就是黄包车，最多时达4000辆左右，这里就是早期最主要的生产地。

2011年的甲工校遗址　杨显峰提供

1935年，省立成都女子职业学校在这里开办，这是成都第一所女子职业学校，开办有会计、统计、染织、家政、日化、图书管理等科，所有费用全免，为当时女性走入社会就业做出了应有的贡献。

1930年，四川饮食文化史上的著名餐馆"姑姑筵"川菜馆由黄敬临开设在包家巷。

黄敬临（1875—1941）本名黄循，敬临或晋临都是他的别号，成都人，毕业于四川法政学堂。自幼好学，而于烹饪技艺有其特别的爱好，真正做到了好学深思、探本溯源，且又喜爱亲自下厨，制作揣摩，年轻时即以美食名家与厨下高手闻名成都，曾被四川省立第一女子师范学校聘为烹饪教师，是四川所有学校中的第一位烹饪教师，也是川菜界最著名的"儒厨"。20世纪20年代初，曾因幼年同学、川军将领陈鸣谦之荐而出任过射洪与巫溪县知事，很快即辞官回蓉。为了维持一家生计，他在时任成都通俗教育馆馆长卢作孚先生的支持下，在少城公园内楠木林东侧开设"晋邻饭店"（这家川菜馆在川菜发展史上甚为重要，但是其名字在近人的不同记载中却有多种写法，此从《吴虞日记》。吴虞在日记中记载有他先后八次在"晋邻饭店"用餐），亲自提调厨务，以以跟随他多年的厨师彭辉廷为"坐押师"，即今天的厨师长。可是他的老朋友如陈鸣谦等竭力劝阻他将一生付与庖厨，并力荐其再度入仕，出任荥经县长。一年多以后他又辞官回蓉，决意永绝仕途，以一生的钻研所得而专心致力于川菜厨艺。此时的"晋邻饭店"由于他大儿子黄平伯的挥霍，已经经营困难，便转让给了温江人陈锡侯，改名为"静宁饭店"（一直经营到抗日战争以后歇业）。而他本人则在包家巷西头路南自己住家的隔壁开设了宅院式的"姑姑筵"川菜馆（按：办"姑姑筵"是四川方言，即小孩子模仿大人做饭请客的游戏，也称"办家家""过家家"。据前辈的回忆，黄敬临对"姑姑筵"的命名来源于他三妹的一句玩笑："看你斯文态态的样子，开啥子餐馆哟，办姑姑筵倒差不多"）。作为诗书俱精的文士，他在大门上挂出了自撰的名联："右手拿菜刀，左手拿锅铲，急急忙忙干起来，做些鱼翅燕窝，供你们老爷太太；前头烤柴灶，后头烤炭炉，轰轰烈烈闹一阵，落得点残汤剩饭，养活我大人娃娃。"在大厅内也挂出了自撰的名联："学问不如人，才德不如人，只有煎菜熬汤，才算我的真本事；亲戚休笑我，朋友休笑我，安于操刀弄铲，正是文人下梢头。"他以家传厨艺与名师高手相结合，主要由黄家姑嫂掌灶，初期所聘用的厨师仍然仅有彭辉廷一人，开发出一批精品川菜，而且拒用味精（当时叫"味之素"，系从日本进口），每天只供应两三桌，最多不过四桌（对于顾客的随从、车夫另设"中席"进餐，这在成都也是首创）。菜单必须由他根据顾客的具体情况亲自安排，而且亲自上菜，主桌上必须给他留一个座位，备一份请柬，以供他亲自讲解。他的这种特别讲究的菜品与特别独特的经营模式很快闻名远近，客人必须在三天以前预订，包括四川军政领袖刘湘也不能例外。由于西较场扩充营地，包家巷西头部分民房被占，"姑姑筵"后来曾几次搬迁，先后迁至暑袜北街、宝云庵马家花园、陕西街和新玉沙街，1938年还应邀去重庆开了"姑姑筵"。他在重庆与在成都时一样，在店堂中都要挂出由他撰写的对联，最有名的一联是讽刺时政的："营业税、印花税、席桌捐、红锅捐，这起去了那起来，弄不清楚；蒸公鸡、炒母鸡、炖牛肉、烤猪肉，肥的精而瘦的嫩，都要整齐。"他的店铺也曾经因为这副对联而被查封，不得不从原来的中营街迁往南岸的汪山。1941年，在日本侵略者对重庆的大轰炸中，已患重病的黄敬临饱受惊吓，病故于汪山。以后重庆的"姑姑筵"迁入城内的民国路营业，改名为"凯歌归"。

川菜名店 "姑姑筵" 王大明提供

在黄敬临的影响之下，他的三弟黄保临（这也是一个辞官下厨的人物，他曾经任过宜宾县征收局长、四川省财政厅科员）先在打金街开设了"古女菜"川菜馆，以后相继在暑袜中街与总府街开了"哥哥传"川菜馆，他的大儿子黄平伯（这仍然是一个辞官下厨的人物，他曾经在川军中任过军部副官）在陕西街开了"不醉无归小酒家"川菜馆，小儿子黄庭仲在祠堂街开了"东风一醉楼"川菜馆。黄氏一门的川菜技艺不仅在当时极受欢迎，而且对后世也有着不小的影响。黄敬临的"唱戏靠腔，吃饭靠汤"的经验总结至今仍是厨师中代代相传的经典之谈。川菜中的著名菜肴开水白菜、软炸扳指、青筒鱼、泡菜烧黄辣丁、豆渣猪头、樟茶鸭、红烧牛头方、麻椒牛筋等，或者是"姑姑筵"的原创，或者在"姑姑筵"有过实质性的改进与提高，至今仍然很受欢迎。后期的"姑姑筵"聘用的厨师中有好几位后来都成了川菜界公认的大师级人物，如北京饭店川菜部与四川饭店的厨师长罗国荣、芙蓉餐厅主厨陈海清、重庆颐之时餐厅主厨周海清等都是。近年来，黄派川菜仍然在各地流传，在日本开有一家"姑姑筵"，在台湾开有三家"姑姑筵"，在成都则有开在草堂北大门的"姑姑筵"和开在陕西街的"不醉无归小酒家"川菜馆。

关于黄敬临的前期生平事迹，过去的有关记载众说纷纭，不少记载都说他是前清秀才甚至进士、在清代供职于北京的皇家接待机构光禄寺，并成为慈禧太后所赏识的御厨，获赠四品官衔。笔者几经考察之后认为不确，此处所述主要依据近年来的新方志。

在包家巷的南面原来还有一条很短的后包家巷，从包家巷通往原来的成都军区被服厂的后门，已经在近年的城市改造中被拆除。

蜀华街

　　蜀华街位于小南街以西，方池街以南，原来是清代满城中的翠柏胡同，又称永升胡同。民国初年更名为厅子街。1921年，辛亥革命时期曾经担任重庆蜀军政府副都督的夏之时（参见"东胜街"）在这条街上创办了私立锦江公学，所以改名为锦江街。1932年，在二十四军副军长向传义和成都回族著名人士马毓智（参见"马家花园路"）主持下，私立锦江公学与私立储才中学（1912年创办于文庙西街，后迁东胜街，再迁燕鲁公所）合并，更名为成都私立蜀华中学，仍在原锦江公学的基础之上开办，故而街名又被改为蜀华街。蜀华中学在中华人民共和国成立之后更名为成都市十四中学，学校扩建之后，大门一度改在相邻的包家巷，现在仍然开在蜀华街，而且在校园内还建有蜀华亭，刻有《蜀华铭》。中国共产党历史上杰出的红色女特工张露萍烈士就是这个学校的学生。

民国时期的蜀华中学　彭雄提供

张露萍（1921—1945）崇州人。本名余家英，在建国中学读初中时认识了同班同学车崇英的父亲、中国共产党的优秀党员车耀先，在其影响下走上了革命的道路。因为积极参加抗日宣传活动而被学校默退，此后跳级考入蜀华中学高中班，继续从事革命活动，并正式参加了中华民族解放先锋队。1937年11月，她在车耀先的帮助下离开成都，1938年到达延安，先后在抗日军政大学与中央军委通讯学校学习。1938年10月加入中国共产党。因为她的姐夫余安民是川军少将，故而于1939年秋受指派回到四川从事统战工作。她回四川以后，根据工作需要，中共中央南方局决定发挥她熟悉无线电报务技术的特长，化名张露萍，潜入国民党特务组织的核心军统局电讯台担任中共特别支部的支部书记，将军统内部的核心机密源源不断地提供给重庆八路军办事处，并利用敌人电台与延安进行联络。1940年冬，因为一位同志不慎被暴露，张露萍等7名革命同志被敌人逮捕。她不仅经受了敌人各种各样的酷刑，而且经受了在贵州省息烽监狱长达四年的折磨，一直没有暴露自己的真实身份和党的机密，是我党在敌人心脏中进行战斗的最杰出的女英雄之一，被后人喻为我党特工的三大女杰之一（另两杰是陈修良与朱枫）。1945年7月14日，她作为"共党重大嫌疑人"被枪杀于息烽快活岭刑场，年仅24岁。

在今天成都十四中校园里、在烈士的家乡崇州市露萍广场都塑有烈士的塑像。

民先队的成员（左一为张露萍）在阅读抗日刊物　建川博物馆提供

方池街

　　方池街在小南街以西、蜀华街以北，中华人民共和国成立以后四川省总工会长期设于此街。

　　清代这里位于满城之内，名叫钟灵胡同，得名于胡同东头有一个钟灵坊。后来把街内原有的一个池塘加以整修，改建为一个方形的池塘，故而胡同也改名为方池胡同，民国时期又改名为方池街。这个方池最大时有 5 亩，栽有荷花，是整个满城中最大的水面。从方池街的方位来分析，街上的池塘极有可能也是古老的内江故道的遗迹，遗憾的是这个池塘早已填平。值得一提的是，附近的老百姓当年把那个池塘叫作"大坑沿儿"（附近的小南街则称为大坑沿后街），很明显是满城中的满蒙同胞的叫法，是北京方言词汇在成都的使用，与今天北京的南河沿儿、北河沿儿相似。

　　从 1982 年到 1986 年，在方池街的基建工地上，相继发现了丰富的古代文化遗存，出土了石器、骨器、陶器、卜甲和卜骨，可以确认这里是一处极为重要的、成都主城区内第一次发现的从新石器时代晚期至战国时期的文化遗址，特别是青石圆雕捆缚人像、陶塑猪龙和三条竹篾笼络卵石砌筑的堤埂（这一治水工程遗迹的时间要早于都江堰几百年）的发现对于古蜀文化的研究有着十分重要的意义。此后在将军衙门、抚琴小区、指挥街相继发现了古蜀时期的笼络卵石埋护岸工程和木桩排列坝体工程的遗迹，表明了成都地区早期水利工程十分普遍。

1986 年的方池街古蜀水利工程遗址　周尔泰提供

　　抗日名将李家钰烈士在成都的住宅有两处，现在都基本保存了下来，而且都在 2001 年被列为成都市首批 22 处文物建筑之一。其中一处是李家钰自己居住的文庙前街 92 号（现由中国共产党四川省委老干部管理局管理使用），另一处就是由李家钰兄弟居住的方池街 22 号（现由四川省总工会管理使用）。

祠堂街

　　人民公园大门外的祠堂街原来位于清代满城东南方的受福门之内，门外就是西御街（所以人们也将这个城门称为西御街小东门）。清初，这条街叫喇嘛胡同，或称为蒙古胡同。清康熙五十七年（1718），八旗官兵在这条胡同中为当时的权臣年羹尧建立一座生祠（位置在今人民公园东北部），并把这条胡同改名叫作祠堂街。年羹尧的生祠在年羹尧获罪死后即被拆毁，以后在原址改建关帝庙（当时在簸箕街也建有年羹尧的生祠，年羹尧死后原址改建为文昌宫），但是祠堂街这个街名一直未改，沿用至今。

　　年羹尧（1679—1726）清康熙、雍正年间著名的大臣。康熙四十八年（1709）任四川巡抚，五十七年（1718）升任川陕总督，先后平定了多次川藏地区的"叛乱"，并成为新即帝位的雍正帝的心腹。雍正初年，又被封为抚远大将军远征西北，受封太保、一等公。由于他自恃功高爵显，骄纵贪暴，专横跋扈，故而被雍正帝逮捕入狱，列出大罪92条，责令自杀。

　　由年羹尧的生祠改建的关帝庙建于乾隆四十八年（1783），光绪年间重修之后更名为武圣宫。在清代初年，满城是按一座大军营来修建并制定有关制度的，满城中供神只能供关圣帝君和观音菩萨（这一规定在清代中期以后逐渐松弛。清代满城之中大小庙宇宫观共有8处，除了关帝庙以外，清初只有宁夏街祭拜奇石的西来寺，守经街上明代双佛寺被改为道教宫观真武宫，西胜街的圣寿寺被迁往君平街，支机石街的严真观被改为关帝庙，其余还有祠堂街的文昌宫和昭忠祠，西来寺侧的欢喜寺，都是清代后期修建的），这座关帝庙就是整个满城中最大的庙宇，左有钟楼和荷花池，右有鼓楼和太极池，大殿三重，金河就从第二重殿前流向半边桥，景色十分别致。由于满城中的旗人不能自由出入满城（外出必须请假），这座关帝庙也就是官员所允许的旗人们游玩娱乐的唯一所在，还建有满城中唯一的一个戏台。特别是其中的荷花池是满城中最大的一片荷花池，在当时颇为知名。时人有《竹枝词》记其事："满洲城静不繁华，种树栽花各有涯。好景一年看不尽，炎天武庙赏荷花。"

祠堂街东头在清同治十年（1871）由四川总督吴棠创建了满城中唯一的书院八旗少城书院，专门培养八旗子弟。这个书院效果不佳，光绪三十年（1904）被成都将军绰哈布下令拆除。

民国初年，满城被拆除之后，祠堂街成了成都市区内东西交通的重要街道，曾经在1936年与1943年两次扩建。前一次扩建时，修成了当时在成都还属于先进施工技术的黄泥灌浆碎石三合土路面，在成都第一次使用了从英国购回的压路机。抗日战争开始之后，成都逐渐成为大后方的文化中心城市，由于祠堂街上有绿树成荫的少城公园，有流水潺潺的金河，还有电影院和川剧院，房租又比春熙路、东大街便宜，所以包括全国著名的生活书店、开明书店、商务印书馆、北新书店、东方书店、大东书局、正中书局、广益书局、儿童书店在内的很多书店的分店都开设在这里，成都本土的普益书社（这家书店以编辑出版活页文选而闻名全市）等书店也开设在这里，不少书店同时兼营出版业务，很多报刊的编辑部也设在这里，故而时人称祠堂街为"新文化街"。由革命烈士车耀先创办的专门出售进步图书的"我们的书店"也开在这里，这家书店的招牌是用美术字体写的，而且是从左到右横排，这在全成都乃是开风气之先的第一家。据统计，从"七七"事变到中华人民共和国成立前夕的12年中，全市共先后开设各种书刊新店267家、文具店54家，而开设在祠堂街的书刊新店就有183家、文具店就有34家。在地下党的组织之下（生活、开明、北新、儿童等书店内都有共产党员），100多名书店店员还组织了图书业工人歌咏团，每天早上在大街上高唱抗日救亡歌曲，晚上进行街头演出和演讲（著名演员赵丹演出过《放下你的鞭子》，白杨演出过《我们大家一条心》，马寅初、李公朴等发表过演讲），被成都市民称之为"晨呼队""晚呼队"。当时的书店都是开架经营，读者可以自由翻阅，一些书店还挂着"欢迎看书"的牌子，甚至免费供应开水，故而每天都有不少爱书人在此阅读学习。《锦城旧事竹枝词》中这样描述："琳琅满目读书香，不逛公园逛店堂。开架任君随意取，一卷忘饥坐中央。"一直到"文革"以前，祠堂街还有古旧书店。一直到改革开放之初，祠堂街还有教材书店和少儿书店。

1942 年的祠堂街的开明书店　杨永琼提供

1938 年 4 月，中国共产党在国统区内唯一被允许公开发行的报纸《新华日报》的成都代订处（也称川西北总分销处或成都分馆，由于这里也出售包括延安出版物在内的各种进步书籍，所以也被称为新华书店）设在本街的 103 号（开办不久改为 88 号，即今祠堂街 38 号），一直到 1947 年 3 月最后撤离，在成都坚持战斗了 8 年，一度成为中国共产党在成都唯一公开的对外联络处。这个当年《新华日报》的革命先辈们工作与战斗过的地方，现在已经成为很多人追寻瞻仰的革命纪念地。需要指出的是，近年成都媒体不少文章对这里的报道多次出现过一些不准确的说明文字，最重要的错误之处是说"周恩来、刘少奇、陈毅等重要人物先后来此工作过"。事实是，刘少奇和陈毅在抗日战争时期根本就没有来过四川，来此工作和视察过的领导同志有周恩来、董必武、彭德怀、林伯渠、吴玉章、邓颖超等。

2011 年的《新华日报》成都分馆旧址　杨显峰摄影

抗日战争时期由中共地下党组织所领导的进步报刊如车耀先主持的《大声》周刊，胡绩伟、熊复主编的《星芒》周报和外围组织星芒社，康乃尔、吴德让主编的成都学联机关刊物《战时学生旬刊》，还有团结在党周围的由周文任主编的中华全国文艺界抗敌协会成都分会机关刊物《笔阵》、由陈思苓任主编的成都文化界救亡协会创办的《金箭》半月刊、杨道生任经理的成都战时出版社、由姚雪岩任经理的莽原出版社、由饶孟文为主编的文化社团群力社等也都设在这里。1938 年 4 月在这里成立了以杨道生为书记的成都图书业支部（杨道生是清华学生，1941 年被捕，1942 年 6 月 3 日牺牲于沙河铺厚生农场）。

由于在文化街上比较容易掩护，所以中国共产党在成都的地下活动据点曾经设在这里。据统计，中共中央南方局、中共四川省委和成都市委先后在这条街上建立过 7 个支部和秘密的联络点、交通站，在国民党发动的 3 次反共高潮中先后有包括罗世文、车耀先在内的 20 多位共产党员在这里被捕，所以这条文化街在当时又有"革命街"之美誉。

"革命街"上当然不止有革命力量。据一个中统特务的回忆，就在祠堂街

88 号对门一个茶楼的二楼上，就是国民党特务在"成都的最大监视哨之一，一些血债累累的特务往来其间，专门监视、守候和盯梢新华书店、生活书店、新知书店、战时出版社、《大声》周刊社、《战时学生》旬刊社、星芒社、群力社的工作人员、读者和与之往来的群众"。特务们"定期在此交换情报，有时还从监狱里带出被捕者坐在茶楼上，指认进出上列书店的人员"。1940 年，被特务误抓的空军军官和特务还在茶楼里发生过一场枪战。

1941 年，由原来的"蜀艺社""蓉社""成都美术协会"合并而成的四川美术协会成立于祠堂街上的少城公园，团结了当时国内一大批知名美术家从事抗战宣传与美术创作活动，以致当时的四川省主席张群也出任了协会的会长，国民党四川省党部书记长罗文谟出任了协会常务理事，不过具体的负责人是担任常务理事兼总务的四川著名画家张采芹（1901—1984）。在四川美术协会的组织与协助之下，张大千、徐悲鸿、吴作人、傅抱石、潘天寿、黄君璧、赵少昂、关山月、吴一峰、岑学恭等的画展相继展出，张大千的各种画展就先后举办了 6 次。成都人十分熟悉的孙中山先生铜像和无名英雄铜像，都是在四川美术协会的大力支持与协助下，由著名雕塑家刘开渠创作的。这个时期是成都现代美术创作最活跃的时期。2005 年，成都市有关部门在人民公园内建成了四川美术协会故址纪念碑。

2010 年的四川美术协会故址纪念碑　杨显峰摄影

在成都市声名远扬的川菜馆"努力餐"，1933年从三桥南街迁来祠堂街137号，直到1983年因为街道扩建才迁与祠堂街相邻的金河路。

还有一件与川菜发展史有关的大事也发生在这条街上。清光绪二十四年（1898），曾经在北京餐馆闯荡10年、在江浙等地长期考察各地名菜的合江人李九如在华兴街开办了近代川菜形成时期最著名的餐馆之一聚丰园，集南北菜肴之精华，又有多项创新（例如今天十分流行的"一鸡三吃"，在当年的聚丰园早就有了，而且是"一鸡六吃"），包席与散客并重，还做满汉全席，一时间轰动全城。经新派官员四川劝业道周善培的安排并得到成都将军卓哈布的支持，聚丰园于光绪三十三年（1907）迁至满城内的祠堂街关帝庙旁，这是清末新政之后汉族人进入满城开设的第一个商铺。聚丰园不仅有当时最高档次的川菜，同时也供应西餐，还有北京烤鸭、生片火锅和绍酒（以后还引入了冰糕和冰淇淋），在店堂布置上第一家使用台布、西式刀叉和高脚酒杯，服务生要经过培训，要讲究迎客站姿，开创了川菜西吃的先例，对后来成都餐饮业的发展产生过重要影响。成都著名文士刘师亮有《竹枝词》写道："聚丰餐馆设中西，布置精良食品齐。偷向玻璃窗内望，何人依桌醉如泥？"被老成都称之为聚丰南堂（清末民初时期，成都人把从江南入川的外乡人开设的具有新式风格的餐馆称之为江南馆子或南堂）的这家著名餐馆一直经营到1944年才歇业。

祠堂街上的四川电影院建于1952年，是成都最有名的电影院之一。这里最早是清代的少城书院，1931年在这里开办了西蜀大舞台，1937年改名天府大戏院。因为新又新剧社长期在此演出川剧，所以又称新又新大舞台，1939年正式改名新又新大戏院。因为两次遭遇火灾，1947年重建之后更名为锦屏大戏院，曾经是成都最有名的剧场之一，也是成都最早修成梯形的前低后高的剧场。从抗日战争时期直到成都解放，其川剧演出的阵容不在悦来茶园之下。更重要的是，在著名剧作家、有"川剧时装戏奠基人"之称的刘怀叙与著名导演与演员周海滨的主持下，这里是川剧界最早、最成功地新编演出现代戏（当时称时装戏）的剧场。刘怀叙一生中先后创作了140多个时装戏，如《哑妇与娇妻》《灵魂的安慰》《农家女》《天字第一号》《自残》（根据话剧《雷雨》改编）等都获得了巨大的成功，抗战戏《滕县殉国记》仅团体票就订出50多场，爱情悲剧《是谁害了她》1981年被犍为川剧团重排后在成都演出仍然受到热烈欢迎。当代川剧演员中的著名前辈如阳友鹤、萧克琴、吴晓雷、刘成基（当头棒）、谢文新、陈书舫等都曾长期在这里演出，阳友鹤与陈书舫都成功地演出过时装戏。1947年刘成基在舞台上自编新词猛烈抨击社会之黑暗，曾遭反动当局拘捕。设于这里的又新科社（过去戏曲界培养学生的机构称为科班或科社，又新科社在中华人民共和国成立以后发展成了现在的乐山川剧团）则是民国时期培养川剧人才最多的科班之一。有不少研究者认为，如果说华新街的悦来茶园是近代川剧形成的摇篮与大本营的话，祠堂街的新又新大舞台就是传统川剧改革与创新的最大一块成功的实验场。中华人民共和国成立以后，锦屏大戏院更名为川西剧院，1952年更名为四川电影院。

民国时期成都最有名的专业童装店"绮罗"开设于此街，女主人曾留学日本，制作出售的童装以高雅与"洋气"闻名全城。

民国时期的少城公园入口处　杨显峰提供

在祠堂街南侧有一块成都市中心最大的绿色景区，这就是全省乃至全中国最早的公园之一的人民公园。人民公园这一大片地区原来是满城中南边的一大块空地，主要是菜园，此外还有稻田、箭厅、马厩、禄米仓（按照清代的规定，满蒙八旗官兵及其眷属均不务农、不经商等，定期由政府发给生活所需要的禄米与银钱，禄米仓就是储存与发放禄米的官仓），也包括永清、永济、永顺等胡同。清代晚期，官方的财政日益困难，原有的各项制度也逐渐松弛，这其中也就包括按"八旗子弟、人尽为兵"的制度而来的满蒙八旗官兵及其眷属均不从事务农经商等产业，定期由政府发给生活所需要的禄米与银钱的制度。北京城中在八国联军入侵之后曾经出现大量旗人因生计无着而卖房卖地乃至卖儿卖女的现象，以至时人有"当年紫气指辽东，武帝旌旗在眼中。三百年来一刹那，日去暮矣更途穷"的诗句。加之国内民族主义情绪高涨，要求"平满汉"的呼声愈演愈烈。1907年，慈禧太后发布了有关"现在满汉畛域应如何全行化除，著内外各衙门各抒己见，将切实办法妥议具奏"的上谕。从此以后，全国各地逐步"平满汉畛域"，满汉分治的严格界限迅速被打破，成都满城与城外汉族居住区最重要的联系通道祠堂街成为第一条出现变化的街道，也就逐渐开设了一些商铺。到清王朝最后一年的1911年，成都将军玉昆与成都劝业道周孝怀决定开放满城，把这一片空地辟为少城公园。其主原因是考虑到1907年清王朝曾经下过《裁停旗饷》诏，只是因为各地旗人的坚决反对才未能真正实行。如果真正要裁停旗饷的话，旗人的终身供给制度就得废除，所以要千方百计为旗人寻找一定的生活来源。公园建成之后，旗人就可以通过出售公园门票和在里面搞一些经营，卖饭卖茶，得到一些收入。辛亥革命之后有《竹枝词》写此事道："八旗坐吃祖宗饭，提笼斗鸟丢江山。六六大顺输到底，禄米官仓变公园。"少城公园最初的大门是开向西侧的永兴街口，即以前使用过的保路纪念碑北边的那道小门的位置。

我国最早的公园于1868年出现在上海的租界里，只供外国人游玩，1886年才对中国人开放，名字一直叫公家花园。为广大市民开放的公园以1907年的北京动物园为最早，但是叫作京师万牲园。据研究，"公园"之称是从日本引进的，全国以公园为名而又对广大市民开放的公园以成都为最早，当时的正式名称就只是叫"公园"，并无"少城"二字。少城公园这一称呼是因为人们以其地处少城之内而加上去的，约定俗成之后才成为正式的名称。从这一意义上说，成都的少城公园是我国最早建成使用的一处公园。1950年，少城公园改名为人民公园。

最初的少城公园的位置是在今天的保路纪念碑以东的一片地区，修建有迎禧楼、观稼楼、松韵楼和湖心亭，面积约50多亩，约占今天人民公园总面积的五分之一。这以后经过多年陆续扩建（最重要的扩建在1914年），渐成规模，成为成都市功能最多的公园。不仅是当年成都市最大的综合性文化设施所在地，又是当年成都市最大的群众活动与集会的场所，民国时期省市各界群众多次的大型集会都是在这里举行的。其中包括五四运动中1919年5月25日成都60多所学校的师生以及各界群众一万余人在这里举行的声援北京学生的大会，1919年6月8日成都各界群众两万多人举行的声讨北洋政府卖国行为、号召抵制日货的国民大会，1924年成都市第一次纪念"五一"劳动节并追悼列宁的群众大会，1925年追悼孙中山先生的群众大会，1928年追悼中国共产党川西特委负责人袁诗尧等14位死难烈士的群众大会，1937年9月5日各界群众5万多人举行的欢送川军出川抗敌的大会（川军出川抗日的先头部队是在9月1日分东、北两路出发的，所以一年后把"九一"定为川军参战永久纪念日），1941年为声讨日本侵略者疯狂轰炸成都（包括少城公园地区）的群众大会……此外，成都市第一届市民运动大会也是于1939年10月14日在少城公园举行的。

成都各界1939年7月7日在少城公园举行抗日救国纪念大会　杨显峰提供

中华人民共和国成立以前，公园内建有四川省立图书馆（初建于1912年，首任馆长为著名学者林思进，因为馆址四周种有松树80棵，故又名八十松馆）、通俗教育馆、金石陈列馆（四川省立博物馆的前身，1941年3月在皇城内明远楼正式改建为四川博物馆，1949年又迁回人民公园，1965年迁至人民南路四段，2002年7月闭馆拆迁，2009年5月1日浣花南路新馆开馆）、音乐演奏室、游艺场、动物园、体育场馆（包括足球场、篮球场、排球场、网球场、田径场）、射箭靶场（成都有名的射德会就设在旁边的茶馆里）、戏园（即万春茶园，这是成都继可园与悦来茶园之后的第三个戏园，建成于1912年，成都最早的话剧团春柳剧社于1918年在此演出过成都最早的话剧，以后还有一九剧社、美化社、四川戏剧协社等话剧团体在此演出话剧，1930年改建为大光明电影院，1941年因为已成危房而拆除）、餐馆（包括著名的晋邻饭店）、少城佛学社与成都佛经流通处（中华人民共和国成立以后出任中国佛教协会副会长的著名佛学大师能海法师是少城佛学社与成都佛经流通处的主持者之一，著名的太虚法师也曾在这里讲经说法），并于小南街引金河水入园再出园汇于半边桥，凿渠的泥土则垒成了假山。这一切，多得力于1924年担任通俗教育馆馆长的著名的爱国实业家卢作孚。

卢作孚（1893—1952）合川人。1908年到成都读书，辛亥革命前参加同盟会。1914年出游全国，返川后在成都任《群报》《川报》的记者、编辑、社长兼总编辑。其间参加少年中国学会，是五四运动的积极参加者。1924年应杨森（时任督理四川军务兼摄省长，简称督军）之邀，出任四川教育厅厅长兼成都通俗教育馆馆长，为少城公园的建设做出了很大的贡献。1926年在重庆创建民生公司，开创民营的川江航运。1927年担任峡防局长，建成了著名的

卢作孚

北碚实验区。1929年出任川江航务管理处长。抗日战争爆发后，他主持了著名的宜昌抢运，开创了川江夜航，将几十万吨军工器材和迁川工厂物资抢运入川，又将20万川中健儿与大量支前物资运往前线。从1935年开始，他兼任四川建设厅厅长，为四川工业建设和水利建设致力不少。通过多年努力，

民生公司成为拥有江海轮船 150 多艘的中国第一航运巨头。中华人民共和国成立之初，他成为全国政协委员和西南军政委员会委员，继续担任民生公司总经理。1952 年，在"五反"运动中不幸逝世。就在他逝世之后不久，毛泽东主席说"中国实业界有四个人不能忘记"，其中之一就是"发展交通运输的卢作孚"。

当年公园中最重要的文化场所就是卢作孚创办并担任馆长的通俗教育馆，内分图书、博物、体育、音乐、讲演、出版、游艺、事务八部，为成都近代文化的传播做出了很大的贡献。通俗教育馆这一名称不是成都自己确定的，而是当时的北洋政府对于全国各地的社会教育机构的统一名称。1934 年，根据南京国民政府的规定，通俗教育馆又改名为民众教育馆，整个少城公园也都由它管理。成都民众教育馆最后一任馆长是曾任《新新新闻》采访部主任的著名记者邓穆卿（1908—2002）。成都民众教育馆一直工作到中华人民共和国成立以后才撤销，其职能由新建立的多家文化机构分担。

人民公园中最重要与最著名的文物首推 1914 年建成的"辛亥秋保路死事纪念碑"，这是当年的川汉铁路总公司为了纪念保路运动中的众多死难烈士而修建的。碑高 31.85 米，由留学日本学习土木工程的双流人王楠设计，胡炳森监督施工，设计时参照了北京白云寺塔和山西凌云寺塔的造型，由基脚、台基、碑座、碑身、碑顶五部分组成，中西合璧，巍峨雄伟，肃穆庄重，宛如一柄长剑直指苍穹，具有浓郁的碑塔一体的传统建筑风格。碑身四周有四位著名学者与书法家书写的"辛亥秋保路死事纪念碑"十个大字，字径一米见方，即名山吴之英的隶书（东面）、华阳颜楷的魏碑（南面）、灌县张夔阶的篆书（西面）、荣县赵熙的汉碑（北面）。1933 年，纪念碑经受了叠溪大地震的考验。1941 年 7 月 27 日日本侵略者对成都进行野蛮轰炸的主要目标之一就是少城公园，除了公园防空壕内的民众死伤几百人之外，纪念碑的宝顶部分也有所损坏。中华人民共和国成立以后曾经进行过修复，1980 年又进行了一次全面的修葺，1988 年被公布为国家级重点文物保护单位。

"辛亥秋保路死事纪念碑"的修建最初选址并不是在少城公园内，而是在督院街的原总督衙门，因为这里是保路运动"成都血案"中成都群众抛洒热血的地方。此时住在原总督衙门中的川军第二师师长彭光烈已经准备将他的师部迁出并拆除周围民房进行修建。由于更多的意见是怕因为拆除民房而引起扰民纠纷，又才重新商议，一致同意了当时的四川巡按使胡景伊的提议，改修在了少城公园之中。

人民公园中原来还有著名抗日将领王铭章的骑马铜像，为著名雕塑家刘开渠塑造，已在中华人民共和国成立之后被拆除。

> **王铭章**（1893—1938）新都人。1909 年入四川陆军小学学习，从此进入川军。1925 年升任师长，1932 年曾兼任成都城防司令，1936 年授中将衔。抗日战争全面爆发之后，他主动请缨杀敌，曾经在德阳的部队誓师大会上慷慨陈词，决心以报效国家的实际行动赎回过去在参加内战之中的罪愆。1937 年 9 月 5 日，他率川军第四十一军一二二师在邓锡侯的指挥之下徒步出川参加抗战。10 月下旬，即在山西娘子关西南部与使用飞机、坦克、火焰喷射器与毒瓦斯的日寇血战 7 天，夺回了平遥县城。然后转往徐州一线，参加了著名的台儿庄保卫战，担任四十一军前敌总指挥，在滕县阻击南下之敌军。1938 年 3 月 14 日，日寇在飞机、坦克、大炮的掩护下疯狂进攻，王铭章率部以步枪与大刀拼死抵抗。当时滕县城内的兵力不到三千，而进攻的敌人超过三万，投弹扫射的飞机有 20 多架。在与敌人血战四天四夜之后，弹尽粮绝，王铭章于 17 日牺牲在电灯厂附近的阵地上，临终时还高呼"拼到最后一滴血""中华民族万岁"（在文艺作品中都说王铭章是举枪自尽，这是不准确的。王铭章是被日寇机枪扫射身中七弹而牺牲的）。第五战区司令长官李宗仁将军说："若无滕县之死守，焉有台儿庄之大捷？台儿庄之战果，实滕县先烈所造成也。"王铭章的灵柩运抵家乡途中，在汉口、重庆、成都举行了公祭，国民政府追授上将衔，毛泽东主席赠送了如下的挽联："奋战守孤城，视死如归，是革命军人本色；决心歼强敌，以身殉国，为中华民族争光。"在将军的家乡新都修建了王铭章墓园，1941 年修建了铭章中学，当时的国民政府主席林森在门额上题写了"壮节殊勋"四个大字。1947 年，成都人民为他塑造了铜像。1984 年 9 月 1 日，四川省人民政府追认王铭章为革命烈士，在新都区新建了

墓园，重建了铜像。当年的铭章中学就是今新都一中，校园内还建有一处
"铭园"。

20世纪40年代的王铭章塑像　建川博物馆提供

人民公园中的鹤鸣茶社沿湖而建，垂柳依依，花木扶疏，最早是一位龚姓
的大邑人开办的，是成都最有代表性的传统茶馆，也是全国最著名的茶馆之
一。凡是过去在成都生活过的前辈回到成都，几乎无一不再到这里一边喝茶一
边回味老成都，包括杨尚昆、张爱萍、魏传统等老一辈无产阶级革命家在内。
1943年，学界泰斗陈寅恪先生曾经与著名学者邵祖平先生在少城公园绿荫阁
茶馆喝茶，邵祖平先生在《培风楼诗存》中留有《初夏同寅恪少城公园绿荫
阁茗坐》一诗记其事："初夏暄风已扇蒸，石榴红破两三棱。茶棚凉对修楠
荫，倦客闲同祝发僧。谈士何妨收稷下，老师应复穗兰陵。少城我亦携家久，
懒惰吟情百未能。"

鹤鸣茶社的开办时间尚待考证，笔者目前所见的有三种说法：1914年、
1920年、1923年。鹤鸣茶社的匾额是由书法家王稼桢于1940年题写的，曾经
在1952年被拆除，1988年又请王老重新题写。成都老茶馆中的形形色色在鹤
鸣茶社中可谓是应有尽有，而具有独特性的文化特色是民国时期在这里进行的
"六腊战争"。

民国时期的少城公园一共有六家茶馆：从祠堂街跨过金河不远就是"枕

流"，"枕流"再往前走几十步就是"鹤鸣"，"鹤鸣"对面一溪之隔是"绿荫阁"，"绿荫阁"东面相邻的是"永聚"，"永聚"北面一溪之隔是"浓荫楼"，保路纪念碑旁边是"射德会"。各行各业习惯分别在此聚会，如"枕流"以学生居多，"绿荫阁"以士绅居多，"永聚"以商界居多，"射德会"以国术界居多，"鹤鸣"的主要茶客是教师与公职人员。当时的教师与公职人员都是聘用制，每逢暑假的六月间与寒假的腊月间，绝大多数教师都会面临着还能不能得到下学期聘书的衣食大事，很多公职人员也有在第二年或下半年还能不能得到聘书的问题。所以，每逢六月与腊月间，鹤鸣茶社中就会聚集着大量的教师与公职人员在这里交流信息、请托关系，为能够拿到聘书、不致失业而千方百计地努力，各校的校长也往往在这里选择他所需要的教师，甚至当场下聘，所以这里就成了充满竞争的人才市场。当时的成都人就把在这里的激烈竞争称之为"六腊战争"，鹤鸣茶社也就成了远近闻名的"六腊战争"的主战场。

当然，少城公园的主要功能是为广大游客提供休闲娱乐服务，正如民国时期的《竹枝词》所写的："丝管东墙聒耳嘈，打球人集笑声高。横生一种郊原趣，短短篱边夹竹桃。""公园啜茗任勾留，男女双方讲自由。体育场中添色彩，网球打罢又皮球。"在当时算是新玩意儿的很多东西，在成都最先都是出现在少城公园之中，例如动物园、喷水池等。民国时期一首记述少城公园风物的《竹枝词》曾这样描述当时难得一见的"喷水机"："喷水全凭压力多，冲天直射怪如何。莲花疑是仙童化，故向荷池尿倒屙。"

1943 年著名学者罗忠恕在鹤鸣茶社　　[英] 李约瑟摄影　杨显峰提供

　　休闲娱乐当然也包括体育活动在内。当年的少城公园是全成都体育场地、体育设施与体育赛事最多的地方，曾经有"体育公园"之称。国内很多体育明星如足球的李惠堂，网球的林宝华，篮球的王玉增、鲍文沛等都曾经在这里显过身手。中华人民共和国成立以后先后担任国家女排主力和教练的我国女子排球的重要奠基者之一的王德芬当年是甫澄中学女排运动员，另一位国家女排主力阚永伍当年是树德中学女排队员，都是在这里培养出来的。而以下的《竹枝词》则应当是成都最早的一首记述足球比赛的诗作："场平草浅夕阳红，如织人来罨画中。学子争夸腰脚健，皮球高蹴篱云空。"从这里可以得知，当年少城公园中的足球场是有草皮的。

20 世纪 80 年代的人民公园航拍图　陈德龙摄影

成都最早的棋社成都围棋社也是成立于少城公园的浓荫楼茶馆中，时间在
1935 年，首任社长是刘扶一，正副会长是黄慕颜与谢德堪（几年之后成都围
棋社迁至提督街三义庙）。当时公园中的另一个永聚茶馆则是成都中国象棋的
窝子。中华人民共和国成立以后还纵横成都棋坛的围棋名家杜君果、象棋名家
贾题韬都是从少城公园成长起来的。

还有一件事不能忘记。1940 年 9 月，少城公园曾经遭到日本侵略者的轰
炸。1941 年 7 月 27 日，日本侵略者轰炸成都时，少城公园以及周围的长顺街、
东城根街一带再遭其祸。侵略者不仅投掷炸弹，还对公园中的游人使用机枪扫
射，使得公园中死伤无数，树枝上遍挂死者腑脏，不少建筑物严重受损，大光
明电影院就是在这次轰炸中因为毁坏严重而拆除的。

柿子巷

柿子巷位于同仁路与金河路之间，是一条 L 形的街道。原来是清代满城之中的太平胡同。民国初年取消胡同的名称，因为街内有一棵柿子树而改名为柿子巷。近年来，因为成都市服务就业管理局职业介绍中心设在这里而为很多成都人所熟知。

闻名全国的四川骨科杜、何、杨、郑四大流派中的两家都出于柿子巷，这就是以杜自明、杜琼书父女为代表的杜氏骨科和以何仁甫、何天祥父子为代表的何氏骨科。他们两家的故宅都在柿子巷。

杜自明（1878—1961）出身于一个满族骨科世家，自幼习武，并随父学习骨科医术。从 1902 年开始悬壶济世，逐渐成为当代骨科泰斗级人物，他的骨科手法与叶心清的金针针刺被时人称为成都的两门绝技。1931 年，成都女子师范学校发生塌楼大事故，伤百余人，经杜自明逐一治疗，没有一例残疾，更无一例死亡，成为中国抢救伤员的一次奇迹。中华人民共和国成立以后被聘到成都铁路医院工作，为当时在修建铁路中大量的骨伤患者解除了病痛。1956 年，因邓小平、贺龙的推荐，以年近80 的高龄进京，在中医研究院创建骨科并

2001 年柿子巷杜自明医馆旧址
冯水木摄影

任主任，以其独特的手法治疗各种骨科难症。铁道兵司令员李寿轩中将多年的脊椎病被他治愈后，下令铁道兵 8 个师各派一名骨科医生来京向他学习。北京很多舞蹈家与著名运动员如陈爱莲、白淑湘、郑凤荣、李富荣等都曾经

接受过他的治疗。他在成都时被选为成都市人民代表，在北京时被选为第三届全国政协委员，有《中医正骨经验概述》《扭挫伤治疗常规》等著作行世。

何仁甫（1895—1969）出身于蒙古族正骨世家，为何氏骨科第四代传人。他武功高强，自制方药，一生中为无数患者解除了病痛，特别是为很多运动员和表演艺术家治好了各种伤痛，往往有手到病除的奇效。撰写有《仁济医话》《无眼斋正骨经验》《特呼尔氏骨科手法》。如今在成都有很高知名度的四川舞蹈损伤研究所所长何天祥、八一骨科医院院长何天佐、四川省中医研究院骨科医院院长何天祺都是何仁甫之子。

将军街

将军街是将军衙门旁边的一条小街，东接东城根上街，西接长顺上街，它的得名却与将军衙门没有任何直接关系。

这条小街原来是清代满城中的永安胡同，因为街口立有一个虎头状的石柱，成都人的口语中把老虎称为猫猫，所以一般人又把这条小街叫作猫猫巷。民国时期，环境幽静、建筑古雅的满城是众多达官贵人选择住宅的主要地区。1925年，另一位川军的主要人物杨森在任四川军务督办时也住进了这条猫猫巷。当他入住猫猫巷不久，就以北洋政府封给他的"森威将军"的名义，下令把这条小街正式命名为将军街。改名的表面理由是因为与将军衙门为邻，而真实理由是因为杨森的绰号叫"耗子精"，在四川方言中"耗子"就是老鼠，所以杨森最讨厌的动物就是猫，故而改名。另有一说是因为"杨""羊"谐音，而"羊"入"虎"口太不吉利，故而改名。

杨　森（1884—1977）四川广安人，1908年入四川陆军速成学堂，毕业后即加入川军，在军阀混战中曾经先后加入多种势力，成为四川军阀中的代表性人物。1920年在任第九师师长、泸永镇守使时，为泸州的建设做过一定的贡献。四川的军阀混战中，杨森在1924年成为北洋政府的陆军上将，担任四川军务善后督办，控制成都地区，在这一时期曾经为成都的城市建设做过贡献。1926年，他以北洋系吴佩孚部四川讨贼联军第一路总司令的身份驻万县与重庆时，英国炮舰在万县制造了著名的"九五惨案"，死伤百姓千余人。杨森在朱德、陈毅的帮助下，扣留英轮并向英舰开战，受到了各界的好评。1926年，在北伐节节

杨　森

胜利的浪潮中，杨森投向国民革命军，任第二十军军长。1933年参加对川陕苏区的"围剿"。在驻防荥经堵截中央红军时，他收到了朱德总司令的信件，于是下令朝天放枪，让红军通过。1937年他率第二十军出川参加抗战，曾在淞沪前线重创日军，名扬全国，以后在湖南与贵州都立有战功。1939年，杨森奉蒋介石密令，制造了杀害新四军干部与家属的"平江惨案"。这以后，杨森于1944年任贵州省主席，1947年任重庆市市长。解放战争中，他的第二十军被解放军痛歼。1949年12月，杨森安排其侄子杨汉烈率重新组建的第二十军在金堂起义，他本人逃往台湾。杨森一生倡导"尚武精神"，提倡"体育救国"，在修建体育设施、组织体育比赛方面有过很多建树，他的部队中专门设有体育处，甚至在1946年担任贵州省主席的时候在贵阳市推行过每天早晨的全市市民的广播体操——复兴操。他去台湾之后仍然一直从事体育事业，长期担任台湾的"中华全国体育协进会"理事长和"奥林匹克运动会"理事长。他本人也身体力行，每周登山一次，70岁学会开飞机，86岁和90岁时两次登上海拔4000多米的玉山。四川军阀之中，杨森是经历最复杂、寿命最长的一位。

将军街40号曾经居住过一个成都当代文化史上最著名的学术之家，这就是赵少咸及其子孙三代。

赵少咸（1884—1966）成都人，年轻时曾因与张培爵（有关介绍见"马镇街"）等缔结反清组织"乙酉学社"而入狱。1918年出任四川省立第一中学校长，此后一直在成都、重庆各校任教，曾任四川大学中文系主任，李一氓、徐仁甫、刘君惠、殷焕先、周法高、李孝定、王利器等均是其弟子。赵少咸一生苦学深研，著述宏丰，是我国著名的古代语言文字学家，特别是音韵学的泰斗级大家，尚未付印的重要著述达800多万字（他与我国另一位古代语言文字学大家黄侃是朋友，他们都特别强调治学的严谨，绝不轻率出版著作，以"50岁以前不言著述"为自律，所以所有的著述都是晚年才修订完成的），其中300多万字的巨著《广韵疏证》、300万字的巨著《经典释文集说附笺》更是在学术界声名远播，著名学者程千帆曾经这样说过："自乾嘉以来三百年中为斯学者，既精且专，先生一人而已。"遗憾的是，他的若干著作还没有来得及出版，就遭遇了"文化大革命"的浩劫。他一生之中的著作手稿与大量藏书共150余箱（其中包括他女婿殷孟伦的藏书）都在1966年秋天被红卫兵抄走，年近八旬的老人气病交加，万分悲痛，于是年12月21日含恨去世。浩劫之中，他的手稿大部分被毁，32册《广韵疏证》手稿仅余8册，30册《经典释文集说附笺》手稿亦仅余8册。他的学生经过整理校订之后，《广韵疏证》和《赵少咸文集》已在近年正式出版。

赵少咸（前中）赵幼文（前左）赵振铎（后右）三代合影

赵少咸一家是当代成都最典型的研究中国传统文化的学术世家，先生的后辈大多学有成就，他的一个儿子赵幼文是中国社会科学院历史研究所研究员、三国史研究专家，另一个儿子赵吕甫是南充师范学院教授、历史学家，他的女婿殷孟伦是山东大学教授、著名的古代语言文字学家，他的孙儿赵振铎是四川大学教授，也是一位著名的古代语言文字学家。

在将军街的东头，今天的成都市儿童专科医院那个地方，原来曾经是当代奇女子董竹君的旧居。

金河路

金河路当然是得名于今天已经不复存在的金河。东起长顺上街口，西至下同仁路口。

金河路原名金河街，是民国初期拆除满城并新开了通惠门之后，从祠堂街到通惠门沿金河新形成的街道。因为与金河为邻，其东段在民国初期还曾有过顺河街的名称。"文革"中因为修建防空洞，金河被毁，但是金河街的街名未改。1987 年，蜀都大道建成之后，改名为金河路，成为蜀都大道的一段。

1990 年金河路成都军区后勤部幼儿园　唐跃武摄影

金河路街北的成都军区后勤部幼儿园旧址是在成都市中心过去很罕见的西式建筑。这里最早是川军旅长杨敏生的公馆，1918 年被日本驻渝领事馆租用作为在成都的办公场所，并以此为基地强行在成都开办驻成都领事馆。按当时有关规定，成都不是通商口岸，不能建领事馆。成都人民为了反对日本帝国主义者在成都开办领事馆，曾经在1926年将这里的领事场所予以捣毁。1931年"九一八"事变后，这个非正式的领事馆在成都人民的强烈抗议之下不得不关闭。以后这处房产是四川军阀王缵绪之子、曾任过国民党军队四十四军中将军长的王泽浚的公馆（王泽浚于1948年11月在淮海战役中被中国人民解放军俘虏，后作为战犯在改造期间病逝于北京秦城监狱），并于1931年改造重建，这就是我们今天所看到的这幢别具一格的楼房。

金河路与小南街交会路口的"努力餐"餐厅不仅是著名的川菜馆，也是成都市重点文物保护单位。1929年5月30日（一说是在1931年）"努力餐"始建于三桥南街南口（位置在今天人民南路的四川剧场对门），1933年5月迁到祠堂街137号，1983年因为扩建蜀都大道，迁到今天金河路的位置，仿其旧貌而重建。"努力餐"餐厅原来是当年中共川西特委负责人车耀先根据党的指示为了掩护革命工作而开设的，得名于孙中山先生遗嘱中"革命尚未成功，同志仍需努力"的名言，是当时中国共产党和各界革命人士进行秘密活动的重要据点，是革命刊物《大声》周刊的编辑部和发行所。成都文化界救亡协会、中苏文化协会成都分会、成都宪政座谈会等革命救亡团体的会议多次在此举行。

"努力餐"餐厅在经营中也很有特色，面向大众，价廉物美。在店堂中挂着这样的对联："要解决吃饭问题，努力，努力；论实行民主主义，庶几（按，即希望能够如此），庶几。"还在店门上写着："包席馆，努力餐，烧什锦，名满川，味道好，精且廉。"每年花会期间"努力餐"都在花会上开设临时餐馆，这时在城墙上打出的广告是"花会场，二仙庵，正中路，树林边。机器面，味道鲜。革命饭，努力餐"。车耀先聘请名厨何金鳌（曾经在滇军中担任朱德的厨师）为首席厨师，价廉物美的特色菜"生烧什锦"是面向大众的名菜，特制的大肉饺子是非拉黄包车的车夫不卖，此外还推出了更加经济实惠的在大米中加入肉粒、笋粒与豆类的碗蒸"革命饭"（这应当视为最早的取得成功的川式快餐），深受广大贫苦大众的欢迎。它的一句宣传广告用语"若我的菜不好，请君向我说；若我的菜好，请君向君的朋友说"至今还以不同的版本被数不清的餐馆袭用，甚至在稍加改动之后为很多服务型企业使用。

2021 年的努力餐　陈轲摄影

车耀先（**1894—1946**）大邑人。1912 年加入川军，在担任川军的团长之时参加革命，1929 年在一片白色恐怖之中加入中国共产党，长期从事党的军运工作，参加策划过 1930 年的"广汉暴动"。1933 年解甲归田，在四川省立成都师范任教。抗日战争爆发之后，他被选为"成都各界华北抗敌后援会"负责人，利用原系川军大邑系的方便和曾经担任二十四军副官长的身份，为党做了大量的工作。特别是他长期从事党的统一战线工作，在社会上有着很高的声誉，被当时的

车耀先

革命同志喻称为"线长"。他所主持的《大声》周刊内部成立有中共党支部，在社会上则被喻为党的"统战部"。《大声》周刊创办于 1937 年 1 月 17 日，短期之内发行量高达 5000 多份，最高时达 7000 多份，并以其读者为主体组织成立了"大声抗日救亡宣传社"（当时简称为"大声社"。社中成立了党支部，社员近千人，分布在省内十几个县），组织了多次《大声》读者座谈会。

《大声》周刊被当局查封后车耀先又出版了《大生》周刊，社址迁到长顺上街益民书店；《大生》周刊被当局查封后车耀先又出版了《图存》周刊，社址迁到中新街 45 号；《图存》周刊被当局查封后车耀先又恢复出版了《大声》周刊，直至 1938 年 8 月被迫停刊为止。三易其名，四次查封，一共出版了 61 期、增刊 7 期，单是毛泽东主席的文章与谈话就刊登过 5 篇。当时在成都的进步人士中流传着这样的顺口溜："要想到延安，去找车耀先。"1940 年 3 月 18 日，车耀先在"努力餐"的楼下被捕，被敌人关押达六年之久，他拒绝了敌人给的四川省政府民政厅长的官职等多种利诱，一直坚贞不屈。1946 年 8 月 18 日，在重庆白公馆监狱的松林坡遇害。

车耀先被捕以后，"努力餐"由其夫人黄体先（车耀先夫妇于 1918 年结婚，当时的农村姑娘一般均有姓无名，故而夫人叫黄三姑娘。车耀先特地给夫人取名叫黄体先，鼓励她身体力行为妇女解放之先锋，放开小足，学习文化，走上社会）与妻弟黄以新继续经营，1950 年交给成都市人民政府。如今在餐厅一楼西头设立有车耀先烈士事迹陈列室。烈士有《自誓》诗一首，值得永远传诵："喜见东方瑞气生，不问收获问耕耘。愿以我血献后土，换得神州永太平。"

东胜街附西胜街

在清代满城之中，长顺街南段的两侧有两条胡同，因为胡同中分别有驻防将军下属的主办吏、户、礼三部事务的右司衙门，和主办兵、刑、工三部事务的左司衙门（吏、户、礼、兵、刑、工这六部是我国古代从隋唐以来中央政府管理天下各方面事务的行政职能部门，清代的驻防将军是皇帝以及满蒙贵族派驻在全国几个军政要地的最高代表，实际上不管理地方的具体政务，这里仿六部而设立的衙门主要是处理满蒙同胞的内部事务和对地方政府进行监督），所以东边的胡同就叫左司胡同，右边的胡同就叫右司胡同。进入民国，废除胡同的称呼，重新命名。为了表示辛亥革命胜利之后的新形势，又因为两条胡同正值将军衙门的两侧，于是就改名为东胜街与西胜街。

东胜街东头北侧的原左司衙门在民国时是民宅，后来由四川军阀唐式遵在这里修建了沙利文饭店（唐式遵的公馆也在东胜街，位置在今四川省文化厅），是民国时期成都最好的西式饭店，当年成都富家子弟的新式婚礼大多在此举行。抗日战争爆发之后，在举国为前线募捐的热潮之中，唐式遵将沙利文饭店的产权捐赠给市政府作为社会公用，由中国共产党地下组织领导的东北救亡总会成都分会曾经设在这里，后来这里设立过美军联络处，抗日名将宋哲元离开军队之后到成都时（宋哲元将军夫人是四川绵阳人，所以他自己生命的最后时光是在四川度过的，死后也葬于绵阳），就曾在此居住。1948年，四川省参议会也曾经迁于饭店内办公。成都解放之初，入城的中国人民解放军负责人与四川地下党负责人正式会师，是在这里举行的；成都市第一届各界人民代表会议也是于1950年3月16日在这里举行的。这以后，成都市政协一直设在这里。

1950 年 3 月，成都市首届各界人民代表会议在原沙利文饭店的这个会议室中召开。

杨显峰提供

沙利文饭店中建有沙利文艺术剧场，1938 年开业，演出话剧、相声、京韵大鼓和各种歌舞，是民国时期成都演艺形式最多的演出场所。

我国当代的传奇女子董竹君在成都的旧居有两处，其一在将军街，另一处就在东胜街。

董竹君（1900—1997）江苏海门人，出身穷苦，13 岁时被卖入妓院为"清倌人"，即卖唱女，学唱京剧。在妓院中结识了在辛亥革命中曾经出任蜀军政府副都督和蜀军总司令、此时正被袁世凯通缉的夏之时，她以心相许，逃出妓院，与夏之时秘密结婚之后到日本留学，时年只有 15 岁。1917 年，她随夏之时回到夏的老家四川合江。1919 年来到成都，先住东胜街，后迁将军街东头今儿童医院处（夏公馆内实行西式的分餐制，这在成都是第一家）。董竹君在成都创办了成都第一个黄包车公司"飞鹰黄包车公司"，又开办了专收女工的富洋织袜厂。因为难以忍受封建大家庭的封闭与桎梏，更不满意夏之时愈来愈严重的消极沉沦，遂放弃了华贵悠闲的生活，与夏之时分手（1934 年宣布离婚），于 1929 年独自带着父母和四个女儿回到上海。她历经艰难困苦，依靠智慧与才能，成为我国现代第一代女企业家，先后创办了群益纱管厂和闻名全国的锦江川菜馆与锦江茶室（以锦江为名，就是她对于十年成都生活的怀念和她自己与锦江边的女诗人薛涛有相近身世的感怀），还创办《上海妇女》杂志。同时她追随革命（她在 1930 年就申请加入中国共产党。党组织从各方面考虑之后劝她以党外人士身份全力办企业，以多种方式支援革命工作，她接受了这种安排），以她的社会关系与经济实力为中国共产党做了很多有益的工作。中华人民共和国成立后周恩来总理曾经专门设家宴感谢她为革命事业所做出的巨大贡献。中华人民共和国成立初期，她将在当时价值 3000 两黄金的所有产业捐给国家，并根据中央与上海市的安排，在锦江川菜馆与锦江茶室的基础之上开办了上海第一家可以接待国宾的锦江饭店，亲自出任董事长与总经理，使锦江饭店成为我国在世界上最为著名的饭店之一，她在有生之年先后接待了 134 个国家的 500 多位元首与政府首脑。她还一直担任全国政协委员，在晚年亲自动笔写作自传《我的一个世纪》。她去世以后，她的祖籍所在地江苏省海门市专门为她建立了董竹君纪念馆。她传奇的一生被拍为 31 集电视剧《世纪人生》，四川省川剧院也演出了川剧《都督夫人董竹君》。

1919 年董竹君（右三）夏之时（右四）与家人在东胜街家中花园。　夏大民提供

四川电视台长期设在东胜街。四川电视台这个位置，曾经是民国时期成都最著名的恶霸与特务头目冷开泰在抗战后期修的公馆。

西胜街在明代有石犀寺，相传其前身是晋代的王羽捐出自己的私宅所修建的龙渊寺，后改名为空慧寺，很可能是成都城区内最早的佛寺。唐代改建之后更名为圣寿寺，是唐代全国七大佛寺之一，也是与大慈寺东西并列的成都第二大佛寺，也和大慈寺一样有大量的精美泥塑与壁画，以有"小李将军"之誉的李升所绘的《出峡图》与《雾中山图》最为出名。玄奘到成都学习佛法时曾住此寺，而且就是在此受戒（有的文章说玄奘受戒是在大慈寺，不确）。圣寿寺内有石犀一座，相传为李冰治水时期的遗物，也是古代成都著名的古迹，所以民间也称圣寿寺为石犀寺或石牛寺，杜甫、岑参、陆游等都有诗咏怀（成都二江在唐代改道之前，内江很可能是从这里流过，所以才会在江边安放石犀，陆游也才会在《谒石犀庙》诗中有"江回陵谷变，碑断市朝非"的感叹）。清代建满城时，石犀寺被迁往南较场侧，在原石犀寺旧址修建了右司衙门，所以李哲生《题咏西胜街石犀》说是"成都古犀今一存，右司井巷西城根"。

光绪末年，在右司衙门旧址开办了第二小学堂。1913 年，初建于玉皇观街的省立第一中学迁到这里，这是四川由政府开办的最早的一所省立中学，成都人一般都称为省一中。五四运动之后，省一中是当时成都革命风气最浓的中学之一，有五分之一的学生加入了共青团，社会上有"要革命，到石犀"的口号，李硕勋（当时名李开灼）、阳翰笙（当时名欧阳本义）都曾经是该校的学生领袖。1928 年，该校师生与反动当局的斗争中爆发了声势浩大的学潮，反对国民党党棍杨廷铨担任校长，并在 2 月 14 日的冲突中将杨廷铨打死，当年称为"一中事件"。2 月 16 日，当局以此事件为由逮捕全市进步师生 100 多人，当天下午将中共党员袁诗荛等 14 人枪杀于下莲池。2 月 22 日，宣布将省一中停办。1933 年，由几位四川地方实力派人物共同开办了协进中学（董事长陈离，董事有张志和、吴景伯、陈书农等，临时校址原来在燕鲁公所），1934 年迁入原省一中校址办学。协进中学仍然是当时革命力量很强的学校，先后有 20 几位中共地下党员在校执教，在教师与学生中都建立有党支部，学生支部成员最多时有 80 多人。特别是在抗日战争时期（为了躲避日本空军的轰炸，1939—1943 年迁到新繁龙藏寺办学），蜀中进步人士将其称为"四川的陕北公学"，成都流传着"要革命，读协进；要救国，到陕北"的顺口溜，龙藏寺被称为"小延安"（据统计，从协进中学走向延安与其他革命工作岗位的学生有100多人）。中华人民共和国成立之后协进中学先后改名为清协联中（由原清华中学与协进中学合并而成）、成都二十八中和金河街中学，1993年恢复协进中学旧名，2009年更名为成都树德协进中学。

李硕勋和夫人赵君陶

李硕勋（1903—1931）高县人，1921年入省立一中读书，1922年6月11日，在四川最早的马克思主义者王右木的领导下，他与同乡、同校又同班的阳翰笙以及高师学生童庸生等在成都《国民公报》上刊登了《四川社会主义青年团成立宣言》（四川社会主义青年团是中国共产党在四川建立组织之前四川最早的党团组织）。1922年11月因被四川军阀刘成勋通缉，乃离开成都到上海入上海大学学习，继续从事革命活动，1924年转为中共党员，从事国共合作工作。他曾经被选为全国学生联合会会长，担任过国民党上海市党部秘书长。1926年担任中共武昌地委组织部长，次年参加南昌起义，任起义军的十一军二十五师党代表兼政治部主任。起义军在广东失利之后，由朱德、周士第和他三人组成了前敌委员会率领部分起义军转入湘南继续活动。10月，他受命潜回上海向党中央汇报工作。此后，他被党中央派往各地从事地下工作，曾经担任中央军委委员、浙江省委军委书记、江南（含当时江苏、安徽、浙江、上海几地）省委军委书记、广东省委军委书记、红七军政治委员。1931 年 7 月在海口被捕，9 月 5 日在海口东较场壮烈牺牲。李硕勋烈士的夫人赵君陶（1903—1985）是中国共产党早期著名领导人赵世炎的胞妹，1926 年入党，曾任湖北妇女协会宣传部长、中共中央妇女工作部负责人。大革命失败后，在成都等地以教师职业为掩护从事地下革命工作。抗日战争时期在中共中央南方局领导下开办保育院，保护和抚育了大批少年儿童。抗日战争胜利以后继续在教育战线工作，1985 年在北京逝世。李鹏同志就是李硕勋和赵君陶的儿子。

阳翰笙（**1902—1992**）高县人，1920 年入省一中读书，与李硕勋同为四川社会主义青年团创始人之一。因为被四川军阀通缉，乃离开成都到上海入上海大学学习，1924 年加入中国社会主义青年团，次年转为中共党员。曾任广州黄埔军校政治教官，参加过南昌起义，任起义军总政治部秘书长。南昌起义失败以后，转入文化战线工作，1928 年任中国左翼作家联盟党团书记、中共中央文化工作委员会党团书记。抗日战争中出任国共合作的国民政府政治部第三厅主任秘书和文化工作委员会副主任。

阳翰笙

中华人民共和国成立以后，曾任政务院文教委员会副秘书长、国务院总理办公室副主任、中国文联副主席和党组书记、中国影协主席。他是著名的剧作家与小说家，电影《万家灯火》《北国江南》，话剧《天国春秋》《草莽英雄》是其代表作。

我国杰出的地质学家黄汲清 1917 年至 1921 年在四川省一中就读。

黄汲清（**1904—1995**）仁寿人，1924 年入北大地质系读书，从此开始了他一生的地质生涯。1929 年至 1930 年，他完成从陕西经四川到贵州的地质考察，写成了著名的《中国南部二叠纪地层》等名著，得到了国际地质界的高度重视，同行多称他为"黄二叠"。1932 年到瑞士留学，获博士学位。1936

年归国后即入中央地质调查所，先后任地质主任、副所长、所长。1937 年组织西北石油考察队到西北考察，发现了我国第一个油田——玉门油田。1938 年又在四川进行考察，在隆昌圣灯山找到并钻井采出了天然气，建成了四川省也是我国第一个天然气田（在此以前，主政四川的刘湘特聘德国地质石油专家萨尔菲尔来川找油找气两年，在多处钻井勘察之后得出的结论是"四川没有有经济价值的油气"）。

黄汲清

这以后，他又考察了著名的四川威远气田、新疆独山子油田，从而在世界上第一个提出了具有重大意义的"陆相生油论"和"多层多期生储油论"。他的工作不仅全面推翻了欧洲地质学家给我国所下的无油无气的错误结论，而且为我国逐步展开的石油天然气开采奠定了坚实的基础，故而被尊称为"中国石油之父""一代地质宗师"。1945 年，他完成了《中国主要地质构造单位》这一世界经典巨著，创立了"多旋回说"等重要理论，建立了中国大地构造理论体系，成为我国历史大地构造学的创始人与奠基人。1946 年，他入选为中央研究院院士，1948 年，主持完成了 1∶300 万中国地质图，对我国的地质工作具有极大的指导作用。

1949 年，他去欧美进行科学访问，国民党方面尽一切力量动员他去台湾，但是他坚决回到了重庆北碚的中国地质调查所，迎接大西南的解放。中华人民共和国成立以后，他作为中国石油地质局总工程师，和另一位地质学家谢家荣一道，领导科技人员先后发现了克拉玛依、大庆、大港、胜利等大油田和四川的大气田，他还主持调查发现了著名的中梁山煤田和东川铜矿。他曾任中国地质学会理事长、中国地质科学院名誉院长、苏黎世大学名誉教授、美洲地质学会名誉会员、苏联科学院外籍院士。黄汲清晚年留给中国科技界的"重磅炸弹"是 1978 年 11 月 14 日在全国科协代表大会上所言："可以得出结论说，大庆、大港、胜利油田的发现与地质力学完全无关。"黄汲清给后人留下的最著名的一句话刻在他自己使用的地质锤上："生不愿封万户侯，但愿一敲天下之石头。"

西胜街东口的少城小学也是一所办学很早的学校。它的前身是清光绪三十年（1904）在满城中拆除少城书院之后，使用拆下来的材料开办的八旗高等小学堂，1912年改名为少城高等小学堂。据有的老人回忆，这个小学内旗杆下的基石就是古老的石犀石破碎之后的残石。

1949年1月，成都地下党的负责人蒲华辅、华健被捕，马识途、王宇光根据上级的安排去香港。10月，在川西的地下党组织成立了川西边临时工作委员会，以李维嘉为书记，主要领导"川康边人民游击纵队"（总部设在雅安，下属有8个支队和两个直属大队）。根据临时工作委员会的决定，11月5日在成都的地下党组织成立了"川西边地下党留蓉临时工作部"（简称"临工部"），由王逸平任书记。"临工部"是中国共产党在旧成都的最后一届地下组织的指挥部，在短时期内为游击队转送成员，筹集武器弹药与药品，保护国家财产和档案文件，策反，准备彭县起义，迎接成都解放，做了大量工作。这个"临工部"就设在西胜街上的金城银行宿舍中进步人士王宏实的住所内。

井巷子

　　下同仁路东侧、窄巷子以南，有一条折弯状的小巷，在清代初年名为如意胡同，后因胡同北部建有明德坊，又名明德胡同。民国初年更名时，因为巷内有一口水井，所以定名为井巷子。

　　井巷子中的这口水井在清代的满城中颇有名气，因为在当地流传着这样一个传说：当清军攻入成都时，很多水井都因为战乱、火灾而被污染或填埋，军队的吃水问题发生了困难。这时，有几匹战马聚在这里用舌头舔着地面不愿离去，清军官兵仔细一看，发现这里的土壤特别潮湿，便向下挖去，很快就挖出了清冽的地下水，解决了军队饮水的困难，于是就在这里凿建了一口水井，还特地用石料修建了井盖。由于这口水井的水质好，水量大，成为满城中最著名的一口水井。

1994 年井巷子中的古井　周孟棋摄影

　　一直到中华人民共和国成立以后，井巷子中的著名水井仍然在使用，而且位置就在巷子的中间。近年来由于水量愈来愈少，已经停止使用。但是为了保留这口著名的水井，又不致妨碍交通，市政部门把井口移向了靠北的人行道上。1990 年，西城区人民政府还在井口旁立了一块石碑，上面写道："此井乃康熙年间满蒙八旗军驻防成都时饮水而凿，地处原少城明德胡同清军营房前。辛亥革命后因巷中有此水井，改名为井巷子。"

2021 年的井巷子　张西南摄影

　　井巷子与邻近的宽巷子、窄巷子一道作为成都市中心的民俗文化街区而进行了整体的改造，成为成都著名的旅游文化区。雕塑家朱成以井巷子南侧原协进中学的围墙为基础，设计建造了老砖艺术墙，在艺术墙上展现了近代成都的民俗文化，成为宽窄巷子民俗文化街区中最有代表性的文化景观。

斌升街

斌升街东为东城根街，西为长顺上街，北为桂花巷，南为东胜街，清代原名斌升胡同，民国时改名斌升街。"斌升"二字乃是一种吉祥用语，"斌"字由文武二字组成，过去称为文武双全，斌升就是寓意文士与武士都能前途远大。

2021 年的斌升街城市艺术壁画　陈轲摄影

中华人民共和国成立以后在斌升街的基建工程中，曾经发现地下有较厚的唐代文化堆积层，其中不仅有开元通宝、乾元通宝等钱币，还有琥珀，估计这一带应当是唐代的南市商业区。

1914 年成都斌升街的德国学校师生合影，这所学校是外国人在四川办的第一所德文学校。　　[德] 魏司摄影

　　清光绪二十九年（1903），在推行清末新政的浪潮中，在街东口建立了第三小学堂，是当时成都最早建立的新式学校之一。

　　1935 年 5 月，著名作家李劼人辞去了重庆民生机器厂厂长职务，回到成都，租住于斌升街 13 号院中。这年夏天，他在这里一口气写出了长篇小说《死水微澜》。这年冬天，又写出了《暴风雨前》的前一部分。次年初，迁居邻近的桂花巷 64 号，写完了《暴风雨前》，并继续写作《大波》。闻名世界的传世之作"大波三部曲"就是在少城之中的这两个小院里问世的。

　　著名学者与诗人庞石帚生前长期居住在本街 5 号。

　　庞石帚（1895—1964）成都人，著名学者赵熙的弟子，其诗名与林思进、向楚齐名，曾任成都师范大学、华西大学与光华大学三个大学的中文系主任，当代著名学者杨明照、屈守元等都是他的学生，中华人民共和国成立以后任四川大学中文系教授、古典文学教研室主任。著有《国故论衡疏证》《养晴室笔记》《养晴室诗录》《养晴室词录》。我国著名的白酒品牌剑南春如今早已闻名遐迩，可是很少有人知道，"剑南春"这个既有历史文化内涵又极有传统酒香的佳名（唐代多以"春"为酒名），就是中华人民共和国成立初期由庞石帚为绵竹酒厂生产的一种优质绵竹大曲酒专门命名的，其根据是唐代李肇在《唐国史补》中的"剑南之烧春"一语。

桂花巷

　　这是清代满城中的一条胡同，因为栽有丹桂而名丹桂胡同，民国初年改为桂花街。因为与南城的桂花街同名（这条桂花街不长，位于指挥街以南，中间以盐道街为界，过去西接东桂街，因为修建岷山饭店而拆除），所以又改名为桂花巷，一直使用到今天。

　　1935年12月，著名作家李劼人从斌升街迁居桂花巷64号"聚园"，在不到两年的时间中，继《死水微澜》之后，在这里写成了他的不朽名著《暴风雨前》和《大波》，著名的《大河三部曲》得以完成。

2021年的桂花巷　陈轲摄影

宽巷子附窄巷子

在清代成都满城的西南角，有两条相邻的胡同叫兴仁胡同和太平胡同，属于当年镶红旗的驻地，因为一条较宽，一条较窄，所以清代就有人将其叫作宽巷子与窄巷子。到了民国时期为满城中的胡同重新命名时，也就将其正式改名为宽巷子与窄巷子。

在过去的满城之中，宽巷子与窄巷子是并不重要的两条胡同，民国时期也少有达官贵人居住，中华人民共和国成立以后也没有机关单位在这里拆除平房改建楼房（据原宽巷子45号的老住户回忆，当时大院内的菜园大约8亩，有一口全城罕见的大口水井用于浇灌，菜农都有好几户。修建体育场时，从东华门迁入了30多户人家前来菜园建房，大院才变成了大杂院）。正是由于这种长期的平民性使得宽巷子与窄巷子基本上没有大拆大改，到了改革开放之后仍然难得地保持了老成都街巷的旧时风貌，保存了一批具有地方特色的小四合院，而没有一幢高楼，使清代至民国时期的建筑风格完整地保留下来，成了成都市中心最有价值的一片老建筑集中区和最有价值的民俗风物保存片区。早在20世纪80年代，成都市有关部门就决定把宽巷子与窄巷子作为城市的特色文化片区加以保护，将其作为供研究者考察和供旅游者参观的窗口。成都市中心一共保留与保护了四个老成都的特色文化片区（宽巷子与窄巷子片区、大慈寺片区、文殊院片区、锦官驿片区），相对来讲，宽巷子与窄巷子片区是保留与保护得最好的一处。无数参观者到此观光，数不清的影视作品在此拍摄，宽巷子与窄巷子已经成为老成都的一个标志。从2005年开始，成都市有关部门对宽巷子与窄巷子（还加上相邻的井巷子）的大多数建筑进行全面重建，为这一片区铺设现代城市的各种管网，修建了地下停车场，并对整个街区进行了全面改造。重建之后的宽窄巷子已经在"5·12"汶川特大地震后的2008年6月正式开街，成为老成都文化的展示区和极有特色的文化旅游街区。

1994 年的宽巷子　陈先敏摄影

改造前的宽巷子　戚亚南摄影

1995 年的窄巷子　张西南摄影

2003 年进行改建的窄巷子　陈先敏摄影

2021 年的宽窄巷子新建砖门　陈轲摄影

我们说宽巷子与窄巷子过去少有达官贵人居住，不是说就没有文化名人和达官贵人居住。例如著名学者张圣奘、李植和徐仁甫，著名民主人士韩文畦、四川师范大学教授郭诚永，还有民国时期成都最著名的恶霸流氓石肇武，都曾经在这里居住。

张圣奘（**1903—1992**）湖北荆州人，张居正十三代孙，自幼随曾担任北洋政府教育总长同时也是著名学者的叔父张国淦长大，在天津南开中学读书时与周恩来同班 4 年。1918 年，年仅 15 岁的张圣奘考入北京大学历史系，成为李大钊的学生、毛泽东的朋友，是马克思主义研究会的 7 名发起人之一。

1922 年，他在上海时以学识与书法被孙中山先生看中，特地让他清抄缮写了著名的《建国方略》。后赴英国、德国、美国留学，精通英、法、德、俄、西、葡、日等国语言和梵文，先后获得了文学、医学、法学、经济学、史学等五个博士学位（值得一提的是，1926 年他在美国俄亥俄州立大学获得经济学博士，论文题目是《计划经济与市场经济的比较研究》，他在牛津大学获得文学博士，论文题目是《杜甫与莎士比亚比较研究》）。在欧洲期间，与周恩来、

张圣奘

邓小平等都是朋友。他还受到过英国女王的接见，和未上台的墨索里尼与希特勒也有过交往。他曾将《周易》译为英文，在英国组织了"神州易经学会"，写有《易经新笺》《易经辩证法》等五部有关周易研究的著作。1929 年回国，先后执教于东北大学（在东北大学期间，他用文言文写成了著名的《回鹘史大纲》一书）、复旦大学、交通大学、重庆大学、中央大学（因为他擅长书画，尤能画马，故与时在中央大学任教的徐悲鸿大师成为至交，当时名噪一时的徐悲鸿与蒋碧微的离婚仪式就是在他家中举行的）等多所学校。因为他精通 9 国语言，开出了 28 门课程，所以被著名学者、中央大学校长罗家伦尊称为"万能教授"，当时的教育部聘他为部聘教授，蒋介石曾经礼请他为其上课，他为蒋介石讲的是《周易》。他是重庆大学的创办人之一，是 1946 年开办在内江的蜀中大学（这是自贡大盐商王、李、颜三家共同出资创办的大学，下设有文学、商学、工学 3 个学院 11 个系科）的主要创办人。1933 年至 1936 年，还曾经在成都主办《新四川报》。1950 年修建成渝铁路时，由他的老朋友邓小平点将，让他出任文物调查征集小组组长，是著名的"资阳人"头骨化石的发现者。1953 年在北京召开"资阳人"学术讨论会之后，毛主席与周总理专门请他在毛主席家中做客，一道进餐，畅叙旧谊。1954 年，他被任命为四川省文物管理委员会办公室主任，主持具体工作，是中华人民共和国成立以后第一次全面考察四川石窟艺术的负责人，发表了《大足安岳的石窟艺术》的重要论文，写出过《编纂中国大百科全书的建议》。1962 年任四川省图书馆研究员，1986 年任四川省文史馆特约馆员、四川省政府参事室参事。他一生喜爱毛主席诗词，曾为 37 首诗词各作唱和 5 首，共得 185 首，精心装裱成卷。"文革"期间他被抄家，诗词手卷竟然被辗

转送到了北京毛主席的手中。毛主席十分高兴，还用铅笔作了圈点。1972年，特地转给章士钊欣赏。章士钊读后又交给了因公到成都的女儿章含之，将诗卷送还给了张圣奘。1991年，他抱病写出了平生最后一篇文章：《我发现资阳的人头骨化石》。他晚年一直住在宽巷子24号邓泽生院中，直至1992年1月7日辞世。

李　植（1885—1975）字培甫，垫江人，同盟会早期会员，辛亥革命元老，曾长期居住在宽巷子19号（晚年居住在焦家巷）。武昌起义之后，他曾在南较场召开万人大会，发表革命演说，同时高悬"同盟会会长孙文"大旗，让孙中山的名字在四川家喻户晓。他曾任大汉四川军政府参赞和四川靖国军总司令部顾问，但是很快就退出了政界。他曾经在日本从章太炎学习国学，是蜀中著名学者，在文字音韵学上有很高造诣，尤其是对"古纽"（即先秦两汉

李　植

时期汉语的声母）的研究有着自成一家的独到见解。中年以后一直在成都各大学任教，曾任成都高师国文部主任、四川大学与成华大学中文系主任，1952年从川大退休。1936年9月27日，四川各界人士公祭于6月14日辞世的章太炎先生，李植撰写的集句联被誉为当代最佳名联之一："富贵不能淫，贫贱不能移，威武不能屈；泰山其颓乎！梁木其朽乎！哲人其萎乎！"

徐仁甫（1901—1988）大竹人，成都高等师范学堂毕业后一直在多所学校执教，潜心于古代汉语的研究，是四川晚清以来"今文经学"派后期的代表学者之一。他一生著述丰富，在改革开放之后的10年间连续出版了《杜诗注解商榷》《广释词》《古诗别解》《广古书疑义举例》等多部学术著作，在学术界影响颇大。笔者在出版社工作时，曾任先生重要著作《左传疏证》一书的责编。

韩文畦（1895—1983）内江人，著名学者、佛学家，擅章草。中华人民共和国成立前曾任西康省教育厅长、西康省通志馆馆长。抗日战争时期在成都创办《重光》月刊，后来成为我国新儒学代表人物之一的唐君毅就是该刊

的编辑。他在 1946 年加入中国民主同盟，曾任民盟成都分部主任委员，为迎接新中国的诞生做了大量有益的工作（有几位前辈在回忆录中都说 1949 年刘文辉等在彭县起义的通电文稿就是由他起草的）。中华人民共和国成立以后，历任川西农林厅副厅长、绵阳专区副专员（笔者那时就读于绵阳高中，曾经听过他给学校师生作的报告）、四川省政协常委、民盟四川省委常委、四川省人民政府参事。他在 1957 年"反右"运动中蒙冤，继而入狱。晚年以"保外就医"名义出狱，就住在窄巷子的女儿家中，直至辞世。

石肇武（？—**1933**）屏山人。自称是太平天国翼王石达开的后代（在四川民间，一直有石达开晚年隐身于江湖，在成都殉难的石达开并不是真正的石达开，而是相貌极似的替身的传说），由土匪而加入川军，拜刘文辉为义父，10 年间官升警卫旅长。他在成都最初的公馆就在宽巷子（时间大约在 1926 年），1931 年才迁往鼓楼南街的新公馆（即有名的"肇第"，两年后即被没收）。石肇武是民国时期成都人最为切齿痛恨的大恶霸、大流氓，奸淫估霸，绑票抢劫，无恶不作，无人不恨，以致在 1933 年军阀混战的"二刘之战"中兵败被李家钰所俘时，刘湘下令立即枪毙，并将割下的首级在人民公园挂笼示众。直到现在，在一些老成都人口中还流传着这样的一个歇后语："石肇武的脑壳——宰了！"

仁厚街

这是原来满城中的仁厚胡同，民国时改名为仁厚街，位于长顺上街与东城根上街之间，北为多子巷，南为桂花巷。

1933 年四川军阀混战时成都市内发生巷战。 此为仁厚街口用街沿石修建的防御工事。　　杨显峰提供

"仁厚"是传统的吉祥语，也是一种道德要求。语出《荀子·富国》："其仁厚足以安之。"

著名国画家陈子庄晚年的住宅在本街 11 号（此前先后在康庄街、宁夏街、江汉路居住）。

陈子庄（1913—1976）号石壶，荣昌人，其父是绘制陶器、纸扇的民间艺人，故而他从小就受到民间艺术的感染。16 岁时来到成都，一边习武，一边绘画，逐渐成为著名的武师与画师，并参加了不少社会活动。1949 年，他协助成功策划了川军王缵绪部的起义，他本人也以国民党军少将的身份起义。中华人民共和国成立以后，他受聘为四川省文史馆馆员，1955 年迁居成都，1963 年成为四川政协委员，长期从事国画创作与授徒。由于他很少与外界交流，所以他的画艺在生前鲜为人知，可是在他死后，尤其在改革开放之后，

却得到了海内外极高的评价，1988 年他的作品在北京的中国美术馆展出时，
被誉为"轰动京华，震惊世界"。在由文化部编辑出版的《中国美术五十年》
中，四川画家列名者只有四人，陈子庄即其中之一（另三人为张大千、石鲁、
蒋兆和），很多研究者认为他是继张大千之后四川画家第一人。特别是他的写
意画中所透出的自然、天真、鲜活的境界，和自成一格的奇兀、峭拔、灵宕
的特色，使很多研究者为之倾倒，被评为"中国的凡·高"。在他的家乡，
已经建成了陈子庄艺术陈列馆。

1976 年 7 月 3 日陈子庄在家中作画

支机石街

　　成都有好几处街道以石命名，可是在成都这个冲积平原上除了河道中的卵石外，不可能有大的石头。成都的建筑用石、园林置石都是从外地运来的。也就是说，大的石头在成都，原本是稀缺的东西，可是成都的历史文化却又与这些外地的大石头有过十分密切的关系。

　　在成都文化公园水池旁，用栏杆保护着一块不规则的方柱形石头，高约两米，上面刻有"支机石"三个大字，这块石头年代久远，大有来历。

放置于成都文化公园中的支机石　杨显峰摄影

　　早在隋代，虞茂就在《织女石》一诗中说："支机就鲸石，拂镜取池灰。船疑海槎渡，珠似客星来。"这是目前在可靠的史料中所见到的最早的关于成都支机石的记载，其中已有很明显的神话色彩。唐代诗人岑参的晚年是在成都度过的，他在成都所留下的诗歌中有一首名叫《卜肆》，其中也说："君平曾卖卜，卜肆著已久。至今杖头钱，时时地上有。不知支机石，还在人间否？"诗中的"卖卜人"与"君平"就是指的汉代成都的著名人物严遵（字君平）。时代稍晚于岑参的赵璘在《因话录》中又说："今成都严真观有一石，俗呼为支机石，皆目云：当时君平留之。"这个神话故事在唐以后多有记载，有多种版本。集大成者应当是明代学者曹学佺在《蜀中广记·人物记·严遵》中所叙述的故事：汉代开通西域的著名大将张骞出使大夏，一直走到了黄河的源头，在归来时乘坐的船中载着一块石头。张骞回家之后，特地请来上知天文下知地理的严君平，问他能否说出这块石头的来历。严君平观察了很久，然后说："去年八月我观察天象，看见有一颗客星进到了牵牛星和织女星的地方，现在看来那就是你行踪的反映了。这块石头就是天上的织女用来垫她的织机的石头，你把它带回人间来了。"张骞说："真是如你所说的那样，我到黄河源头时，看到有一个女子在织布，一个男子在放牛。我问，这是什么地方？织布的女子说这里不是人间的地方。她把一块大石头放在我的船上，叫我回家之后去找成都的严君平，说你一定会把真情实况告诉我。"从此，这块天上织女星织机下面的支机石就留在了成都。

这个神话说明，这块石头在成都人眼中是天上神人送来的不一般的石头。所以，从历代记载中可以清楚地知道，最晚从唐代开始，这块被称为"云藏海客星间石"的石头就被供奉在祭祀严君平的严真观中，上面刻有"支机石"三个篆文大字，原来的高度在两米以上。严真观毁塌之后，仍然立在严真观旧址的空地上。明清时期，这里建成了街道，明代街名不详，清代是满城之中的仁里二条胡同，是个很典型的北方街道名称。但是因为原来曾经有著名的严真观，所以也称为君平胡同。民国时期则改名为支机石街。支机石街原来的严真观旧址在清代改建为关帝庙（按清代的有关规定，满城中只准供奉观音菩萨和关圣帝君，这个规定在清代前期一直被严格遵守，后期才有所松动），成都人也称为支机石庙，支机石就立于庙中。到了清末，庙宇被毁，支机石又立于露天。1924年，兼任成都民众通俗教育馆馆长的著名实业家卢作孚先生曾经打算建立一个支机石公园，但是在那军阀混战不断的年月，他这一愿望未能实现。1985 年，支机石终于得以移入文化公园，实测高度为 2.05 米。原石上所刻的"支机石"三字早已磨灭不显，现在石上的"支机石"三字是移入之时补刻的，书法为著名书画家伍瘦梅手书。

根据学术界基本一致的认识，古蜀时期的成都人有一种对大石的崇拜理念，他们往往在墓地或其他的重要建筑物之前树立着特地从山区运来的一块巨石。古代蜀人的主要先民是羌人，在已经发现的无数古代羌人的石棺墓的葬俗和今天茂县、汶川羌族同胞中仍然保持着白石崇拜的习俗中，完全可以看到这种大石崇拜的影子。所以，成都在今天还保存下来的几处古代的大石崇拜物，以及由此而命名的街道或地名，也就可以找到答案了，原来这些都是古蜀先民大石崇拜的遗迹。由于祖先过去所选择并运来平原地区的这些大石都是要竖立起来用为某种标志的，所以大多是碑状、笋状。清人的《竹枝词》有这样的记载："华阳尉左武担山，别有天涯石可攀。评古吊今情不已，支机石在满城间。"对于这些大石的用途，古人有一些很有价值的判断。例如清代著名诗人吴伟业在《成都》一诗中所说的"鱼凫开国险，花月锦城香。巨石当门观，奇书刻渺茫"。他所说的"门观"，与今天历史学家认为是大型建筑之前的标志物（四川是我国著名的汉阙之乡，汉阙也就是汉代大型建筑之前的标志物即门观）的判断基本上是一致的。

为了今天仍然能够在成都人的心目中继续保持对于古老的大石文化的点滴记忆，成都在近年来的城市建设中以不经意的方式做了许多工作。例如，在府河与南河的综合整治中，特地在两岸绿地中以园中置石的手法安排景观工程，摆放了若干巨石；在琴台路的改建工程中，特地在南头设计了若干块高大的石碑；在浣花溪及其下游南河之侧，特地把一条由滨江路向西延伸新建的长街命名为大石东路与大石西路等等，这些都是有意而为之的对古老历史的回顾。

现在支机石已经移到了文化公园，但位于老满城之中的支机石街仍然存在，东接长顺街，西接同仁路。相传这条街的西段就是汉代严君平读书授徒卖卜的地方，在唐代被称为君平卜肆。唐代建成了严真观，宋代的吕公弼在《严真观》一诗中写道："卜肆垂帘地，依然门径开。……空余旧机石，岁岁长春苔。"可见当时的支机石就在严真观中。

2006 年，在支机石街与同仁路的交会处，新建了一个小游园，按目前文化公园中的支机石的形状复制了一个支机石，作为支机石街的标志。

有一点需要说明的是，在目前成都的很多书籍、地图与公共标志中，包括具有权威性的《四川省成都市地名录》，都是把"支机石"写作"支矶石"。这是不对的，应当写作"支机石"。一来在古代文献中就是写的支机石，二来这个机原本就是纺织机的意思。1987 年版《成都城坊古迹考》一书中就一直写为"机"。1992 年，《成都城区街名通览》一书在"支矶石街"之下明确指出"'矶'应是'机'之讹"，可是这一错误一直未能得到纠正。笔者在本书中对于街道名称的写法，是严格依照具有权威性的《四川省成都市地名录》，但是在这里却是一个例外，所以有必要加以说明。

民国时期成都名医张先识所创的"汲古医学社"开办在支机石街。

民国时期政坛著名人物李璜的故宅在支机石街。

李　璜（1895—1991）成都人，13 岁入成都洋务局英法文官学堂，以后就学于上海震旦学院，1918 年在北京与王光祈、李大钊等共同组建少年中国学会。1919 年赴法国留学。1923 年在巴黎与曾琦等创建中国青年党，提倡国家主义，反对共产主义。1924 年回国后历任北京大学、成都大学等校教授，著作有《法国文学史》《欧洲远古文化史》《国家主义的教育》等。与此同时，创办《醒狮》周报，宣传反共反苏，成为"醒狮派"的代表人物。抗日战争时期追随

李　璜

国民党，曾出任国防最高委员会参议、国民参政会参政员并任国民参政会主席团主席。1945 年任联合国制宪大会中国代表团成员。国民党政府曾任命他为经济部部长，因病未就任。1949 年去香港，后去台湾，名义上任台湾"总统府"国策顾问，实际上未从事政治活动，而从事中华民国史研究。

多子巷

今天的东城根上街与长顺上街之间，有一条多子巷，共青团四川省委办公楼就在巷子的东头。

作为满城的众多胡同之一，多子巷原名太平胡同，里面有一些为满蒙八旗制造刀枪兵器的匠铺，到了民国时期，就改称为"刀子巷"。川军首领刘湘（关于刘湘的介绍见"体院路"）的宅院就在这条巷子里。1935年，刘湘听从了著名学者张圣奘（当时刘湘正聘请张圣奘来成都主办《新四川报》，住在刘湘公馆中。关于张圣奘的介绍见"宽巷子"）的建议，将刀子巷改名为多子巷，一来是因为刀子巷的名字暗藏凶机，太不吉利；二来是因为刘湘的长子与次子均早逝，当时只有一子一女，为了求得多子多福，所以改名为多子巷。

成都城内过去还有一条刀子巷，就是今天位于大业路与青石桥之间的向阳街，因为与满城中的刀子巷重名，所以在民国时期就改名为向阳街。

多子巷中的刘湘公馆　杨显峰提供

著名的书法篆刻家余中英的故宅就在多子巷的东头（去世之前住在支机石街朋友家）。

余中英（**1899—1983**）号兴公，成都郫县人。从成都陆军小学毕业之后，一方面在川军中任职，一方面醉心于金石书画，曾在辞去军职之后专门到北京向齐白石大师学习，成为白石入门弟子。他在书法艺术上的造诣很深，是现当代成都籍书法家中成就最高的一位。抗日战争开始之后，曾任第七战区中将副参谋长、四川行营副参谋长、成都市市长等职。他在 1940—1944 年担任成都市长期间，对市政建设多有建树，如开办了第一所市

余中英

立公立医院和第一个市立公办中学，开建了自来水厂，开通了从牛市口到茶店子的私营公共汽车等。中华人民共和国成立以后，被聘为四川省文史研究馆馆员，并被选为四川省政协委员，中国书法家协会四川省分会副主席。

泡桐树街

泡桐树街位于实业街与支机石街之间，原来是清代满城之中的仁里胡同。民国初年取消胡同的名称，因为街内有一棵大泡桐树而改名为泡桐树街。

创建于 1961 年的泡桐树街小学是教育部授牌的全国现代教育技术实验学校，位于本街的东头，是四川省和成都市最负盛名的小学之一。

2021 年的泡桐树街小学　陈轲摄影

四川省第一条公路成灌公路的修建与管理单位成灌马路总局当年就设在泡桐树街。据笔者所知，我国所筹划修建的第一条公路不是在沿海，而是成都的成灌公路。1912 年，护理四川都督胡景伊采纳了一些新派人物的建议，决定在成都与灌县之间修建一条可以通行汽车的公路（当时叫马路），委派巡警总监戴鸿畴为总办，聘请刘锡松为主任技师。测出的线路就是今天的老成灌路，全长 55 公里。修筑是从灌县首先开工。因为沿途均有人以"破坏风水、有扰墓地"等种种理由坚决反对，特别是沿途四县（成都、郫县、崇宁、灌县）的哥老会全部不予支持，所以只修了一公里示范性的路基到赵家院，就不得不全面停工，已修的这一公里也在以后恢复为农田。而在第二年，即 1913 年，湖南从长沙到湘潭的公路就修成了，成都的这个"第一"，就只能留在文献记载之中。成灌公路停工以后，就开始了讨袁之战，然后就是无休止的四川军阀混战。一直到 1924 年，杨森主政四川，他决定把官办改为官商合办，招募商股，最大的股东是江津人张鹿秋。于是张被委任为成灌马路总局会办，办公机构也由灌县迁到成都泡桐树街张鹿秋的家中。与此同时，又组建了商办的成灌马路长途汽车公司，共有汽车 9 辆。

四川著名爱国民主人士张为炯在成都的故居就在泡桐树街。

张为炯（1888—1972）四川德昌人，在西安陆军中学读书期间参加同盟会。因为他是德昌人，又与刘文辉在保定军校同学，所以长期是刘文辉的重要助手。西康建省后，他担任省政府秘书长，只要是刘文辉不在西康，他就代行省政府主席职务，故而长期被称为"代主席"。他一生信佛，清廉自守，在西康地区有很高的声望。1949 年 12 月 12 日，他根据刘文辉与他商议好的决定，在雅安宣布西康省起义，接受北京中央人民政府的领导（当时刘文辉在成都举行彭县起义，不在西康）。由于当时由他指挥的兵力有限，解放军一时又不能到达，国民党军队田中田部进攻雅安，原刘文辉部师长唐英又意图叛变。紧急时刻，张为炯以坚定的立场和沉着的毅力，率领省府人员避走灵官寨（今宝兴县灵关镇）固守，一直等到解放军进入雅安。他的这一举动受到了党和人民高度的赞扬，被选为西康省人民政府副主席。西康与四川合并之后，他又担任了成都市副市长、四川省副省长和民革四川省委主任委员。

商业街附实业街

　　商业街位于原来的皇城之中，在清代因为设有副都统衙门，所以本名副都统胡同。清代八旗制度下每一旗的最高长官是都统（一般都由亲王兼摄），副都统为副长官。在全国各地的驻防八旗官兵中所设的副都统实际上是该地八旗官兵的最高长官，地位只在驻防将军之下。成都是在乾隆年间才开始设驻防将军，所以这个衙门在清代前期是成都满城中官职最高的衙门，中期以后也是成都满城中仅次于将军衙门的第二大衙门。民国时期在原副都统衙门的地方兴办了商业专门学校，所以这条胡同在民国时期就叫作商业街。

　　商业专门学校办校的时间不长。据前辈的回忆，川军一位旅长强纳民女为妾，而这位民女又一直爱着商校学生金灿，婚后仍有往来。旅长遂以强奸罪名抓捕金灿，酷刑拷打。金灿拒不承认罪名，并通过校友控诉旅长强占民女，舆论一时哗然。军方悍然将金灿枪杀于西较场，商校师生即采取各种方式表示抗议，军方遂将商校封闭，师生均被赶出。从此之后，商校也就未能复校。1931年在原地开办了励志社成都分社。励志社原本是1929年在蒋介石倡导下于南京成立的，全称"黄埔同学会励志社"，是以文化活动来加强蒋介石嫡系军政高层人员内部联系的机构，以后在各大城市都有设立，实际上就是国民党军政警特界高级人员的一个联络处和吃喝玩乐的高级招待所。1937年，由著名建筑学家杨廷宝设计，修建了一座成都在民国时期唯一的宫廷式建筑风格的钢筋混凝土大楼（今天南京中山东路的金山宾馆就是民国时期的南京励志社总部大楼，也是由杨廷宝设计的，所以由他在晚些时候设计的成都励志社大楼与南京的励志社总部大楼建筑风格十分相近，只是体量稍小），并用作美国援华军事顾问团驻地，同时也是在蓉援华美军招待所，著名的飞虎队（即陈纳德志愿航空队）成员轮休时曾在这里居住，美国副总统华莱士在这里接见过飞虎队成员。1941年6月，美国著名作家、诺贝尔文学奖获得者海明威以记者身份偕夫人来成都了解美国援华情况，也曾经住在这里，写下了他对成都的观感

（最有趣的记载是行走在成都街头的骆驼商队）。这座大楼至今仍在。中华人民共和国成立以后，这里一直是中国共产党四川省委机关办公地。四川革命前辈张秀熟曾用一首诗概括了商业街的历史："商业学堂民元开，坊巷锡（按：同赐）名商业街。抗战楼高迎远客，今日省委指挥台。"

励志社大楼　杨显峰提供

抗日战争期间，美国驻华大使馆新闻处成都分处较长期间驻于商业街的励志社中（最初在春熙路青年会，以后又迁西御街），该处主任福斯特是秘密的美国共产党党员，所以他所聘用的工作人员如汪骏等都是中共地下党员或进步青年，他们利用美国驻华大使馆新闻处的有利身份，为推进反法西斯战争，为宣传中国共产党的主张做了许多有益的工作，毛泽东的《论联合政府》一书在成都主要就是由他们传播出去的。

商业街上的省委机关的对面，有一片包围着的绿地，这就是曾经使全国文物考古界为之震惊的战国时期特大型成都船棺群的发掘现场。

船棺是古代巴蜀地区一种特殊的埋葬形式，就是用很大的整体木头挖空成船的形状，将死者与随葬物品放在里面下葬。中华人民共和国成立以来，在四川的很多地方都发现过这种船棺葬，改革开放以后成都开发居住小区，在青羊小区、抚琴小区、白果林小区、石人坝等地的建筑工地都发现过船棺，时期大多是在古蜀王朝中后期，即相当于中原的春秋战国时期。2000年7月29日，省委机关食堂进行改建时，打算修建一个储藏食物的地下室，向下挖掘中发现了这个史无前例的特大型船棺葬遗址。在一个长约30米、宽约20米的巨型竖穴式墓坑中有17具船棺，全部用巨大的楠木做成，最大的一具竟然长达18.8米，直径1.7米，下面还垫着众多的枕木，是我国也是全世界最大的船棺王。在船棺中还发现了精美的漆器、陶器、铜器和陈放编钟的木架与击打编钟的木槌，遗憾的是青铜编钟早在汉代就已经被盗墓贼盗走。在这个墓坑之上还发现了大型木结构建筑的遗迹。据初步研究，这里很有可能就是古蜀王朝中开明王朝的皇家墓地，它与古蜀时期的三星堆遗址、金沙遗址一同构成了古蜀文明中迄今为止最为重要的三处大发现，也是成都市中心最为重要的考古发现（根据探测，大型墓坑四周肯定还有未发掘的地下宝藏，将在今后适当时机继续发掘）。商业街大型船棺群已经列名于全国重点文物保护单位，根据有关部门的决定，这里将建成我国最大的原址保护的船棺博物馆。

2000年商业街船棺葬发掘现场　李绪成摄影

与商业街紧邻的实业街原来是满城中的甘棠胡同。这里的"甘棠"源于《诗经·召南·甘棠》。因为宋代大学者朱熹对这首诗歌的解释是："召伯循行南国，以布文王之政，或舍甘棠之下，其后人思其德，故爱其树而不忍伤也。"所以后人用"甘棠"来表示地方官员有惠于民的德政。因为这里当年开设有八旗官学，是培养八旗子弟读书的地方，所以就取了"甘棠"这样一个很文雅的名字。清乾隆十六年（1751）在这条街上开设了皇城中第一所学校"成都八旗官学"（不久又在包家巷开设了第二所八旗官学，1871年两校合并，只保留了实业街的这一所）。民国初年，在八旗官学的地方开办了一所女子实业讲习所，所以就把这条街改名为实业街。

1917年，由成都文化界著名人士、"五老七贤"中的徐子休等人发起并集资，在实业街的北侧重建了原来建在文庙西街的六先生祠，又名六公祠（六公祠始建年代不详，最早建在江渎祠侧，所祭祀六公是李冰、文翁、廉范、张咏、赵抃、崔与之），祭祀四川宋代六位著名学者范镇、范祖禹、张栻、李道传、魏了翁、谯定。因为各方面的原因，六先生祠难以维持，不久即废。但是，这是成都近代文化史上为四川的文化先贤集中修建的最大的祠庙（在簧门街上，清末民初的存古学堂中曾建有四先生祠，祭祀的是范镇、范祖禹、张栻、魏了翁四人）。现将六先生祠中供奉的四川六位先贤简介如下：

范　镇（1008—1089）成都人，北宋著名政治家、史学家，参与修《新唐书》《仁宗实录》。曾任翰林学士、端明殿学士，封蜀郡公。

范祖禹（1041—1098）成都人，北宋著名史学家，著有《唐鉴》《帝学》，是司马光修《资治通鉴》的主要助手之一，世称"唐鉴公"。曾任礼部侍郎、陕州知州。

张　栻（1113—1180）绵竹人，南宋著名学者，与朱熹、吕祖谦并称"东南三贤"，主讲岳麓书院多年，是湖湘学派的主要开创者，世称南轩先生。曾任吏部侍郎、江陵知府、右文殿修撰。

李道传（1170—1217）井研人，南宋著名学者，以朱熹后学为己任。曾任真州知州、提举江东路常平盐茶公事。

魏了翁（1178—1234）蒲江人，南宋著名学者，建立并主讲鹤山书院，是南宋时期四川学术的主要代表，世称鹤山先生。曾任礼部尚书、签书枢密院事、资政殿大学士。

谯　定　生卒年不详，涪陵人，南宋学者，曾从程颐学《易》，后隐居青城山讲学授徒，蜀人尊为"谯夫子"。至今仍在流传的"易学在蜀"一语与他对《易》学在巴蜀的传授有很大关系。

实业街小学（今泡桐树小学实业街校区）的前身，是 1904 年开办在支机石街的公立第三小学，1905 年迁斌升街，1906 年迁实业街，1909 年改名为三英小学。三英小学所以知名，是因为清政权被推翻之后，四川军政府代表与成都的满蒙同胞代表的重要会谈就是在三英小学中举行的，而这次重要的会谈使得成都得以和平易帜，在解决满城这个十分棘手的问题上没有出现暴力（有关情况参见"同仁路"），极大地减少了可能出现的损失。三英小学这个"三英"不是三个英雄的意思，而是满语"善""美"的对音汉写。当年曾有满族文士吴俟庵撰文立碑阐释其义，这块碑过去立在实业街小学中，1960 年被毁。

1926 年 4 月，中国共产党在成都建立了第一个地方组织成都特支，特支的机关就设在今天实业宾馆对面钟善辅的家中。特支所办的刊物《火星》也是在那里编辑的。钟善辅是成都最早的青年团员和共产党员，当时正负责全市的工人运动工作。

1926 年 1 月 28 日，成都历史上第一家公共汽车公司华达汽车公司就开设在实业街。华达公司的实际创办者是从法国归国的留学生何嘉谟，他说服了父亲何羽仪与何羽仪的朋友胡又新共同集资成立了华达汽车公司，又请何羽仪的同乡、川军著名将领邓锡侯出任名义上的董事长。何嘉谟从上海购买了全套部件，运回成都组装了 7 辆 1.5 吨福特汽车，木制车厢中有 20 个座位（因为车厢颇似小房子，所以当时的成都人把这种汽车称为"洋房子走路"，这一说法在成都曾经流行了很久）。华达汽车公司设计了以下公共汽车线路：老东门到老西门、北门到南门、商业场前门到实业街、商业场后门到槐树街东口。在培训了驾驶员之后于 1926 年 1 月 28 日开业运行。由于当时街道太窄，车行不畅，易出事故，一些守旧者就以声音太大、速度太快、破坏市容、吓坏老人等种种理由，上书当时的成都统治者刘湘，以汽车如虎伤人为由，要求下令禁止。当时有位侯幼坡写了名为《汽车》的《竹枝词》，反映了成都市民对这一新生事物"市虎"的反感与抵触："万树芙蓉绕郭生，新潮高涨旧潮平。城居却是山居样，昼夜都闻'市虎'声。"当时一位文士在给当局的上书中还有这样的文字："盖城内面积不过十里，有何急务，如斯奔忙？且乘此汽车者，强半喜其新奇，姑一驰骋，惟因此闲游之举，而撞毙触伤之事层出不穷，使行人有举步之惧，栗栗若临深渊……"全城黄包车夫也群起阻挠，见车就抛石掷瓦。在这种情况之下，市政当局下令禁止公共汽车在城内开行，只保留了一条从春熙路出南门再到青羊宫的路线，每人收厂版铜圆一个，故而又有《竹枝词》写道："便利交通说有年，汽车今日见吾川。春熙路到青羊去，厂板才收一块钱。"就是这样，仍然不被守旧派所容许，仍然有人继续告状。华达公司只得把这一条线路也完全改为城外，从柳荫街到青羊宫，专门为花会服务。花会结束之后，又被迫停运，于是又只得改驶成都往新津一线的长途。由于道路太差，乘客太少，只维持到1927年，成都第一次开办的汽车公司就因严重亏损而不得不停业倒闭。在此之后，一直到抗日战争时期，成都人口愈来愈多，又才在1942年底成立官商合资的成都市公共汽车公司，有烧木炭的汽车12辆，开设了两条线路：沙河铺到茶店子、红牌楼到驷马桥。但是因为不堪兵痞流氓的骚扰，不到一年即亏本停业。1947年又曾恢复，有车7辆，只开行沙河铺到茶店子一线，一年多以后完全倒闭。一直到中华人民共和国成立以后，成都才在1952年7月1日开始发展愈来愈完善的公交事业。

在实业街的西头，抗日战争期间由我国著名公共卫生专家陈志潜（时任四川省卫生实验处处长）建立四川省传染病院，由留学美国的杜顺德医生担任院长。这是成都第一个专业的传染病院。传染病院后来迁出城外，将这里改建为妇婴保健院，1950年又改建为成都市第二妇产医院。经过多次扩建之后，目前已经成为成都市最具规模的妇幼保健院之一。

娘娘庙街

位于今天的大慈寺路以北、书院西街以东的书院东街，过去曾经叫娘娘庙街。娘娘庙街的得名是因为在这条小街上曾经有一个广生宫，又叫娘娘庙。

广生宫中供奉的是在古代社会中很有影响的子孙娘娘，即保佑妇女多生儿女、顺利生儿女的民间神，四川也叫送子娘娘。正如清人的《竹枝词》所描述的："大慈寺后广生庙，送子催生各位神。蜜意痴情都可述，娘娘也是女儿身。"由于是民间神，所以古代的子孙娘娘很多，诸如王母娘娘、天妃娘娘（即妈祖）、九天玄女娘娘、泰山娘娘（又称碧霞元君）等等都是，另外还有著名的送子观音。供奉子孙娘娘的庙宇也多，很多庙宇中都可能建有娘娘殿，甚至在有的关帝庙中都有。由于广生宫早已不存，娘娘庙街的广生宫中究竟供奉的是哪一位子孙娘娘，是多少位子孙娘娘，现在已经不明。

成都人还有另一种说法，说这个娘娘庙中供奉的娘娘不是子孙娘娘，而是帝王娘娘，她就是蜀汉的北地王刘谌的妻子。

三国时期的蜀汉政权自诸葛亮去世以后就开始走下坡路，原因虽然很多，但是当朝皇帝是刘备的不肖之子、被后人称为"扶不起的阿斗"的后主刘禅，他的无所作为，应当是主要原因之一。当魏军攻来的时候，刘禅开城出降，不仅当了亡国的俘虏，还到洛阳去摇尾乞怜，吃喝玩乐，留下了一个"乐不思蜀"的千古臭名。刘禅一共有7个儿子，除了一个刘琼早夭之外，当魏军攻来时还有6个，5个都跟着刘禅举手投降，只有一个被封为北地王的刘谌成了坚决不降的硬骨头。据《三国志·蜀书·后主传》注引《汉晋春秋》的记载，当刘禅决定向魏军主将邓艾投降的时候，"北地王谌怒曰：'若理穷力屈，祸败必及，便当父子君臣背城一战，同死社稷，以报先帝可也。'后主不纳，遂送玺绶（按：即向魏军送上代表国家政权的大印）。是日，谌哭于昭烈之庙（按：即祭祀刘备的宗庙，也就是今天的武侯祠的前身），先杀妻子，而后自杀，右无不涕泣者"。在古代，凡是决定要自杀以保全名节者，大多要先让妻子自杀或是先杀妻子，也就是古人所谓的"满门自尽"，其目的是为了妻子不被敌人欺辱。刘谌的这一壮烈之举，长期受到后人的尊崇，他殉义的妻子也一样受到后人的尊崇。

关于娘娘庙，必须提到成都还有过另一座娘娘庙和另一条娘娘庙街。

在今天文殊院的后面有一条西马道街，西马道街 50 号在今天已经是一个普通的民居大杂院，但是在过去却是个娘娘庙，也曾经叫作广生宫。坤道孙至兴从 7 岁开始就在此出家，直至 2006 年以 86 岁高龄羽化，如今她的徒弟陈理清仍然住在这里，在一间小屋（当年曾经是娘娘庙的三官殿）内守着七星灯，延续着娘娘庙的香火，与前来进香的道友们敲着钟鼓，祭拜着北地王刘谌和他的崔氏娘娘的塑像。崔氏娘娘的塑像前写着"蜀汉北地王妃崔氏娘娘"的牌位是在 2008 年 9 月 16 日娘娘庙开始整修之后才树立的。

2009 年西马道街 50 号内的娘娘庙　林立摄影

考察上述两个娘娘庙中的娘娘，笔者认为应当是子孙娘娘而不是帝王娘娘。据孙至兴老人回忆，当年的西马道街娘娘庙中有三清殿、真武殿、观音殿、斗姥殿、皇经楼等 29 个殿堂，娘娘殿只是其中的一个殿。每年办"喜神会"时，都要把两个用白果木雕成的娘娘像从神龛上请下来，清洗之后穿上漂亮的衣服用轿子抬着游街，叫作"送娘娘出驾"。清末的《成都通览》说："俗传三月三日为送子娘娘生辰，省城之延庆寺、娘娘庙各处演剧酬神（按：

这就是成都人所称的'喜神会'，年年都要举行，中华人民共和国成立以后中止。近年在武侯祠正月初一举办的"游喜神方"定诸葛亮为喜神，形式有所不同，大家都抢摸三义庙的'喜神碑'，以求当年喜事多多）。会首则大肆饕餮，并用木雕之四五寸长童子童女若干，在神殿前抛掷人丛处，待人争抢。抢得童子者即于是夜用鼓乐旗伞灯烛火炮，将童子置于彩亭中……比真正得子者尤为热闹。"由此可以确知上述两处娘娘庙应当都是供奉祭祀子孙娘娘的娘娘庙。但是由于成都人对于北地王刘谌的尊崇，于是就将娘娘庙视为供奉刘谌夫人的娘娘庙。这是一种值得注意的民俗现象，是成都人尊崇忠臣烈士的一种民心民意的表现。2010 年的"三月三"，西马道街娘娘庙恢复了传统的"童子会"。只是所抢的不是木雕的大"童子"，而是用布做的与红枣、花生一样大的小"童子"。

在今天所看到的清代重建的武侯祠（同时也是祭祀刘备的汉昭烈庙）的刘备殿中，除了刘备的塑像之外，刘氏皇族就只有一位刘谌，而没有曾经当了多年皇帝的蜀后主刘禅。据说过去曾经有过，因为被众人唾骂，挨口水，所以被拆去了。

还值得一提的是：邓小平同志曾经五次来到武侯祠。第三次是在 1963 年，他是与其他中央领导一道来的。他当着众多陪同人员说："刘备是儿子坏，孙子好，诸葛亮是三代都好。"邓小平同志所说的"孙子好"，就是指的刘谌。

今天的商业后街过去是没有的，是在中华人民共和国成立以后城市改造的时候拆除了一条叫娘娘庙街的小街和原来的大部分黄瓦街以及小部分的长发街之后形成的。这条娘娘庙街原来叫作积善胡同或育婴胡同，清代后期在胡同的东口建有一座娘娘庙，所供奉的就是人人皆知的送子娘娘。

中国共产党早期的四川省主要领导人杨闇公于 1921 年至 1924 年间曾经在这条娘娘庙街 24 号居住，1924 年 1 月 12 日，他与吴玉章发起组织的"中国青年共产党"就在这里宣告成立，还创办了机关报《赤心评论》，开展了不少革命活动。中国青年共产党并不是真正的中共党组织，而是在探索革命道路中成立的以马克思主义为指导思想的地方革命团体，因为杨闇公与吴玉章当时不知道中国共产党已经在上海成立，而又认为四川应当有一个马克思主义政党，吴玉章又因为年龄偏大不宜参加成都已经有了的中国社会主义青年团，于是就成立了这个革命团体。当他们很快分别在上海和北京找到并参加中国共产党之后，就立即解散了中国青年共产党。

杨闇公（**1898—1927**）潼南人，早年留学日本时开始学习马克思主义并参加爱国运动。因为声援国内的五四运动被日本警察逮捕判刑，出狱后即回成都，与吴玉章、刘伯承等人开展革命活动。1924 年 9 月，他参加中国共产党，并担任社会主义青年团重庆地委书记。1926 年任中国共产党重庆地委书记，与刘伯承一道策划并领导了泸州、顺庆起义。1927 年 4 月 6 日，壮烈牺牲于重庆浮图关。

1922 年杨闇公（右一）与廖划平（右二）、童庸生（左二）、吴玉章在成都。　中共成都市委党史研究室提供

杨闇公本名杨尚述，是杨尚昆同志的四哥和革命引路人（在杨闇公的引领下，他的家人有 6 人参加了中国共产党）。杨尚昆同志于 1921 年 14 岁时来到成都，先入成都高等师范学校附属小学补习，1922 年考入高师附中，并在此参加革命活动，1925 年毕业之后去重庆。他在成都期间就住在娘娘庙街他四哥家中。

抗日战争结束以后，国民党最大的特务组织国防部保密局的蓉站就设在娘娘庙街 38 号。国民党特务的"十二桥大屠杀"的决定与部署就是在保密局局长毛人凤的主持下于 1949 年 12 月 3 日在这里做出的。

栅子街

在长顺中街与中同仁路之间有栅子街与栅子西街，两条街原来是一条街，因为当年扩建中共四川省委第三招待所（今实业宾馆），中间被隔断，就成为两条街。

在红星路二段以西、布后街以北有双栅子街。前面已经介绍过的中新街过去也曾经叫作中栅子。

栅子街在清代是满城中的一条胡同，因为胡同中建有一座里仁坊，所以叫作里仁胡同。进入民国以后，"胡同"这一名称不再使用，因为还保留着栅子，故而被称为栅子街。双栅子街则是因为街南端的确有两道栅子而得名，因为这里距藩库街很近，藩库是省里的官家库房，建有官栅，街道上又建有街栅，所以就有了双栅子的街名。

"栅子"是四川方言，就是木制的栏杆门。清代的成都每条街都有栅子，栅门边都有更棚。夜晚三更时栅子一律关闭上锁，钥匙由更夫掌握，居民有紧急之事要进出栅子必须请更夫开锁。这种办法事实上是实行了全城的宵禁，对于维护社会的治安具有积极的作用。1905年成都有了警察之后，社会秩序由警察负责，栅子不再上锁，栅子也就逐渐失去作用。1924年杨森主政四川时，曾经对成都市政建设采取过一些"新政"，其中一项就是宣布取消街巷中所有的栅子。但是这以后凡是到了城内出现秩序不安、治安不良之时，各条街巷总会在街巷两端重修栅子。

成都最后一次大规模修建栅子是在成都临近解放的1949年11月中旬。由于此时国民党军队节节败退，成都的散兵游勇、匪贼流氓愈来愈多，由进入成都的国民党军队第三军军长盛文担任司令的成都防卫总司令部立足未稳，只知如何保卫刚到成都的蒋介石等少数国民党要人的安全，根本无心也无法维持愈来愈乱的社会治安。在这种情况之下，为了保卫全城百姓的生命财产安全，在中共成都地下组织的支持下，由已参加中共外围组织"新民主主义实践社"

的"成都民众自卫总队"副总队长乔曾希出面（"成都民众自卫总队"是当时
在四川地方实力派支持之下，由成都市政府出面组织的维持地方治安的不脱产
的民众地方武装，按全市 14 区 147 保进行编制，共有队员 3 万多人，长短枪
4000 多支，总队长由市长冷寅东兼任，此时的冷寅东也已经接受了中共成都
地下组织的指导），发动全市市民出钱出力，在十几天之内，全市所有的街
口、巷口和城墙缺口都建起了木制的栅子。不在本街巷居住的陌生人进出栅子
都要受到盘问，在重要街口还安放了枸槎和沙包。这一措施为增加市民的安全
感、防止兵痞盗贼起到了相当重要的作用。包括蒋介石、顾祝同、盛文在内的
国民党头目认为这一措施会造成城内军政力量的分割，影响军队的调动，三次
下令拆除栅子，但是由于冷寅东、乔曾希等人的暗中抵制，由于全城老百姓的
软顶硬抗，成都全城街巷的栅子一直保持到 1949 年 12 月 27 日解放军先头部
队入城之时才全部拆除。从此以后，成都人就再也看不到栅子了。

我国现代著名学者吴虞在成都居住时间最长的故居是在栅子街 50 号，并
将之命名为"爱智庐"，吴虞与夫人曾兰也是病逝在这里（吴虞在成都还有一
处故宅是在文庙后街）。

吴　虞（**1872—1949**）新繁人。1891 年入尊经书院学
习，但是他对西方新学更有兴趣，时人称他是"成都言新
学之最先者"。1905 年去日本留学，1907 年回到成都，发
表了一系列非儒反孔、抨击专制主义的议论与文章，又公
然因为家庭问题的冲突而与父亲打官司对簿公堂，故而被
保守派称为"名教罪人""士林败类"。四川教育总会将他
"逐出教育界"，四川护理总督王人文更是下了逮捕令，他
只得逃至乡下避难。辛亥革命之后，他在成都新闻界、教

青年吴虞

育界十分活跃，在北京的《新青年》等刊物发表了大量震撼全国的反对封建
礼教的文章，与陈独秀南北辉映，被胡适誉为"四川只手打孔家店的老英
雄"（按：在很多介绍吴虞的文章中都把此话误写为"打倒孔家店"，原文见
《吴虞文录》胡适序，这里有无"倒"字是含义有别的）。特别是在 1919 年
第六卷第六号《新青年》上发表的《吃人的礼教》一文，与鲁迅的《狂人日

记》一起在全国产生了空前的影响。1921 年去北京，先后在北京大学、中国大学等校任教。1925 年回到成都，在成都大学、四川大学等校任教，仍然坚持他一贯的非儒反孔的学术观点，反对国民党当局尊孔读经的教育方针，以致被特务邮寄左轮枪子弹以进行恫吓。吴虞晚年基本上退隐于家，趋于消沉。1941 年"皖南事变"爆发之后，他写下了《读廉颇列传》一诗对国民党反动派的倒行逆施加以申斥。1949 年 4 月 27 日病逝，与夫人曾兰合葬于新繁龚家碾。

曾 兰

曾 兰（1875—1917）吴虞夫人曾兰也是一位在成都现代文化史上值得纪念的人物。她出生在文庙前街，是一位著名的女诗人、小说家、书画家，与吴虞比邻而居，青梅竹马，15 岁时嫁入吴家，是吴虞一生中倡言新学、反抗旧礼教的支持者。1912 年出任过由孙少荆主办的成都第一张妇女报纸《女界》的主笔，撰写了一系列倡导女权的文章，有的还发表于著名的《新青年》杂志上（当时全成都的《新青年》订户只有 5 家，她家就是其中之一），是引导四川女界登上社会舞台的重要推动者。例如，由于《女界》的呼吁，四川省临时参议会专门设置了接待女记者的会议室，第一张入场券就是送给曾兰的。1914 年，成都的《娱闲录》发表了她的白话短篇小说《孽缘》，次年由著名的上海《小说月报》转载，这是我国最早的现代小说作品之一（比《狂人日记》早 3年）。他们夫妇及其两个女儿吴楷、吴桓都能诗，而且一家四口都参加了著名的文学团体"南社"，被"南社"盟主柳亚子委托为"南社"在四川的联络人，成为成都文化史上的一段佳话（当时全川参加南社者约有 20 人）。有不少研究者认为，吴虞所以会在晚年消沉乃至颓废，应当与曾兰的过早病逝、缺乏支撑有很大的关系。曾兰一生著述有《定生慧室遗稿》二卷传世。

吴虞在成都的故居已经不存，但是他于 1938 年在故乡新繁正北街买的一处命名为"爱智庐"的住宅至今仍在，是新都区文物保护单位。

抗日战争结束以后，国民党最大的特务组织军统改名为国防部保密局，原军统的"川康区成都站"改名为保密局成都站,是成都地区最重要的特务机构,中华人民共和国成立前夕发生在成都的很多罪恶活动都是该站干的,其站部就设在栅子街 44 号。1949 年 1 月 13 日夜,当时的川西地区中共地下党主要负责人蒲华辅就是在这里的审讯室中叛变的。

小通巷

这是少城中的一条半截小巷，位于奎星楼街以南、中同仁路以东，清代名仁风胡同，民国初少城中各胡同改名时，因为这条胡同的巷道狭窄，有如一条通道，所以就命名为小通巷。

1992 年的小通巷　陈锦摄影

小通巷中曾经住过一位今天几乎已经快被人遗忘的我国现代文化史上的先辈曾孝谷。

曾孝谷（1873—1937）成都人。幼时随父在山东与北京读书，1906 年考取官费留学日本，与著名学者、艺术家李叔同（即后来的弘一法师）一道进入东京美术学校西洋画选科，并与李叔同、唐肯等人创立了我国第一个话剧团体"春柳社"。1907 年 2 月，曾孝谷翻译了著名话剧《茶花女》，并在公演中扮演亚猛的父亲，这是我国演出的第一出话剧。1907 年 6 月，他根据美国斯陀夫人的小说名篇《汤姆叔叔的小屋》创作了话剧《黑奴吁天录》，并在公演中饰演黑奴之妻。《黑奴吁天录》是我国第一个话剧剧本，被公认为是中国现代话剧诞生的标志，著名戏剧家田汉曾经说过，曾孝谷的创作"展开了中国话剧运动的第一页"。2007 年，在纪念我国话剧诞生 100 周年的活动中，北京人艺与国家话剧院还专门编写并上演了《寻找春柳社》以作纪念。曾孝谷

1906 年曾孝谷（右）与李叔同在日本组织春柳社时的剧装照

1911 年从东京美术学校西洋画选科毕业之后，曾经读了一年研究科（这也是我国第一个攻读西洋画的研究生）即退学回国。在上海短期生活之后回到成都，于 1915 年在成都高等师范学校担任图画教授，是成都最早教授西洋美术的教师，也是成都的第一个油画家。他又在成都组织了成都第一，也是全国最早的话剧团体之一的成都"春柳剧社"，组织一批成都县中的中学生在 1918 年进行了成都历史上的第一次话剧（当时俗称为"幕表剧"）演出，剧目仍然是《黑奴吁天录》。这以后，他曾经担任过少城公园中通俗教育馆的第二任馆长（第一任馆长是创立者卢作孚兼任的），做了大量的文化普及工作。曾孝谷后来做了中学教师，晚年生活清苦，把自家在小通巷的独院"梦明湖馆"大部出租以维持全家的生活，死后的安葬费都是靠包括当代成都著名画家屈义林在内的一些学生凑集的。著名文士林思进赠他的挽联是："杜甫一生逢乱世；郑虔三绝少知音"（按：唐代大画家郑虔擅长诗、书、画，被时人誉为"郑虔三绝"）。曾孝谷的诗作有《梦明湖馆诗》一书传世，由他的老朋友谢无量作序。

黄瓦街

黄瓦街原来是清代成都满城中的松柏胡同，在今天的商业街后面。因为有两位没落的贵族用红墙黄瓦修建了自己民居的围墙，这在当时的成都是十分罕见的，故而民国时期就叫作黄瓦街。

2021 年的黄瓦街　张西南摄影

中国共产党在四川的早期重要领导人刘愿庵生前家住黄瓦街，中国社会主义青年团成都地方委员会（也称特别支部）的机关 1926 年 4 月以前就设在刘愿庵的家中。

　　刘愿庵（1895—1930）陕西人，自幼随父在成都长大。辛亥革命时期投身军界，为人正直，同情贫穷。1922 年在任丰都县长时，因为惩治贪官污吏、废除苛捐杂税而被军阀上司撤职，可是老百姓却给他树了德政碑。回到成都后，他结识了四川无产阶级革命的先行者王右木、恽代英、吴玉章等，开始学习与宣传马克思主义，并以四川省

刘愿庵

议会秘书长的公开身份投身革命运动。1925 年，他加入了中国共产党，并于年底任中国社会主义青年团成都地方委员会书记，次年任中国共产党成都特支书记。1927 年调往重庆，任中共四川省委秘书长。1928 年 3 月，在省委书记傅烈牺牲之后，任代理书记。不久即去上海向中央汇报工作，并去苏联出席中国共产党第六次全国代表大会，被选为中央候补委员。1928 年底回到成都，在新省委中任常委兼宣传鼓动部主任。1929 年 6 月，任省委书记。1930 年 5 月 5 日，因为内奸的告密在重庆被捕。军阀刘湘派刘愿庵的亲属劝降，许以"院长""厅长"等高官，但在刘愿庵面前完全无效。5 月 7 日，刘愿庵英勇就义。

1938 年夏天，中共成都市委的秘密机关曾经从忠孝巷转移到黄瓦街的一处二楼上，那里是当时的市委宣传部部长张宣租用的临时住房。

红墙巷

与黄瓦街相似，红墙巷原来也是清代成都满城中的一条胡同，位于长顺上街以东、东马棚街以北，原来名叫普安胡同，又叫吉祥胡同。因为街上过去有一座关帝庙，庙外的围墙涂成红色，红墙也就成了这条街的景色特征。民国时关帝庙已不存，但是仍然改名叫红墙巷。

著名的四川小吃担担面在今天几乎是处处可见，但是老成都过去最有名的担担面就是在红墙巷的东头北侧，一直到1956年才从这条小巷迁往提督街。

1995年的红墙巷　陈先敏摄影

奎星楼街附裤子街

老成都的满城中有一条光明胡同,因为西头原来曾经有一座关帝庙,关帝庙中后来又增加了一座奎星阁,所以在清代时就又名奎星楼胡同,民国时改名为奎星楼街。

奎星也称魁星,按我国古代天文学的正式叫法应当是奎宿,为二十八宿之一,共包括十六颗星,因为这十六颗星"屈曲相钩,似文字之画",所以在古人眼里奎星或魁星被认为是主管文运之神。唐宋时期的科举考试以五经(即《诗》《书》《礼》《易》《春秋》)取士,每一经的第一名叫"魁首",共有五经魁首(今天人们饮酒划拳时喊的酒令中的"五魁首"就是这样来的)。这个"魁"就是来自于古人对于文运之神的崇拜,以后又加上了凡是科举考中者都是"魁星点斗"的更多的神话,所以在我国各地过去都有奎星阁、奎星楼(也有的叫作魁星阁、魁星楼),专门供奉决定科举考试命运的文运之神奎星(奎星塑像也不是一般的端坐神像,而是站在地上、手握巨笔、正要"点斗"的很有动感的雕塑),是过去的读书人经常去顶礼膜拜的地方。

奎星楼街在清代建有一座牌坊叫里仁坊,上面有"里有仁风,探花及第"八个大字,应当是表彰这条胡同中出过一位探花(科举考试中殿试的第三名),可是在各种文献中对这位探花却没有任何记载,这件事至今还是成都地方史上的一个谜。

奎星楼街过去还有过一个别称叫裤子街,这是因为清初的奎星楼街的东头曾经分为两个出口(如果从清代遗留下来的几种地图加以考察,清代满城中的胡同有两个出口者不只这一处,这是什么原因造成的,目前还不清楚),有如裤子的两个裤管。民国时期建房多了,这个裤管形的两个出口也就见不到了。

2021 年的奎星楼街　陈轲摄影

著名数学家魏时珍曾长期居住在奎星楼街 13 号自己设计修建的寓所中。

魏时珍

　　魏时珍（1895—1992）蓬安人，1908 年考入四川高等学堂分设中学，与郭沫若、王光祈、周太玄、李劼人、蒙文通等同学。1913 年入上海同济医工学院（同济大学的前身）学习。1918 年加入少年中国学会，以后又介绍张闻天、沈泽民、宗白华等参加了少年中国学会（根据笔者所见到的资料，魏时珍是最后一位辞世的少年中国学会会员）。1920 年与王光祈一道留学德国，是当时有"数理王国"之称的哥廷根大学的第一个中国留学生。他在与科学泰斗爱因斯坦通信并得到支持之后，于 1923 年在《少年中国》月刊开办了《相对论专号》，将自己的两篇文章与爱因斯坦给他的回信一并发表，为相对论在我国最早的传播起到了重要的作用。1925 年获哥廷根大学博士学位，是四川省第一位数学博士。在哥廷根大学期间，还曾经辅导初到德国留学的朱德、孙炳文学习德语，时间延续近两年，所选用的教材就是《共产党宣言》（这本教材已入藏中国国家博物馆）和布哈林的《共产主义 ABC》。1955 年朱德来成都时，曾经两次会见并宴请他的这位老朋友。魏时珍于 1925 年回国之后，长期在四川各大学任教，担任过成都大学理学院院长和四川大学理学院院长，是我国偏微分方程和理论力学学科的奠基人，是主张文理不分家的先行者，主张给学生吃"复合维生素"。在他1946年所创办的成都理学院（这所大学的前身是他在1939年创办的川康农工学院，成都理学院在中华人民共和国成立以后并入了四川大学）中，特聘彭芸生主讲古典文学，吴天墀主讲中国通史。1949年，他拒绝了国民党当局要他去台湾的安排而留在了成都。他不仅是我国现代早一辈的数学家，是第一本《偏微分方程》的作者，还是一位长期研究哲学的学者，1937年就发表了《康德与马克思对话》的论文，1958年主编了哲学杂志《相对论》，1980年写了《孔子论》一书。1984年，哥廷根大学向这位在60年前第一个荣获博士学位的中国人颁发了"金禧博士学位特别纪念奖状"，以表彰他在教育科研工作与促进中德文化交流中所做出的巨大贡献。

长发街

这是清代满城中的一条胡同,原来就叫长发胡同,民国时期改名为长发街。如今位于长顺中街以东,东门街以南。

长发胡同的得名是出于这样一个传说:这里过去曾经有一个尼姑庵,庵里有一个长发尼姑,她不仅可以预示庄稼的丰歉,而且每根长发都可以祛病避邪。这当然是一种表达美好愿望的传说,因为在不同的清代地图上,我们可以见到对这条胡同的三种不同的称呼:长发胡同、长法胡同、长陵胡同。就以长发胡同的得名也有两种说法:一说是因为当年在胡同的西头有一个牌坊名叫发育坊;另一说是出自《诗经·商颂·长发》中的"长发其祥"的诗句,是一种吉祥语。

1940年5月,经中共地下党组织的安排,周恩来与川军将领刘湘去世后的刘湘系继任领袖潘文华在长发街32号乔毅夫私宅中进行了一次十分重要的会谈,建立了双方长期的声气相通的统战关系。此后,中国共产党先后派唐午园等人到潘部做联络员,派到潘部担任各种职务的中共地下党员近20人,汪导予、苏爱吾出任顾问,田一平出任机要参谋。所有这些,为中国共产党在国统区的各项工作,为日后的成都解放都起到了十分重要的作用。

吉祥街

在同仁路与长顺街之间、槐树街以南的第一条小街就是吉祥街。吉祥街原是清代满城中的众多胡同之一，原名通顺胡同，又名吉祥胡同。民国初年改名新巷子，后来又改名为吉祥街。

1995 年的吉祥街 严永聪摄影

1919 年 7 月，由李劼人主持的少年中国学会成都分会创办的周报《星期日》就在吉祥街 8 号创刊，经理孙少荆，编辑李劼人。《星期日》是成都第一家以宣传新思想、批判旧制度为主要目的的周报，提倡"劳工神圣"，宣称社会主义是"人类的福星"，刊载过毛泽东、李大钊、陈独秀等人的重要文章，是五四运动时期与《每周评论》《星期评论》《湘江评论》齐名的四大刊物之一。

1946 年，四川省第一所会计专业学校在这条街开办，名为四川省立会计专科学校，其基础是原来的四川省立教育学院会计专修科。此校初创于 1943 年，第一任校长王荫初，当时没有自己的校址，是利用青龙街成都县中的校址

（当时成都县中已疏散到郊外），1946年由杨佑之接任，迁入吉祥街的专用校址。

　　杨佑之（**1893—1971**）南京人，在北京大学商科就读时成为我国经济学泰斗马寅初的高足。1938年来到成都，此后一直在四川大学、华西大学、四川财经学院等各大学任教，直至辞世。他是在四川第一个讲授高等会计学的教授，他写成的《会计学》《会计学纲要》《高等会计》《高级统计学》《审计学》等著作被认为是我国会计学领域的权威性著作，他也被认为是我国会计学科的"祖师爷"，在52年的执教生涯中培养了数不清的专业人才。

杨佑之

　　也是在1946年，由著名幼教专家陆秀主持的四川省立成都幼稚师范学校在吉祥街开办，其校址是当时的四川省参议会议长向传义借出的公馆。

　　陆　秀（**1896—1982**）女，江苏无锡人，1932年赴美留学，专攻幼儿教育，获哥伦比亚大学学前教育硕士学位。1934年与著名学者、后来的四川省博物馆馆长冯汉骥结婚。抗日战争全面爆发以后，夫妇俩回国入川，她全力投身于四川婴幼教育事业，传播西方最先进的婴幼教育理念与方法。她在茶店子筹建了成都实验幼稚园（园中设有当时极为罕见的婴儿部），主编出版《实验幼稚教育》杂志，在华西大学担任家政系教授，成为当时在大后方实验探索现代婴幼教育的开拓者与引路人。中华人民共和国成立以后，她在担任四川省妇联副主任、成都市民政局局长的同时，继续关注婴幼教育，特别是她在1958年以自己的积蓄在老马路开办的婴儿之家先后免费托收了100多名婴儿（其中包括三胞胎、早产儿、体弱儿），百分之百健康成长，对全省的婴儿保育做出了杰出的贡献，在全国也产生了很大的影响。1964年，她的老同学邓颖超来到她的婴儿之家，赞不绝口，当场以自己的工资作为捐赠。她开办的成都实验幼稚园几经演变，成为今天位于茶店子的成都第四幼儿园；

原来的婴儿部几经演变，成为今天位于新南门的四川省省直机关实验婴儿园。
她开办的婴儿之家在1966年"文革"初期结束。

1940 年成都实验幼稚园　杨显峰提供

　　国民党元老戴季陶在成都的公馆就是在本街中段，当年的成都市政当局特
地将戴公馆的门牌号码定为"新一号"。戴季陶在广州自杀之后遗体运回成都
时也就是在这里装殓的。

东门街

如今被成都市民俗称为羊西线的第一段就是东门街。这条街在清代是满城中的五福胡同。民国初年改名时，因为它是出入满城东门的胡同，所以改名为东门街。

清代满城共开有五道城门，东边有两道，靠北的叫迎祥门（门内是五福胡同和长发胡同，门外是羊市街和五福街），靠南的叫受福门（门内是祠堂街，门外是西御街），成都市民一般简称为大东门和小东门。东门街东口所在的东门，就是满城的大东门。

东门街今天有成都著名的成都市第一骨科医院。这家医院是著名的成都杜氏骨科传人杜琼书与郭钧主持建立的，最初是设在柿子巷的西城区骨科联合诊所，1957年迁往东御街，1959年迁至东门街，改名为西城区骨科医院。杜琼书本人则先后被调入四川省人民医院与四川省中医研究所。

槐树街

　　槐树街原来是清代满城中的槐树胡同，民国时期改名为槐树街，位于长顺街和同仁路之间。改革开放之后新建从羊市街向西出城的通道，当时的工程名称是羊市街西延线，简称"羊西线"。整个新通道建成之后分段命名，从东到西分别是东门街、槐树街、永陵路、抚琴西路、蜀汉路、蜀西路、西芯大道。成灌高速建成以后就是成灌高速的主入口。由于羊西线这一非正式的工程名称早已在人们的口中普遍传用，槐树街这一正式名称反而被羊西线的俗称代替而少为人知。

　　当年的槐树胡同有过好多老槐树，还有一片槐树林，今天只剩下几株，但是还有几株高大的老银杏树立在车水马龙的大街之旁。在成都市区的主要交通干道上还有几棵高大老银杏树的，也就只有这条槐树街了。

1910 年的槐树街　杨显峰提供

　　民国时期著名法学家、吴虞的堂弟、担任过北京大学教授、成都大学教务长、四川大学秘书长与法学院院长的吴君毅（1886—1961）的私宅就在当年槐树街西头的 34 号。著名学者向宗鲁 1935 年至 1941 年在成都时期也居住在本街的李炳英宅（李炳英也是一位著名学者，曾先后担任四川大学、光华大学、川北大学、四川师范学院中文系主任）。

向宗鲁（1895—1941）重庆人，自幼饱学，《昭明文选》这样的大部头典籍可以全书背诵，人称"向书柜"。在成都存古学堂求学时为廖平的得意弟子，也是非正式的学术秘书。生前长期担任重庆大学与四川大学教授，抗日战争时期在峨眉山伏虎寺卒于四川大学中文系主任任上。向宗鲁是蜀中著名的古文献学家，所校注的文史典籍多达十余种。由于他具有蜀中前辈学人轻易不言著述的严谨传统，故而他的研究成果在生前多未问世。直至他去世之后多年，《校雠学》《说苑校证》《周易疏校后记》《月令章句疏证叙录》等著作方由其弟子屈守元、王利器等整理出版。

向宗鲁

民国时期，有 3 位蜀中文史名家英年早逝，这就是 36 岁的刘咸炘、36 岁的吴芳吉、46 岁的向宗鲁。

东马棚街附西马棚街

　　东马棚街和西马棚街在清代都是满城中的胡同，东西相邻，当时名叫仁德胡同和广德胡同。这里是满蒙旗兵养马较多的地方，原来有很多竹木搭建的马棚，少有住户。民国时期不再在这里养马，并逐渐修建了若干民房，并把街道名称改作了东马棚街和西马棚街。

　　1912年四川外国语学校从昭忠祠街迁到东马棚街，1914年改称为四川公立外国语专门学校。1919年9月，15岁的巴金以李尧棠的名字与他的三哥李尧林一同考入此校读书，从补习班到预科、法文本科，直到1923年春天离开成都取道上海去法国留学。因为巴金自幼在家读私塾，没有上过小学和中学，没有中学的毕业文凭，所以被学校列为旁听生，没有得到毕业文凭。但是，四川公立外国语专门学校是巴金青年时期所上的最重要的一所学校，他不仅在这里初步掌握了英语、法语和世界语（巴金是我国世界语运动的先驱者之一），他的第一篇公开发表的文章与最早的一批文学作品也都是在这一时期问世，他所参加的第一次社会斗争（为反对军阀刘存厚而举行的罢课与请愿活动）和参加社团、编辑杂志也都是在这一时期。所以，四川公立外国语专门学校对于巴金的成长具有相当重要的作用。

20世纪60年代东马棚街四川公立外国语专门学校旧址

　　长期在东马棚街办学的成都市第一中学现与树德中学合并，称为成都树德实验中学，就是开办在当年的外国语专门学校的旧址上（这个旧址还包括1914年开办在这里的四川省立第一师范学校，省一师于1919年迁盐道街）。而成都一中的前身又是1931年在这里开办的四川省立女子中学（另有省男中在五世同堂街）。正因为这里过去办的是女子中学，所以成都一中在建校后很久仍然是中华人民共和国成立以后成都仅有的两所女子中学之一（另一所是成都十一中），现已改为男女合校。

　　民国时期，东马棚街上的一个宅院中出售一种由家庭主妇自己制作的豆瓣酱与红豆腐，颇有口碑，人们都称之为"太太胡豆瓣"。

2012年的西马棚街　杨显峰摄影

　　抗日名将孙震在成都城内的故宅在今西马棚街小学校园内。

焦家巷

焦家巷是原来满城中的上升胡同，东起长顺上街，西到同仁路。因为原来巷中有一位满族的官员额苏里氏的住宅，民国时改名为焦家巷。这与清代后期满族改用汉姓有关。

1986 年的焦家巷　张西南摄影

满族同胞在清初入关之时，都用的是原来的满族姓氏（满族的姓与氏不分，在满语中称为"哈拉"，在汉译中可以称为姓或氏，也可以称为姓氏），如叶赫那拉氏等。按照满族的传统习惯，对满族男子是只称名而不称姓氏，如努尔哈赤、纳兰成德。在受到汉族文化的影响之后，一些满族人就把汉译名字的第一个汉字作为新的姓，当时叫作"以名若姓"。再进一步，就干脆改满姓为汉姓。到了清末，几乎绝大多数都改成了汉姓，如爱新觉罗氏改为姓"金"、姓"赵"，完颜氏改为姓"王"、姓"汪"，瓜尔佳氏改为姓"关"、姓"管"，博尔济吉特氏改为姓"白"、姓"尹"等。成都的这家额苏里氏把他们家改为姓焦，周围的人就称他们一家为"焦家"，因为他们家是全巷中名气最大的一家，所以就把上升胡同改称为焦家巷。

1940 年前后的一段时期，中共川康特委机关曾经设在焦家巷 20 号。焦家巷中曾经居住过不少成都的文化名人，如藏学家张怡荪、文字音韵学家李植（见宽巷子）、古典文学家屈守元、神话学家袁珂等。

　　张怡荪（**1893—1983**）蓬安人。曾任清华大学、山东大学、四川大学教授，四川大学文科研究所所长。1922年，他作为刚从北京大学毕业的学生，面对名满天下的梁启超的老子研究成果写出《梁任公提诉老子时代一案判决书》，得到梁启超的高度评价，被收入了著名的《古史辨》，在学术界产生了很大的影响，以后即入清华大学执教。1928 年，他开始在北京圆恩寺与雍和宫中研究藏学，学习藏语文，开始做编写《藏汉大辞典》的准备工作，出

张怡荪

版了《藏汉集论词汇》和《藏汉语对勘》二书。1937 年，他来到成都，在厅署街开办西陲文化院（为了躲避日寇的轰炸，曾一度迁往崇庆县大北街的刘家祠），继续《藏汉大辞典》这项工程，成为我国最著名的藏学家之一。中华人民共和国成立以后，他受命担任主编，再次编写了我国第一部共收词 5.3 万条、总字数达 350 万的《藏汉大辞典》。为了保证辞典的编写质量，他于 1958 年以 65 岁高龄到当时生活与工作条件都十分艰苦的西藏工作了两年。《藏汉大辞典》是我国目前水平最高、收词最多的藏汉辞典，出版之后获奖无数，几乎被全世界各大图书馆所收藏。英国藏学专家说"《藏汉大辞典》远远不止是藏、汉两种语言的字典，它是由藏、汉族学者编纂的有关藏族宗教文化的一部综合性的百科全书"。遗憾的是，此书 1985 年才得以出版，此时张怡荪已去世两年。

　　屈守元（**1913—2001**）成都人。蜀中研究中国传统文化的著名学者，长期在四川师范大学执教，曾任中文系主任、图书馆馆长、古代文学研究所所长。他博闻强记，具有蜀中前辈学者较为共通的两大特色：一是治学面广，对于古代文化具有通识，从来不拘于一朝一代，无论是研究或是教学都

屈守元

可以从先秦直到近代；二是治学严谨，慎于著述，他的著作如《中国文学简史》《文选导读》《韩诗外传笺疏》《经学常谈》等都是到了晚年在各方的催促与力劝之下才交付出版。屈守元先生晚年最重要的著述是由他主编的《韩愈全集校注》。

袁　珂（**1916—2001**）新繁人，1941年毕业于华西大学中文系，终生研究中国古代神话，是我国最负盛名的神话学家，曾任中国神话学会主席，生前为四川省社会科学院研究员。主要著作有《中国神话传说》《中国神话传说辞典》《古神话选释》《中国神话通论》《山海经校注》等。

袁　珂

焦家巷东口有民国时期成都著名的"马红苕"。今天遍布街巷的大炉烤红苕当时全城就只有这一家，很受群众喜爱。周菊吾先生当年曾有诗写道："滑滑焦家巷口泥，忍饥客散雨丝丝。红泥炉子通红火，番薯浓香透鼻时。"中华人民共和国成立以后，马红苕不再经营。有记载说，朱德和邓小平这两位四川老乡在中华人民共和国成立以后回成都时，都曾经提出希望能再品尝"马红苕"的烤红苕。

过街楼街附过街楼横街

　　过街楼是我国古代城镇中修建在不大的街巷之上的通道，其使用性质好似今天的跨街天桥，但是上面有屋顶，颇似河流之上的廊桥。过街楼街原来是清代满城之中的集贤胡同（又名永兴胡同），就是因为有一座这样的过街楼而在民国时期被改名为过街楼街，在旁边还有一条过街楼横街。成都城内的过街楼直到中华人民共和国成立以后还有好几处（骑楼也是过街楼这种建筑形式的一种），都已经在街道的扩建之中被拆除，现在是一座也见不到了。

1987 年的过街楼街　张西南摄影

上半截街

在原来满城中长顺下街的两侧有几条半截巷。东半截巷在民国时期即已不存，西半截巷一直存在，到前几年旧城改造时才被拆除。上半截巷一直存在，民间长期只名叫半截巷，现在名叫上半截街。下半截巷这个名字自改名以来一直不被当地的居民所接受，因为在成都方言中把人的下半身也呼作人的下半截，用作街巷名称就颇为不雅。当时在下半截巷中住有一位祖籍安徽桐城的姚姓人家，是我国著名的桐城派文学家姚鼐的族孙、曾经任过左都御史的清代学者、著名书画家姚元之之后。姚元之家修有竹叶亭（竹叶亭旧居今天仍在，即桐城市北街小学所在地，是桐城市市级重点文物保护单位），自号竹叶亭生，其著作以《竹叶亭杂记》最为知名。所以这户姚姓人家就以自己是桐城竹叶亭后人的名义，于1923年向市政当局提出建议，申请将下半截巷改名为"竹叶巷"。这一申请得到了批准，从此以后成都就有了一条竹叶巷。竹叶巷的位置就在长顺下街以西、四道街与焦家巷之间，已经在城市改造之中拆除。

中国共产党第一个成都市委员会是在1927年冬天建立的，第一任市委书记是张秀熟。这个成都市委机关的办公处与联络点，就设在竹叶巷8号李静轩（当时是川军刘文辉的参谋长，已经加入了中国共产党）的私宅里面。

关于上半截街与半截巷，有几点需要说明：第一，由于"半截"与"半节"读音相同，意义相近，所以上述的几处半截巷在成都不少地方也写作"半节"。不妥，应当是"半截"。第二，中华人民共和国成立以后，陈毅同志的三弟陈季让住家在原四川电影院侧的另一条半截巷（现已拆除），所以曾经有一些文章把上半截巷误认为陈毅同志在成都的故居，这也是不对的。第三，上半截街目前仍在，位置在长顺下街东侧，东二道街与过街楼街之间，街道标牌写着"上半截街"，而且真是一条很短的半截小巷，门牌号码只有12—20号。可就在这8个门牌上，却有"上半节街""上半节巷""半节巷"三种错误的写法（原因应当是成于不同的时期），多年未改正，是成都街道门牌中错误最突出的一处。

二道街附三道街 四道街

在今长顺街北端的两边，清代时是满城中的几条胡同，到民国时期，胡同名称不再使用，逐渐都有了新的名称。由于这几条街地处满城的北端，从北往南数的第一条胡同，就是今天的西大街。为了方便，就把当时没有较为明显特征的第二条、第三条、第四条胡同分别叫作二道街、三道街和四道街。

二道街以长顺街为界分为东二道街和西二道街。东二道街向东原来是接东城根街的，中华人民共和国成立以后东城根街重修时将过去的斜街取直，在新建的取直后的东城根街北端以东，就出现了一段斜行的老东城根街。与此同时，取直后的东城根街北端又把东二道街截去一段，这一段街的东头仍然与老东城根街相接，西头就与新建的取直的东城根街相接了。这一段连接在老东城根街与新建的东城根街之间原来的东二道街的一段，就被命名为横东城根街。

设在郫都区古城填的阳友鹤纪念馆

当代川剧一代宗师阳友鹤生前就住在西二道街。

　　阳友鹤（**1913—1984**）彭州人，原名阳永清，8 岁入金兰科社学习川剧，工旦角，艺名筱桐凤。他在川内多处搭班学艺，广采博收，悉心出新，在剧本、唱腔、表演、服装、化装等多方面都有所改革。1931 年在重庆演出时即名噪一时，1938 年被百代公司请至上海录制唱片。1940 年演出新排的《凤仪亭》，受到郭沫若、田汉、阳翰笙等人的高度赞扬。中华人民共和国成立以后，1952 年在第一届全国戏曲观摩演出大会上得一等奖。1956 年赴京参加第二届戏曲观赏讲习会，讲解《川剧旦角的基本功训练与表演要求》，以后由中国戏曲研究院派专家记录整理出由梅兰芳作序的《川剧旦角表演艺术》一书，再版三次，在全国产生很大影响，全国多种地方戏曲都请他讲课或者传授技艺。他先后担任西南川剧院实验学校教务主任、成都戏曲学校校长、成都市川剧院副院长、中国戏剧家协会四川分会名誉主席。他文武兼备，唱、做、念、打无所不精，是公认的川剧一代宗师，为川剧艺术的发展做出了杰出的贡献。1980 年，中华人民共和国文化部、全国文联、中国戏剧家协会及省、市文化部门在成都联合举办了"阳友鹤舞台生活六十年纪念"活动。

20 世纪 50 年代阳友鹤授徒　张蜀华摄影

三道街本来应当以长顺街为界分为东三道街和西三道街，东边的仁里胡同原来就是分为两截的，而且有上半截巷或东半截巷的名字，所以民国时期仍然保留了上半截巷的旧名而没有改为东三道街，以后就只有西三道街被称为三道街。

四道街本来也应当以长顺街为界分为东四道街和西四道街，东边的胡同原来就分为集贤胡同和永兴胡同两段，而永兴胡同因为有木质的过街楼，所以民国时期就把永兴胡同改名为过街楼街，而把集贤胡同叫下半截巷。这样就只有一条四道街了，这就是西四道街。

1918 年 5 月 15 日，《戊午周报》（后改名《戊午日报》）在四道街 45 号创刊（后迁刀子巷今多子巷 46 号）。该周报的主要支持者是老同盟会员和当时拥护孙中山先生的部分川军将领，在全国主要城市和海外近 10 个大城市有代派处和特约记者，稿源丰富，反帝爱国立场鲜明，很受读者欢迎。每期发行 3 万份以上，巴黎和会期间超过 4 万份。该报在 1918 年 9 月 24 日的"新论"栏目中刊载了世界著名马克思主义者河上肇的《马克思社会主义之理论的体系》一文，向四川人民全面地介绍了《共产党宣言》。

成都中医学院附属医院原来就设在四道街，后迁至西一环路以后，又在原址设立了四川省中医中药研究院。此外四川省皮肤病防治研究所也设在本街。

RECORDS OF
STREETS AND ALLEYS
IN SHAOCHENG

少城街巷志

The Qing City and the Manchu City

After the Tang Dynasty (618 ~ 907 AD), Chengdu continued to follow the pattern of an inner-city wall surrounded by an outer-city (*luo*) wall. Following the Five Dynasties (907 ~ 979 AD), in the Shu period, an immense outer fortification was built within the northern and western sections of the outer city to serve as the *luo* wall's boundary, a perimeter of 21 kilometers. However, as it was made entirely out of rammed earth rather than bricks, the wall was destroyed during the Northern Song Dynasty (960 ~ 1127 AD). Throughout the Song Dynasty (960 ~ 1279 AD), there were five restorations to Chengdu's city walls, but in the late Song and early Yuan dynasties (1279 ~ 1368 AD), the majority of the *luo* wall was destroyed in war, along with the entire inner city. During the Ming Dynasty (1368 ~ 1644 AD), a larger city called Fucheng was built over the remains of the *luo* city. Shu Palace[1] or the Imperial City, as it was typically called—was then built on the foundations of the inner city. Although the city always had remained the irregular shape and skewed orientation in the past, Shu Palace was more like a typical Chinese city—a planned city, square and oriented perfectly south-north. Although the new city wasn't very large, it was encircled by a city moat, beyond which lay a large outer wall, known as the "spirit screen". In terms of the present city, this wall extends approximately east to Shuncheng Street, south to Dongyu Street and Xiyu Street, west to Dongchenggen Street, and north to Yangshi Street and Xiyulong Street.

As the Ming Dynasty collapsed in 1644 AD, Zhang Xianzhong led an army of peasants against the city. They went on to occupy not only Chengdu but the majority of the Sichuan Basin. With Chengdu designated as the Western Capital, Zhang Xianzhong proclaimed himself Emperor of the "Great Western Empire" and set up his palace in the palace of the former Shu. However, when Zhang Xianzhong commanded his armies northward to resist the Qing Army in 1646, the entire city of Chengdu, including the palace, was destroyed in the fire of war.

---

[1] Shu Palace (*Shu Wangfu*) was not a single building but an enclosed complex of buildings for use by the royal family and scholar-officials. [Translator's note]

When Qing soldiers occupied Chengdu in the fourth year during the reign of Emperor Shunzhi (1647) , it was already overgrown with grasses and brambles, a pile of ruins inhabited only by grazing deer. Not only were there no residents, but no structures to provide shelters. For the time being, the Qing government could only relocate the government to the city Langzhong. This arrangement continued to the seventeenth year during the reign of Emperor Shunzhi (1660) , during which the Sichuan capital was moved back to Chengdu. Starting with the official offices, step by step, the Qing set out to restore the city and rebuilt the city wall in 1665. In the fifty-seventh year during the reign of Emperor Kangxi (1718) , the Qing government accelerated the process, mobilizing the administration authorities of all counties, districts and prefectures in the province to take respective responsibility for building segments of city walls and streets in Chengdu. The city was essentially completed the following year. In the fifth year during the reign of Emperor Yongzheng (1727) , the city underwent a repair. Then in the forty-eighth year during the reign of Emperor Qianlong (1783) , under the direction of Sichuan Governor Fu Kang'an and by the collective power of the province, the city and walls were entirely rebuilt with bricks. This would be the last and most important rebuilding event for Chengdu's major city structures. Prefectures and counties from all over the province were responsible for the project and they constructed it according to unified standards. Two and a half years later, the project was completed (by that time Fu Kang'an had left office and been succeeded by Li Shijie). Therefore, to put it more accurately, the latest construction of the ancient walls of Chengdu which can still be seen today was made in the fiftieth year during the reign of Emperor Qianlong (1785). From then on, all of Chengdu's walls, avenues, bridges and principal urban structures have been basically retained until today.

The layout of Chengdu in the Qing Dynasty differed from past dynasties in certain respects. What remained the same was the skewed orientation of the area enclosed by the city moat, a trend established with the "Turtle City" in the Qin Dynasty (221 ~ 207 BC). Thus Chengdu's four main roads do not run down to east, south, west and north, but to southeast, southwest, northwest and northeast. This helps to explain why Chengdu's old-timers give or ask for directions, they prefer to say "left-hand" or "right-hand" rather than say east or west. (The "left-hand" and "right-hand" habit of speech was probably introduced to Chengdu by migrants from Huguang—i. e.

present day Hubei and Hunan provinces. ①)

Chengdu in the Qing Dynasty was largely analogous in shape and scale to the Chengdu of the Ming Dynasty, while the extent of the city expanded just slightly. According to written records, the city wall had a perimeter of 22 *li* and 8 *fen*② at that time. Measurements undertaken following the founding of the P. R. C. found it to be a little over 12 kilometers in today's terms. As for its height of 3 *zhang*, it was equivalent to about 10 meters. Although the walls of the Qing Dynasty have already been demolished, the city moat structure was still retained from the Tang Dynasty, with the Fuhe River and Nanhe River embracing the city. Therefore, the layout of Chengdu in the Qing Dynasty was basically visible as the inner boundaries of the Fuhe River, Nanhe River, and Xijiao River (there was no inner boundary line on the west side; it roughly conformed to the direction where present-day Tongren Road runs to the Xijiao River).

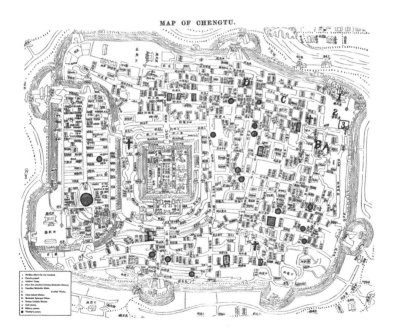

MAP OF CHENGTU.

Map of Chengdu printed by foreign missionaries, 1895 Courtesy of Yang Xianfeng

---

① Mass migration events (mainly) from Huguang occurred in both the Ming and Qing Dynasties following population depletions in the war-torn Sichuan Basin. [Translator's note]

② One *li* is equivalent to 500 meters; one *fen* is equivalent to 50 meters.

One often hears old-time Chengdu residents say that "it's nine *li* and three *fen* to pass through the city". This goes back to a record in the "Western Regions" of the *Sichuan Tongzhi* (the official annal of Sichuan) which describes Chengdu as "nine *li* and three *fen* east to west, seven *li* and seven *fen* south to north". However, initial studies conducted after the founding of the P. R. C. shows that the city runs 4.6 kilometers east to west and 3.85 kilometers south to north. Thus the "nine *li* and three *fen*" record and the local saying are merely an approximation.

According to the typical ratio of ancient city constructions, the width of the city wall base in the Qing Dynasty was approximately the same as its height at 3 *zhang*, or about 10 meters. The width at the top of the wall was 1 *zhang* and 8 *chi*, about the width of a city avenue in that period, or 6 meters in today's terms (this measurement refers to the width of the original construction, as the wall was enlarged during each of its subsequent reconstructions). People living around Chengdu had a custom that the entire family members should make "a trip for cure-alls" to the city on the sixteenth day of the first lunar month, believing that a visit on this particular day can keep disease at bay throughout the remainder of the year. Since the Ming and Qing dynasties, this custom could be found across the country, variously referred to as the "a walk for cure-alls" or "an outing for cure-alls" or "crossing the bridge", or "ascending the city wall". On this occasion, the government would permit commoners to freely enter the city. One Qing-period *Bamboo Branch Verse*[1] (*Zhuzhi Ci*) describes the customs:

> An outing for cure-alls prevents the sores;
> Travel with their children out of the doors.
> On the 16th day of the lunar New Year,
> Everyone agrees to meet on the city wall.

By the late Qing Dynasty, the political system had essentially collapsed. The city wall, originally built for protection, was no longer maintained. At relatively thick sections of the wall, people gradually began to build rooms section by section, and the makeshift shelters came to be formed something like the shanty towns of today. Even some official organizations built their offices on the top of the city walls. For example,

---

① *Bamboo Branch Verse* (*Zhuzhi Ci*) is a genre of poetry/folk song with a four-line structure that typically describes folk customs and everyday life. [Translator's note]

on the southern wall at the Gongbei Bridge, the Sichuan Machinery Bureau opened an industrial school for training skilled workers. The school, which enrolled over fifty students, sat entirely at the top of the southern wall in the city. These add-on structures remained in place until the demolition of the walls in 1958. Today their final remains can still be seen at 4 Xialianchi Street (i. e. the Xinnanyuan residential complex).

Compared with the Ming Dynasty, the most significant chang that took place in Chengdu was the construction of the Manchu City in the west during the Qing Dynasty. The Manchu City was where the Manchu and Mongol Eight Banners[1] officials, soldiers, and their families took up residence. In a sense, it marked a return to two thousand years ago, in the Qin Dynasty, when a smaller city adjoined a larger one (although examination halls were rebuilt at the site of the Shu Palace in the Ming Dynasty, their scale was much smaller, and this complex was not regarded as a "city" during the Qing Dynasty). Thus, the structure of the ancient city of Chengdu can be characterized as undergoing a cyclical journey: from containing an off-center small city to a centered small city, then to an off-center small city again. Yet over the course of more than two millennia, the basic layout of the two concentric cities remained unchanged, which is unique in China. This special characteristic has drawn the attention of all ages. For instance, a line in "*Climbing Chengdu's Baitu Tower*" by Zhang Zai of the Jin Dynasty (266 ~ 420 AD) —the earliest poem known to describe Chengdu—refers it to as "a twin city". In the poem titled "*Chengdu Prefecture*" written by master poet Du Fu when he arrived in Chengdu, he referred to it as the "two-city", too. Chengdu's famous poetess Xue Tao also depicted it as the "two-city" in her poem "*Attending Xichuan's Commander, Minister Wu Yuanheng*".

In the fifty-seventh year during the reign of Emperor Kangxi (1718), the Qing government specially arranged for the long-term residence of the Eight Banners in Chengdu, but the number of officials and soldiers was small. Three years later, a defensive force of 3,000 bannermen originally stationed in Jingzhou, Hubei were relocated to Sichuan. After participating in military activities to quell the Dzungar Khanate, a troop consisting of 1,600 cavalries, 400 infantry, 74 officers and 96 laborers remained in Chengdu; thus the city came to be known as "Camp Jingzhou".

---

[1] The Eight Banners were the empire's top-ranking military and administrative units, a system of organization unique to the Qing Dynasty. [Translator's note]

People of that period recorded the event in the *Bamboo Branch Verse*:

> In the west of the city lied the Manchu City,
> Which was built for bannermen with public funds.
> When did it turn out to be a military camp?
> In Autumn 1718 of Emperor Kangxi's reign.

According to the data from the sixtieth year during the reign of Emperor Kangxi (1721), stationed banner troops numbered over 3,000. From then on, the Eight Banners continued to expand, so that by the thirtieth year during the reign of Emperor Guangxu in the late Qing Dynasty (1904), there were over 5,100 Eight Banners households incorporating over 21,000 people. In Chengdu, the Eight Banners were a Manchu-Mongol composite establishment. The banners were divided into three ranks, wherein the top and mid-ranking spots went to Manchus and the lowest-ranking to Mongols. Eight Banners troops all brought their wives and children with them and thus required permanent residences for them. On top of that, ethnic conflicts stemming from the early Qing still ran rather deep[①]. Therefore, Nian Gengyao, the Inspector General of Sichuan at that time, requested that the Qing court build a new city in Chengdu specifically for the residents of the Eight Banners. Construction began on this city-within-a-city in the sixtieth year during the reign of Emperor Kangxi (1721) and continued for over 20 years. The result is what would come to be known as the "Manchu City" or the "Small City".

The Manchu City's walls extended approximately 2.7 kilometers around. Within it, there were eight streets for Eight Banners officials, 42 streets of soldiers' garrisons, and five connecting channels (However, regarding the exact number of streets within the Manchu City, various records show some discrepancies. The figure used here is taken from the *Chronicles of Chengdu Manchu-Mongol*). In present-day terms, it extended east to Dongchenggen Street, south to Junping Street, and north to West Street, and its western wall was the same as that of the larger city. The main

---

① Unlike the Ming Dynasty, which was ruled by a lineage of China's majority (Han) nationality, the Qing Dynasty was established by conquest from the outside. The rulers of the Qing Dynasty were from Manchuria, had their own language and traditions, and constituted a minority ethnicity within their own Qing Empire. Resentment against the violent conquest and ensuing Manchu rule was amplified by the group's cultural and ethnic differences. The Manchu adapted to Chinese systems in many respects but maintained a certain distance from the majority-Han populace. [Translator's note]

thoroughfare ran south-north through the center of the Manchu City, which is today's Changshun Street. To either side of Changshun Street were rows of *hutongs* formed by the walls of joined courtyard homes. The Manchu City thus resembled a centipede with its head at the *yamen* (bureaucratic office) of the garrison's highest official—known as the "General's Yamen—and legs extending east to west. The term "hutong" was introduced to Chengdu from Beijing during this period. And, also as in Beijing, they were named with numbers—the first *hutong* was called "No. 1 Hutong", the second "No. 2 Hutong", and so on. After the founding of the Republic of China (1912), however, they were renamed as streets and alleys according to the customs of southern China. The names of alleys were once compiled to form various rhythmic chants like "yellow tile (Huangwa Street) facing the red wall (Hongqiang Alley), and long hair (Changfa Street) facing good fortune (Jixiang Street)..."

A street in Shaocheng in the late Qing Dynasty Courtesy of Yang Xianfeng

Within the Manchu City, the residences of the Eight Banners officials, soldiers, and their families were arranged according to the three ranks within the banner system: the three upper banners, the three middle banners, and the two lower banners. Each household group was allotted a plot of land corresponding to their ranks. It was called a *jia* (as in *baojia*) and was a standard for land distribution among the Eight Banners. Thus a "one *jia*" plot varied in size. For example, a cavalry *jia* was larger than an infantry *jia*. Cavalry soldiers among the highest three banners were allotted approximately 80 square *zhang* of land (about 882 square meters), while infantry soldiers among the lowest two banners were allotted approximately 40 square *zhang*. Officers, meanwhile, might be allotted several, perhaps even several tens of *mu*[①] according to their ranks. In general, the Eight Banners were arranged with the solid yellow and bordered yellow banners residing in the north of the city, the solid white and white-bordered banners in the east, the solid red and red-bordered banners in the west, and the solid blue and blue-bordered banners in the south. More specifically, according to the layout of Chengdu today, the solid yellow banners' residences were located from West Street to West Mapeng Street, with the officers on East Mapeng Street. The bordered yellow banners could be found from Babao Street to East Mapeng Street, with the officers on East Mapeng Street. The solid white banners were situated between Dongmen Street and Shangye Back Street, with the officers on Shangye Street. The bordered white banners' residences extended from today's Shangye Street to Dongsheng Street, with the officers on Dongsheng Street. The solid red banners were to be found from today's Huaishu Street to Shiye Street, with the officers on Shiye Street. The bordered red banners resided from Paotongshu Street to Xisheng Street, with the officers on Xisheng Street. The solid blue banners could be found from today's Jiangjun Street to the People's Park, with the officers on Cangfang Street (now incorporated into the People's Park). The bordered blue banners lived from Shizi Alley and Jinhe Road to Baojia Alley, with the officers on Shuhua Street.

The Manchu City in the Qing Dynasty was rather insular, closed off from the larger city with its own set of four gates. Han people from the outside could not enter the city without permission. As for the Manchu people within the city, they could not go out of the city unless they asked for leave. On the east side of the Manchu City, the northern gate was Shoufu Gate—customarily referred to as "Small East Gate" —and was located at the corner of today's Citang Street, while the south-east gate was called Yingxiang Gate or Big East Gate, and was located at the corner of today's Dongmen Street. Anfu Gate or "Small South Gate" was located on the southern wall at the corner of today's Xiaonan Street. The north wall had Yankang Gate at the corner of today's Ningxia Street. On the west, as the western border of the Manchu City was also the western border of the larger city, no gate was opened there. Instead, the Manchu City shared Instead, the Manchu City shared with the larger city the Qingyuan Gate, which was located at its northwest corner, the west end of today's West Street. The Manchu City's main gate, however, was the "Small East Gate" located at the junction

---

① One *mu* was then equivalent to 614. 4 square meters.

of today's Citang Street and Xiyu Street. Two pillars flanking the gate were once adorned with a pair of giant plaques that respectively read "Small City, Ancient Rule" and "Beautiful and Lofty". The Manchu City was rather sparsely populated (never exceeding twenty thousand residents), so there was quite a lot open space. Moreover, the bannermen liked to plant trees and flowers, such that the city came to be abounded with flora and was shrouded in the shade of thick branches. A Qing Dynasty *Bamboo Branch Verse* writer describes it:

> Manchu City is quiet and secluded,
> Where trees and flowers are planted.
> You can hardly enjoy all the scenery in a year,
> But you may enjoy the lotus at Guandi Temple in summer.

As late as 1945, renowned writer Ye Shengtao also said: "The trees in the Small City are truly luxuriant, to exaggerate slightly, it looks as if the houses are hidden among the trees instead of the trees being planted around the houses. "

Because the Manchu City was originally intended to serve as a glorified army camp, it consisted only of houses, offices and warehouses. The installation of shops, teahouses, or taverns was forbidden. For the most part, all necessary provisions transported into the city through the Big East Gate would be stored in one of the Small City's large warehouses. These warehouses were grouped on a large stretch of land close to the Big East Gate (within today's People's Park). In such a huge Manchu City, most of its buildings were residential. Their interiors were quiet and comfortable. Apart from the *yamen*, where homes might be joined to form courtyards, most of the households lived either in rows of three-room, single-story houses or in three-sided semi-courtyards with two side buildings flanking the main one. Residents could construct flower gardens and low walls in front or behind their homes, but none formed a pure four-sided courtyard. Today those buildings we can see from the Manchu City are those that were renovated in the Republican period (1912 ~ 1949 AD). They are composed of street-facing houses and some small, three-sided courtyards with small wells, but very few four-sided courtyards, which reflect an important feature of Manchu City's architecture.

In line with Chengdu's long-established layout of a larger city enclosing a smaller city, Chengdu people generally refer to the Manchu City as Shaocheng *or* Small City. The name is still in use today—not only as a habit of speech among long-time Chengdu

residents (for example, many continue to call the People's Park "Shaocheng Park"),
but also used in certain places, including government offices and businesses
(Shaocheng Sub-District Office, Shaocheng Restaurant, and so on). At the outset of
the Reform and Opening-up era, Chengdu's first large-scale road construction project,
carried out between 1981 and 1984, was to connect east and west with construction of
Shudu Avenue. Shudu Avenue consists of eleven sections all together; among them,
the section from Dongchenggen Street to Xiaonan Street is known as "Shaocheng
Road". For the most part, this section was built upon the original foundations of
Yongxing Street, Paifang Alley, and Citang Street; thus it once laid within the bounds
of the Small City in the Qing Dynasty.

Wenchang Palace in Shaocheng, 1906 Courtesy of Yang Xianfeng

The Manchu City was no longer retained after the Xinhai Revolution (the
Revolution of 1911). Demolition began in 1912 with the gradual removal of its
northern wall, and continued until 1935 when the final section along Xiaonan Street
was taken down. At the same time, although there was no massive demolition to bring
down the larger city wall, the city's more powerful classes would continuously pilfer
bricks from its bases, tops, and parapets to contribute to their own residences.
Because most of the demolished bricks were concentrated on the inner base of the
larger city wall, a number of areas were totally stripped to expose soil slopes covered
in various weeds and even small trees. Some of these sites were referred to as
"collapsed walls".

The final restoration of the larger city wall took place in 1935. The goal was not to
protect the historical landmark but rather to build the defense project for the battle. By

that time the Fourth Front Red Army had incorporated Tongjiang, Nanjiang and Bazhong counties into its Sichuan Shaanxi Revolutionary Base. Crossing west over the Jialing River, they had then occupied Jiangyou and other places in the Mianyang area. Fearing that the Red Army would attack the city, Chengdu's government and business circles established a "City Wall Engineering Committee" to carry out restoration work, focusing particularly on the comprehensive restoration of the battlements (i. e. crenellations or parapets) and the construction of several watchtowers. This project marked the last maintenance work to be conducted on Chengdu's city walls. Once the War of Resistance Against Japanese Aggression broke out, the old wall was soon riddled with gaps again to take shelter from air raids. Meanwhile, some refugees arriving in the city constructed simple houses on the wall, forming several "shanty towns".

Moso bamboos in Shaocheng, 1910 Courtesy of Yang Xianfeng

Immediately following the founding of the P. R. C. , the city wall was retained. There was a discussion at the Sichuan People's Congress on whether the wall should be demolished or not. Because of different opinions among them, no decision was made about it. Then in March 1958, Chengdu hosted China's Central Economic Work Conference, for which Chairman Mao Zedong came to the city (for only time in his life). When he arrived in Chengdu on March 5th, accompanied by Zhou Yi, the Under-Secretary-General of the CPC Sichuan Provincial Committee, he toured the city by car. During the tour, Chairman Mao expressed (roughly) his thoughts on the Chengdu city wall: "Why can't it be torn down? Beijing's wall has already been demolished. This wall is unattractive, and holds up the traffic, too. City walls are backward things. When they're torn down, people can go in and out of the city easily.

The soil can be used as fertilizer, and the bricks can be used to renovate buildings. Demolishing walls is progressive; while keeping them still is backward". At this, the Chengdu People's Committee (the equivalent of today's municipal government) issued a notice on April 11 [th], 1958: "For the sake of city's environmental hygiene and further construction, all existing sections of the city wall are to be torn down in stages. The wall's soil will be used to fill ditches and ponds while eliminating the grounds for preventing mosquitos; the wall's bricks will be used in urban construction..." According to records, the city wall (including both standing sections and ruins) extended 12.33 kilometers in length with 22 openings and relatively complete segments being 7.5 meters high. Its average width was 14.5 meters at the top and 18.5 meters at the base. All in all, the wall contained about 50 thousand stones, 6.02 million bricks, 1.32 million cubic meters of soil, and its walls and feet provided a home to 40 thousand square meters of makeshift buildings.

In June 1958, Chengdu established the City Wall Demolition Headquarters. According to the subdivision of labor, even some schools near the city wall were assigned to remove a specified number of bricks every day (for example, students at Chengdu No. 16 Middle School had to take down 10 pieces of brick per day). In less than half a year, 297,160 "citizen soldiers" had done their part. The original Qing wall had essentially been torn down, of which the stone and brick components were then used for urban construction projects or "small blast furnaces" of various work units for China's period of intensive steel production. For example, a large number of bricks from the city wall were used for the construction of Jinjiang Bridge on South Renmin Road and the eastern suburb sewerage system. Meanwhile, the soil from the wall was used not only to fill in 365 ponds and lowland areas, but also to fire bricks (according to one record, 110 kilns were constructed and 7.6 million bricks were made of clay). This is how the Wangjiaguai Brick and Tile Plant, the Chengdu's first large-scale brick factory, came to operate in 1958 (it merged with the similar Jinhe Brick and Tile Plant in 1960, and was renamed Chengdu No. 1 Brick and Tile Plant. Once the last of the soil had been excavated from the walls, the factory went through a number of product changes, at last becoming the Chengdu Safe Factory, still located at the same site—12 Chengbian Street). Of course, for a long time, some residents had been excavating bricks from the walls. According to one elder's recollection, the wife of a pedicab driver on Shangchizheng Street was digging bricks from the base of the city wall, when a collapse buried her in the soil; she lost her life there. Finally, because of the mass mobilization for baking "bricks prepared for war" in the 1970s, most of the wall's earthen remains were dug out. Today, there are only a few broken sections of the wall remain. According to my investigation, remains of the wall can be found at the following locations:

South of Wuding Bridge at the northwest corner of Beijiaochang: This section of the old city wall, about a hundred meters long, is quite stunning and complete, as reconstruction has been built upon the remnants of the original site. Most of its bricks were collected from those of the old wall. It is the only section of Chengdu's old city walls that can be visited by the public now. Moving east from this section, there is another portion: the two sides of the main gate of the north wall; this is also a remnant of the old city wall.

In the Jinjiang Huating Community on Huaxing Road, west of Mengzhuiwan: This section of wall stretches several tens of meters. Although it was added to and was repaired during the new housing construction, the form of the old city wall is still clearly visible.

Yingxixia Street: This section of wall had been hidden behind residential buildings and was only exposed in the process of road construction. Forty-some meters long, it is quite complete—it even retains some stone stairs once used for ascending and descending the wall. Most likely, this section once flanked the old wall's eastern floodgate. The government restored it and still continues to protect it. And it is now a landmark in the Jiaoziyuan residential complex at the back of North Dong'an Road.

Remains of the city wall in the Jinjiang Huating Community, 2013. Photo by Yang Xianfeng.

The north section of West Jinli Street: Behind a long row of residential buildings lies the former Xijiaochang (West Military Field), which is the present site of the Joint Logistics Department of Chengdu Military Region. Between the residences and the military compound, one finds intermittent remnants of the old city wall spanning over 1,000 meters. In some places, it serves as the back wall of the residences, and some parts of the wall have rooms built on its top. This section of the wall has been preserved because of its location between these residential buildings and the Joint Logistics Department. It is now the longest existent section of the old wall of the Qing Dynasty.

West Jinli Street's Qing City Wall, 2009. Photo by Yuan Tingdong.

On either side of Xinnanmen (New South Gate): Twenty-some years ago, there was still a section of the wall extending over 140 meters, with some simple houses built on it. This wall was listed as the "East Jianguo Street Wall" on the list of the Chengdu Cultural Relics Protection Unit. In the recent urban reconstruction, it has mostly been demolished, but today there are still some sites where the wall can be seen. For example, there are old walls of several tens of meters long at 4 Xialianchi Street (i. e. Xinnanyuan), where several buildings were built directly upon them. One can find remnants of the southernmost section of Chengdu's city wall at 12 Xialianchi Street (formerly Jiaolian Gongsuo Street).

Inside the former Chengdu Water Meter Factory at the intersection of Tongren Road and Shiye Street: A section of old wall here reaches 30 meters in length and 9 meters in height. Of particular interest is this section of the wall which plays a role in the War of Resistance Against Japanese Aggression. At that time, the Sichuan Air Defense Command carved a 170-square-meter cavity into the wall that was able to fit about 100 people. This air-raid shelter was the place where the Sichuan Air Defense Command was situated during the war. After the founding of the P. R. C. , the shelter was used by the water meter factory instead as a warehouse for storing gasoline. Chengdu lies on flat land, with the water table even higher, so one could find groundwater simply by digging down a few inches, and this made it extremely challenging to build air-raid shelters. To my knowledge, there are only three sites in present Chengdu where one can find air raid shelters during the War of Resistance Against Japanese Aggression—one at Citang Street, one at Front Wenmiao Street, and one here.

The south end of Tongren Road: To the west of Tongren Road lies a small section of ruins. It is close to the wall's western floodgate with the three characters *Shui Xi Men in chinese* (West Water Gate) carved there. The ruins have undergone restoration in recent years, but most people don't get the chance to see them because they are hidden inside the Jindu residential complex.

Upper Qinglian Street: This section of the wall in the Qing Dynasty may also witness the location of the city wall in the Ming Dynasty (for details, see "Upper Qinglian Street").

The layout of the Manchu City underwent few changes in the Republican period. At the time of liberation of Chengdu, there were 49 streets in the former Manchu City. Due to changes following the founding of the P. R. C. , there are now 47 streets.

The Jinhe River

The Jinhe or Jinshuihe (meaning "river of golden water") is a small waterway that once flowed west to east across the entire city of Chengdu. It was constructed over existing channels in the city in the seventh year during the reign of Emperor Xuanzong in the Tang Dynasty (853) under the direction of Bai Minzhong, the Military Governor of Xichuan and Magistrate of Chengdu Prefecture at the time. It provided a water source for a large number of city residents and a means by which they discharged rainwater and sewage in the city. Because its source came from the west, the river was named "Jinshuihe" or "Jinhe" for short, for the traditional Chinese thought associates *jin* (gold/metal, one of the five elements) with the west. Sands and pebbles silt up quite easily in urban rivers, so it must have been dredged periodically. The location of the Jinhe River in the Tang Dynasty is unclear, and multiple dredging projects have resulted in small changes in its watercourse, making it hard to say whether the Jinhe River of the Ming and Qing dynasties has followed the same path as that of the Tang Dynasty. When the Chengdu's West Trunk Road was constructed in 1984, archaeological excavations uncovered the ruins of an ancient riverbed on the southwest corner of Dongyu and Citang Streets. Piles of wood were found in the river, suggesting that this was most probably the location of the "Jinhe Road" in the Tang Dynasty. By the Ming and Qing dynasties, the river had already deviated from the south, roughly parallel to its course during the Tang and Song dynasties. We know this from records of a large-scale renovation project supervised by Sichuan Inspector General Tan Lun and Chengdu Magistrate Liu Kan in the forty-fifth year during the reign of Emperor Jiajing in the Ming Dynasty (1566). Upon the completion, the channel was approximately 10 meters wide and 3 meters deep.

The Jinhe River flowing through southeast Chengdu in the Late Qing Dynasty. Photo courtesy of Jacques Dumasy〔France〕.

Initially, the Jinshuihe flowed into the city from the Pijiang River outside the west of the city wall after the latter changed its course from the Xihao (Xihao was a small canal dug in western Chengdu to maintain the city moat after the Pijiang changed its way; it becomes the Xijiao River downstream). In the Qing Dynasty, Chengdu shared its western wall with that of the Manchu City. To guarantee the safety of the Manchu City, the Shuiguan (checkpoint) on the western wall was fortified with an iron gate—known as the "water gate", which was under the military guard. It would only open to the passage of small boats. A sluice was also installed on the gate to control flood in summer. In the parlance of Old Chengdu, this place is known as *Shui Xi Men* (West Water Gate). After the founding of the P. R. C. , its exact location was encompassed by the Sichuan Fire Fighting Machinery Factory. Today it falls within the premises of Changfu New Town (a residential complex). From the western wall, the Jinhe River flowed east, spanning the entire city and passing through the eastern wall at the south of present-day Dongmen Bridge, where it met and emptied into the Fuhe River. Unlike its western-wall counterpart, the Shuiguan at the eastern wall was open; and small boats could reach the city by working their way upstream. As with the western gate, however, old-time Chengdu residents referred to it as *Shuidongmen* (East Water Gate). Somewhat confusingly, there was a Shuidongmen Street on Chengdu's east side; and the road was set down in the early years of the Republican period following the construction of Wucheng Gate (colloquially known as *Xindongmen*, "New East Gate"). However, this Shuidongmen Street is named for a sewer line that drains into the Fuhe River at that location, and has nothing to do with the Jinhe River.

The remains of Shuiximen Photo by Yang Xianfeng

According to the *Chronicles of Chengdu County*, Vol. 1 during the reign of Emperor Tongzhi (r. 1862 ~ 1875) in the Qing Dynasty, the Jinhe River was 1,526 *zhang* or 5,087 meters in length. The volume of the river changed from one period to another depending on the dredging situation (following the reign of Emperor Yongzheng in the Qing Dynasty, the Jinhe River was dredged every year in the absence of any limitations. Project funds were contributed by sub-prefectural Yamen for water conservancy, who took these from the balance of yearly fees paid by Dujiangyan. Dujiangyan's annual fees were shared equally among the nine water utility counties in Chengdu on a per-*mu* basis, and basically guaranteeing the dredging funds). Over the Ming and Qing dynasties, the Jinhe River was consistently navigable for small vessels (except for a short period in the late Ming and early Qing dynasties when the channel was ruptured and boat traffic was blocked. During the reign of Emperor Yongzheng in the Qing Dynasty, Chengdu Magistrate Xiang Cheng had the waterway dredged to restore the river to navigability). Boats traveling into the Jinhe River from the Fuhe River would have to work upstream to ship their wares into the city. In the Ming Dynasty, all the provisions required for the Shu Palace could be transported on the Jinhe River to Sanqiao Wharf. In the Qing Dynasty, boats would come instead to Banbian Bridge just outside the water gate on the eastern wall of the Manchu City (by land or water, the permission for Han people to enter the Manchu City was not given at all). At that time, the Manchu City's wood and grain warehouses were all located in the area of the People's Park today. Those warehouses' stores have largely been shipped into and through the city via small boats on the Jinhe River. According to interviews conducted with elderly residents in the spring of 1950, the government organized a collective dredging of the Jinhe River as well as the Yuhe River. They also widened the banks and erected a retaining wall. Up until 1958, small boats could still be seen passing over the Jinhe's waters.

Considering how narrow it was, the kinds of vessels traversing the Jinhe River were different from those on the wider Jinjiang River. First of all, they were small, only taking on loads of three to four hundred *jin* (1 *jin* = 0.5 kilograms) at a time. Second, they used neither rudders nor oars, propelled only by short bamboo poles. Third, there was no differentiation between the bow and stern—earning these boats the nickname "looking both ways" —in which case there was no need to turn the boats around, only to decide whether they were coming or going. For the sake of urban sanitation, boats travelling on the Jinhe River should also abide by a customary rule: All food-bearing vessels were to enter the city by morning or midday, while those transporting human waste were only to enter around five in the afternoon.

Over the years, we've read many poems and prose extolling the beauty of the Jinjiang River, but in the past time, Chengdu's Jinhe River was also a beautiful "mother river" supporting the flourishing of countless homes. After major renovations to the river were completed during the reign of Emperor Jiajing in the Ming Dynasty (r. 1522 ~ 1566) , Chengdu Magistrate Liu Kan wrote a piece called *On the Reopening of the Jinshuihe*, providing a detailed and vivid account of the Jinhe River: " The ripples of the Jinhe River expand, permeating the marketplace. Shu (Sichuan) people rush and gather to watch, wondering at its magical allure. The potsmiths fetch water, the filthy are cleansed, the thirsty take drinks, silk is rinsed, and gardens are irrigated. Officials in brocades and exquisite women mix and jostle, a thousand voices are raised in cheer, and every spirit is lifted. " Inside the Manchu City in the Qing Dynasty, there were few structures on either bank of the Jinhe River; mostly it was flanked by farm and vegetable plots. Thus, up until the early years of the Republican period, articles continued to refer to the area as "fields and thickets".

Perhaps, the most surprising thing in the history of the Jinhe River is that a water turbine was once put to use there around 1880 in the late Qing Dynasty. Ding Baozhen, a firearms manufacturer working at the Sichuan Machinery Bureau—which was located along the Jinhe River near Gongbei Bridge—enlisted Zeng Zhaoji, an eminent technician from Shandong Province, specifically to build a small-scale water turbine on the Jinhe River. Water stored in the river during the summer and autumn drove the turbine to generate electricity; only in the winter and spring did the use of electricity rely fully upon coal. This was able to save more than 500 kilograms of coal per day, and more than 4,000 silver taels per year. One time, Ding Baozhen even reported to Emperor Guangxu specifically on this matter. Unfortunately, the details of the small hydropower station were never recorded. (Looking back, we can infer that this was a pilot seasonal power station and experimental in nature. Chengdu was also the site of Sichuan's first genuine full-fledged hydropower station built in 1929 at Hualong Bridge. Its founder, Zou Xinkai, born in Zhonghechang, studied hydropower in Lyon, France, and then returned to establish Zhongheminyou Hydropower, Inc. The small hydropower station had an installed capacity of 3 kilowatts and continued to operate. Until 1934, it was forced to close over water disputes).

The Jinhe riverbank, 1935. Photo courtesy of Sang Yichuan.

There was also a time when the Jinhe River served as a firefighting reservoir for the entire city. In 1940, in preparation for preventing fires resulting from Japanese air raids, four floodgates were built on the Jinhe River to store and separate a large supply of water, essentially forming a series of massive reservoirs.

In 1971, amidst the "Cultural Revolution", orders came down demanding that air raid shelters must be built for preparations for the battle. At this point, the government determined that it would construct a long "air raid tunnel" by cutting off the Jinhe River's water supply, adding brickworks, and building an arched roof overhead. I took part in this project, laboring along Longwangmiao Main Street with teachers and students from History Department of Sichuan University. Destroyig a portion of the Jinhe River with my own hands, I built an "air-raid shelter" that couldn't really shelter at all. I can recall how that year both banks of the river were lined with weeping willows, and how the Jinhe's water babbled as it flowed past. Those who lived nearby washed clothes there. Though there were few fish to be found, a number of ducks flitted freely about.

Throughout the devastating "Cultural Revolution", three major acts of stupidity were committed in Chengdu's city planning. The first was destroying the Jinhe and Yuhe rivers. The second was destroying the Imperial City. And the third was destroying Zhaojue Temple to create a zoo. Just try to imagine if Chengdu still had a lovely river lined with weeping willows—if it still had the majestic Imperial City seated at its city center, encircled by the Yuhe River—and if it had something so grand and ancient as the former Zhaojue Temple! How beautiful it would be!

Yet the Jinhe River was not completely destroyed. As a part of the river happened to cross through the People's Park, leaving it alone was a preferable alternative to extending the "air raid tunnel" through the park instead. Thus it lives on as those few-dozen meters of streams passing under the bridges of the park. Although one no longer hears any "babbling" from the flow of its waters, one can still see a little trace of history there. Elderly Chengdu residents still remember how, all the way up until the founding of the P. R. C. , tourists could rent a small boat in "Shaocheng Park" and row it all the way to Tonghuimen.

Although today Chengdu lacks a Jinhe River, it still has a Jinhe Road, as well as a Jinhebian ("Jinhe Riverside") Street, with the famous Jinhe Hotel located on the former site. As long as one hears such names, one can be sure—the Jinhe River once passed by there.

Flowing through the densely populated districts of the city center, many bridges were built across the Jinhe River during the Qing Dynasty. Some of their names are still used as street names in today's Chengdu. Walking west to east, one encounters Banbian Bridge Street, Old Wolong Bridge Street, Jinjiang Bridge Street, Qingshi Bridge Street, Xiangrong Bridge Street, Yuqing Bridge Street and Gongbei Bridge Street. All of these streets still in use today were named after the bridges they bore back then. Apart from these memorialized bridges, however, there were yet more once spanning the Jinhe, now absent in both form and name—for example: Qingyuan Bridge outside the city wall (which had Kuixing Pavilion built upon it), Jinhua Bridge at the entrance to today's Tongren Road (most likely the location of Chengdu's famous City Bridge of the Han and Jin dynasties), Hongban Bridge at the entrance to today's Shizi Alley, Jielü Bridge on the south side of the General's Yamen (also known as "Jieli Bridge", it was the Jinhe River's only wood plank bridge without rails, and continued to be used after the founding of the P. R. C.), Tongshun Bridge at the north entrance to today's Xiaonan Street, Xieban Bridge leading to the side entrance of the People's Park, Gongbei Bridge and Yinding Bridge within the People's Park, Sanqiao Bridge at today's Tianfu Square, Jinjiang Bridge at the east entrance to today's Ranfang Street, Taiping Bridge and Yidong Bridge on today's New Banbian Street, the Old Wolong Bridge on today's Hongxing Road, Banban Bridge and Jingyun Bridge on Longwangmiao Main Street, Jinjin Bridge on today's Xialianchi Street, Tieban Bridge beyond the old city's exit gate, Puxian Bridge on today's Qing'An Street, Da'An Bridge on today's South Tianxianqiao Road, and a few more 22 bridges in total. In the Qing Dynasty, to accommodate boat traffic on the river, every bridge downstream Banbian Bridge was originally an arch bridge. Elderly denizens recall the height of Old Wolong Bridge—more than a *chi* (or a third of a meter).

The West Gate

Just the same as the East Gate, people in Chengdu refer to the West Gate as the old West Gate because the New West Gate was built on the western end of Chengdu City.

It is still unknown that how many West Gates were built in Chengdu in the Qin Dynasty for the lack of historical materials. In the Han Dynasty, there probably used to be two West Gates, but only one of them was called Shiqiao Gate. It was clear that there were two West Gates in the Tang Dynasty whose names were "the Bigger West Gate" and "the Smaller West Gate". The location of "the Smaller West Gate" was roughly the same as the one of the Shiqiao Gate during the Qin and Han dynasties, so the name of this gate was also changed into "the Smaller Shiqiao Gate". In the Former Shu Kingdom (891 ~ 925 AD) among the Five Dynasties, all the names of the gates were changed. The Bigger West Gate was changed into Qianzheng Gate and the Smaller West Gate was changed into Yanqiu Gate. When it came to the Song and Yuan dynasties, the former names of the Bigger West Gate and the Smaller West Gate were both restored. In the early years of the Ming Dynasty, there were five city gates in total along the city wall of Chengdu with one gate on each end of the city except for the west end where there were two gates whose locations were approximately identical to that of the Bigger West Gate and the Smaller West Gate in the Tang Dynasty. Among the two gates, the one on the north side was named Qingyuan Gate and the other one on the south side was named Yanqiu Gate whose location was roughly equivalent to that of today's Tonghui Gate. In the twenty-ninth year during the reign of Emperor Hongwu in the Ming Dynasty (1396), the Smaller West Gate was closed and only the Bigger West Gate was left as Qingyuan Gate. In the Qing Dynasty, the city pattern of the Ming Dynasty was inherited with only Qingyuan Gate left on the west end which still stood on the north side but was located at the northwest corner of the city, namely the location of Xiyuecheng Street. A building called Jiangyuan Tower was also built on this gate.

The west city wall of Chengdu in the Republic of China with an advertisement of a watch shop on Chunxi Road. Photo courtesy of Jacques Dumasy [France].

The western part of Chengdu City in the Qing Dynasty was the Manchu City, so the larger city and the Manchu city shared the same west city wall and the same west gate. Due to this fact, the West Gate of Chengdu City in the Qing Dynasty was actually used by the Manchu City. The Han people at that time were not allowed to go through this gate. People who wanted to travel to Pixian County and Guanxian County could only go through the North Gate or the South Gate. This was why the place outside the South Gate was more bustling than that outside the South Gate.

Tonghuimen and Tonghuimen Road

In the Qing Dynasty, Chengdu's west gate in the Manchu City was situated rather far to the north, making it highly inconvenient for the residents (including the Manchu and Mongol bannermen) to set out from the city in a south-westerly direction. This was particularly vexing for attendees of the flower festival held each year at Qingyang Temple. To get there, city dwellers would have to leave Chengdu either by the Old South Gate or the North Gate, walking around the city wall. Just as one of *Bamboo Branch Verses* during Emperor Tongzhi period in the Qing Dynasty (r. 1862 ~ 1875 AD) reads:

> A path winds its way to the distant Wuhou Temple,
> A roundabout route by the way of the Wanli Bridge.
> I'm going to the flower market at Qingyang Temple,
> Where the flower festival will be held tomorrow.

But in the early years of the Republican period, when the Manchu City's walls began to be torn down, exiting the city from the southwest became possible. In 1913, Hu Jingyi, Sichuan Tuchun (Military Governor) ordered the opening of a new city gate. It would be situated behind Xijiaochang and face out in the direction of Qingyang Temple and Erxian Temple (Temple of Two Immortals) to facilitate transportation to the flower festival. The name of the new gate—Tonghuimen or Tonghui Gate—was taken from a line in *The Commentary of Zuo: Second Year of Duke Min* (660 BC), a history of the Spring and Autumn period. "*Tong*" refers to trade interrelations, while "*Hui*" means benefit, so the name expresses convenient circulation and mutual gains. Indeed, the new gate immediately made it convenient for the public. As a *Bamboo Branch Verse* from that period expresses:

> A shortcut opens where Tonghuimen lies;
> Wagons shuttle like the clouds in the sky.
> Carts carry women like carrying flowers,
> Raising a whirl of red dusts flying high.

A well-known literary critic and historian Tang Zhenchang (1922 ~ 2002) grew up in Chengdu. In a pair of essays recalling his hometown, he said that when Tonghuimen was being built, there was a giant banner hanging from one of its towers. It's a phrase written by Zhou Shanpei, who had made many contributions to Sichuan's modernization in the late Qing Dynasty. The banner reads:

Beautiful and lofty, its name is Chengdu. Build up civilization, go beyond the past.

I couldn't find much records of this in other anecdotal accounts of Chengdu, but it does fit with the overall strategy of city planning at that time.

The older generation who grew up in Chengdu tend to refer to Tonghuimen As Xinximen ("New West Gate") , and the original West Gate as "Old West Gate".

As there are no city walls or gates in Chengdu today, Tonghuimen no longer exists in that form, but there is still a Tonghuimen Road. After the Tonghui Gate was built, the path leading there from within the city gradually came to form a street— "Tonghui Street", which continued to be called so after the founding of the P. R. C. , until a place-name survey in 1981 adjusted it to Tonghuimen Street. It ran from Tongren Road in the east to Shi'erqiao Road in the west. After the construction of Shudu Avenue and subsequent sectioning of roads, it was renamed Tonghuimen Road.

To the south of Tonghuimen Road is former Xijiaochang. In the Qing Dynasty, it was a field where the Manchu and Mongol Eight Banners conducted drills, and it continued to be used for military purposes throughout the Republican period. Likewise, the Logistics Department of Chengdu Military Region (now the Joint Logistics Department of Chengdu Military Region) was also stationed there for a long time following the founding of the P. R. C.. During the War of Resistance Against Japanese Aggression (1937 ~ 1945) , as Chiang Kai-shek's central forces slowly gathered in Sichuan, a special operation base was set up there diagonally across from the General's Yamen. Together, they came to serve as the base camp for Chengdu's Kuomintang (KMT) military police intelligence. To dress itself up in front of the city residents, Xijiaochang's gate was engraved with the same famous couplet that could be found on the main gate of the Whampoa Military Academy (the military academy for the Republic of China, located in Guangzhou) :

If you look for promotions and wealth, please go elsewhere.
If you cling to life and fear death, do not pass through this door.

But Chengdu residents only turned up their noses at such hypocrisy, circulating a joke made by changing a few characters of the saying:

If you look for promotions and wealth, please come this way.
If you cling to life and fear death, hurry through this gate.

As the day of Chengdu's liberation (by the People's Liberation Army) drew near, Sheng Wen, a Commander of the Third Army under Hu Zongnan's Division, set up the "Chengdu General Defense Command" at this site, issuing "ten lethal orders" (actually 12) and sending soldiers across the city to violently subdue or massacre anyone they found suspicious. As news of killings on Chunxi Road spread among the people, they began referring to the Xijiaochang military encampment as "a butcher's table for chopping flesh". And it was precisely from this "butcher's table for chopping flesh" that Sheng Wen—in compliance with Hu Zongnan and Chiang Kai-shek— deployed two units on a mission to blow up the entire city. Detailed plans had already been put in place, and it was only because underground forces were able to incite defection within the two units that Chengdu narrowly escaped this colossal disaster.

Shi'er Bridge outside of Tonghuimen (Tonghui Gate), in the early years of the Republican period. Photo courtesy of Yang Xianfeng.

Changshun Street

There is a very long road in Chengdu's inner city called Changshun Street. Although it was an extremely important road in the Qing Dynasty, it was one without a name.

In the Qing Dynasty, the Manchu City was constructed on the near-west side of Chengdu. It had a central axis with many *hutongs* extending from its sides. This layout prompted some to describe the Manchu City as a giant centipede: the General's Yamen was its head; the long central lane was its body; and the *hutongs* were its many legs. Because each *hutong* was the dedicated living area for some part of the Manchu and Mongol soldiers and their families, each one had a name; it was only the main thoroughfare connecting them because it was for public use, thus was never given a name. When the Manchu City was dismantled in the Republican period, its various *hutongs* were renamed as streets and alleys; meanwhile, the main street was also given a name. Initially it was called Tongshun Street, as *tongshun* expresses longevity and smooth connection, but as there was already a well-established Tongshun Street in the north of the city—and even an East Tongshun Street—it was ultimately renamed to avoid repetition. The name Changshun was chosen as it still conveys the originally intended meaning (*chang* means "long"; *shun* means "smooth").

Changshun Upper Street, 2020 Photo by Zhang Xinan

Changshun Street is indeed long, totaling approximately 1,700 meters. Thus it is divided into Upper Changshun Street, Middle Changshun Street, and Lower Changshun Street from south to north. Among these, Upper Changshun Street has a rather unique trait—its southernmost section splits off into two directions, forming a "Y" shape. This is because Changshun Street originally terminated at the General's Yamen—the Manchu City's highest military and political office. Although the General's Yamen naturally had roads within it—one principal north-south road on each side—neither of them had names. It was only in the early years of the Republican period when Changshun Street was named that both of the road became "Upper Changshun Street", with the eastern branch designated as the main one. The branches of Changshun Upper Street adjoin at their north ends where they meet Zhijishi Street. This layout has been maintained until today (though strictly speaking, it is the most illogical). On either side of the Jinhe Hotel, one can find two separate places, each marked by a street sign, where Jinhe Road intersects with Upper Changshun Street. In the course of my investigations, I have found no other such case among the streets of Chengdu.

Likely following the Manchus' and Mongols' dietary habits, two of Chengdu's most famous beef dishes originate from Changshun Street, which lies in the heart of the Manchu City. Since the founding of the P. R. C. , these two beef dishes have each graced the tables of the Banquet Hall of the Great Hall of the People.

Inventors of *fuqi feipian* ("husband and wife lung slices") : Guo Chaohua and Zhang Tianzheng couple

One Sichuan dish that would gained nationwide popularity started out as the *mala feipian* ("hot and numbing lung slices") sold by a married couple Guo Chaohua and Zhang Tianzheng at a small roadside stand on Upper Changshun Street in the 1930s (some elderly residents recalled that before setting up their roadside stand, they'd sell their dishes from a pushcart, calling out as they went up and down the lane—hence the saying: "The cart travels halfway down the street; the scent of meat pervades the neighborhood"). The dish gained popularity for its superior flavor, and people gradually began to call it *fuqi feipian* ("sliced beef lungs sold by husband and wife" or "sliced beef and ox tongue in chili sauce"). As their reputation grows, the couple was able to transform their business into a small shop. As described in the *Memories of Old Jincheng*① *Bamboo Branch Verses*:

> A mom-and-pop shop they run as the Sima's② do,
> Operating it with a joint effort all to the good.
> Husband cuts meat while wife manages the sauce,
> Mixing green onions to season a wonderful food.

After the founding of the P. R. C. , the *fuqi feipian* shop moved first to Banbianqiao Street, then to a large restaurant on Tidu Street, hence its fame spread far and wide.

Early on, *fuqi feipian* had another popular name: "looks both ways". This is because the early "lung slices" actually evolved from *bobo* beef (another Sichuanese dish) and it didn't have a particular name in its own right. The "lung slices" *feipian* were originally a different *feipian*, meaning "leftover cuts" —in other words, scraps of beef offal and tripe. These *bobo* beef leftovers were cooked in brine, cut into big slices, mixed with spices and seasonings, and put into large earthenware bowls that were then hung on the side of the street. With a few pairs of chopsticks stuck inside, those strapped for cash—including young children—bought these *feipian* by slice. I was just such a customer in my own youth. Yet there was something rather inelegant, if irresistible, about eating *bobo* beef while standing in the street, such that those diners who cared about their reputations would always look both ways before digging in, making sure that no one they knew was around to see them. That's where the nickname "looks both ways" came from; only later was it to win the more refined title

---

① Jincheng is another name for Chengdu.

② Sima Xiangru and Zhuo Wenjun are poet lovers during the Western Han Dynasty (202 BC − 8 AD). After eloping, they ran a pub together.

of "*fuqi feipian*". Regarding the transformation of this famous dish's name in Sichuan, the 1943 publication of "*New Chengdu*" explains the problem best: its name in the book is "beef lung slices", with the alternative name "*panpan* beef" (*panpan* refers to a container for beef) in parentheses.

Originally at the intersection of Changshun and Kuixinglou Streets, Zhidehao was founded by Yao Shucheng in 1934. The shop primarily sold braised beef noodles and *xiaolong* (bamboo basket) steamed beef—the latter earned them citywide fame. The primary means of *xiaolong* steamed beef consumption at the time was to pile it up in a baked wheat flatbread called a *guokui*. Basically it was Chengdu's take on the sandwich. After the founding of the P. R. C., Zhidehao's *xiaolong* steamed beef became a famous Chengdu snack. The flagship store used to be on West Renmin Road and then relocated to Yinsi Street before moving to its current location on Sandongqiao Street.

There are three main streets running from south to north on the west side of Chengdu. From east to west there are: Dongchenggen Street, Changshun Street, and Tongren Road. Because of their length, all three have been segmented into upper, middle, and lower sections. The thing to be noted here is that *Dongchenggen* and Changshun Streets' upper, middle and lower sections go "up" as one goes south (the southernmost are the "upper" sections and the northernmost are the "lower" sections). Also, the segment name goes after the street's name—e. g. Upper Dongchenggen Street and Lower Changshun Street. For Tongren Road, however, the order is reversed, and the sections go "up" as one goes north. Not only that, the name of the section goes before the name of the street—as in the Shangtongren Road ("Upper Tongren Road"), the Zhongtongren Road ("Middle Tongren Road"), and the Xiatongren Road ("Lower Tongren Road"). This discrepancy is the result of history rather than any sort of logic, but it is necessary to add a reminder here for those friends unfamiliar with the streets, lest they keep confusing the north/south location of their upper, lower, and middle sections.

Dongchenggen Street

Literally meaning "at the foot of the city", *chenggen* is an ancient term—appearing, for instance, in poet Wei Yingwu's *"Appreciating Poems from Minister Qin and Minister Shu on a Beautiful Spring Day"* : *"Chenggen is* halfway up the mountain, the pavilion reflected in the center of water. " In modern times, *chenggen* is used in Beijing dialect to refer to streets. The term was not initially used in Chengdu dialect, but was introduced in the Qing Dynasty via Manchu and Mongol bannermen who continued to speak Beijing dialect in the Manchu City. In fact, today's Beijing still has a place called *Huang Chenggen*—literally "at the foot of the imperial city" —though these days it's been changed to its homophone meaning "at the foot of the yellow city". As for Chengdu, there is only one instance of *chenggen* still used to name the contemporary street. There is also a discrepancy between how the term is used in Chengdu compared with Beijing—in Beijing (as well as nearby Baoding) , one absolutely must add the nonsyllabic " er" suffix (*chenggenr*) , but not do so in Chengdu. A number of words appearing in Chengdu's place names bear the obvious influence of Beijing—*hutong*, *pailou* (ceremonial archway) , *xiao naoba* (pool) , and *dakeng yanr* (pondside) —then, of course, there is the one well-known street that retains its original *chenggen* name, and that's *Dongchenggen* ("East Chenggen") .

Dongchenggen Street refers to the east wall of the Manchu City in the Qing Dynasty. Built early in the Qing Dynasty, once west outer wall in the Ming Dynasty—which served as the spirit screen'was completely demolished. Some of the bricks used in the east wall's construction came from the outer city wall that once surrounded Shu Palace; in fact, the east wall of the Manchu City used the very same foundation as the former Shu Palace wall. The Qing bannermen referred to the road at the foot of the eastern wall as *Dongchenggen*, such that the road forming in the same location where once the wall was torn down in the early years of the Republican period took the same name: Dongchenggen Street.

Constructed in stages over the early years of the Republican period, Dongchenggen Street was the city's first road construction project after the fall of the Qing Dynasty. In 1913 demolition started on the Manchu City wall. The old revolutionary and famous educator Zhang Xiushu wrote a *Bamboo Branch Verse* titled

Memories of Dongchenggen Street:

Speaking of the Chengdu's city infrastructure,
I witnessed its construction in the fiftieth year[1].
At the junction of two streets at Citang east gate,
Wall was torn up while road was under repair.

Road construction began over the founding of the torn-down eastern wall in 1916. Early after its completion in 1918, Xiong Kewu (the then-commander of Sichuan's military and a veteran of Sichuan's Xinhai Revolution) renamed Dongchenggen as "Jingguo Road". This was to commemorate the site where supporters of Sun Yat-sen had formed the Sichuan Jingguojun ("National Pacification Army"). There was once even a stone tablet at where Dongchenggen intersected today's Dongsheng Street that bore the three characters "*Jing Guo Road*" —these were written by Dan Maoxin, another Sichuan Xinhai revolutionary and officer in the Jingguojun (General Dan was quite well-known for his calligraphy, especially his large-character inscriptions; he was also responsible for the large stone inscriptions at the entrances to King Wang and King Cong's tombs at Wang and Cong Memorial in present-day Pixian County, Sichuan.) Because nearby residents were already accustomed to calling this place Dongchenggen, however, the name "Jingguo Road" never caught on. In 1924, Sichuan Tuchun Yang Sen targeted a number of sites in the city center for a road expansion project. Dongchenggen was among the streets to be broadened and was lengthened at the same time. Stretching over 1.5 kilometers from Citang Street in the south to Qinglong Street in the north, it was subdivided into outh, upper, middle and lower sections of Dongchenggen Street. This four-segment naming conventions survive to this day. Today's Lower Dongchenggen Street, however, is different from the original Lower Dongchenggen Street. The new lower street was constructed to straighten out the original's bending course. One can still find the bend located at the juncture of the original middle and lower sections, but the original lower street is now called Old Dongchenggen Street to differentiate it from the newer and straighter extension of Lower Dongchenggen Street.

---

[1] The fiftieth year in the sexagenary cycle (in this case, 1913)

Market on Dongchenggen Lower Street in the 1980s. Photo courtesy of Yang Xianfeng.

West of Old Dongchenggen Street and east of the new Lower Dongchenggen Street was a short "Dongchenggen Cross Street". This was originally the eastern part of East Erdao Street, broken off when the new Lower Dongchenggen Street was constructed after the founding of the P. R. C. The resulting layout meant that this separated section of East Erdao Street now ran east-west to connect two different Dongchenggen Streets, so it was named Dongchenggen Cross Street.

Dongchenggen Street was a new street in the Republican period, and the business there was far from booming. Yet in the cultural life of old Chengdu, a teahouse located at the intersection of Dongchenggen and Xiyu Streets left an indelible impression. Jinchun Teahouse's wide-reaching fame came from the "Three Wonders of Jincheng" (or "Gang of Three"): Blind Jia, who sang *zhuqin* (Sichuan bamboo drum)[1], Pock-faced Zhou, whose artistry in tea-pouring was unmatched, and Fatty Si, who sold shelled peanuts. [In the later years of the Republic, Chengdu also had a somewhat different list of the "Four Wonders of Jincheng"; they were the city's four most famous folk artists: "Blind" Jia Shusan (*zhuqin*), Li Decai (*yangqin*, dulcimer), Zeng Bingkun (*xiangshu*, vocal imitation), and Li Yueqiu (*qingyin*, Sichuan ballad singing).]

---

① *Zhuqin* is an ancient musical genre in Sichuan where rhythms beaten on bamboo tube drums are accompanied by the sung rhymed prose. [Translator's note]

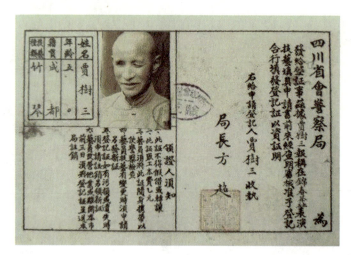

Jia Shusan's registration certificate for engaging in art, 1941

Perfectly reflecting Chengdu's spirit as an immigrant city, Jia Shusan skillfully employed multiple regional dialects in his performances—including Cantonese, Shaanxi dialect, and Lower Yangtze Mandarin. This ability was rare among Chengdu's late-Qing artists.

Blind Jia (1894 – 1951), actual name Jia Shusan, a member of the Hui people, and was born and raised in Chengdu's Hui district, Huangchengba. He was orphaned when he was one year old and went blind at the age of three, after which everyone called him "Blind Jia". His family background and resulting destitution forced him into selling pear-syrup candies on the street since the age of six. At the age of ten, he began to learn *zhuqin* from an herbal doctor named Li, after which he successively studied under Ma Shaocheng and Cai Juezhi. He also innovated a one-person version of the traditional five-person band①, singing and performing all the traditional theatrical personas himself. He absorbed the essence of Sichuan opera and *yangqin* masters' vocal arts and gained fame throughout the province for his unique gifts for the bamboo drum, effectively starting the "Jia school" of *zhuqin*. Since early 1930, with major support from Tan Chuangzhi, Chengdu cultural celebrity and editor-in-chief of the *National*

---

① Literally "five person sit-and-sing"; this method of performance is still used for Sichuan *yangqing* (dulcimer).

Gazette, he was booked permanently for nightly performances at the Jinchun Teahouse (only during the War of Resistance Against Japanese Aggression, the venue was temporarily moved to a tea shop outside the Old West Gate in order to avoid being bombed). His special act continued for 20 years—exceptionally rare for a folk artist, and a brilliant addition to Chengdu's modern cultural history. Just as Tan Chuangzhi wrote after he watched Jia Shusan's performance: "Hearing the vicissitudes of life through his songs, I gazed at the extraordinary Blind Jia for a long spell; his performance had aroused all the human emotions to surge and clash in my heart, where can I find such a soul as to harmonize with Li Guinian[1]?" His singing was not only popular among all manner of Chengdu people; he could also count military leaders from the north like Feng Yuxiang, well-traveled journalists like the renowned Hu Yuzhi, and famous actors like Xie Tian among his "fans". Feng Yuxiang once said: "I believe that Beijing's Liu Baoquan (that era's "King of Jingyun Drum"[2]) and Sichuan's Jia Shusan are a perfect double in skill". During the War of Resistance Against Japanese Aggression, famous modern author Mao Dun once said: "No visit to Chengdu is complete without hearing Blind Jia's *zhuqin*". The former Sichuan Tuchun Yin Changheng, a political giant among Chengdu's older generation, once honored Blind Jia with the following couplet: "Those great works of the glory days are heard but rarely now, yet today has brought the second coming of Shi Kuang[3]". The blind man's talent is matchless, with his best works being "Chu Dao Huan Ji" ("The Road to Chu Leads Back to My Lover"), "Li Ling Jian You" ("Farewell to Li Ling"), "Xun Yang Song Ke" ("Seeing off Guests in Xunyang"), and "Zi Xu Du Lu" ("Zi Xu Crosses the Reeds"). He expertly moves between the expressions of each Chinese opera character, and his impassioned performance dazzles the crowd.

Pock-faced Zhou, whose true name has been lost to the past, was an outstanding representative of Chengdu's traditional tea art. When serving guests, he would always

---

[1] Li Guiyuan, composer and musician in the Tang Dynasty.

[2] Jingyun Drum is a folk art from Beijing where a performer matches drum and vocal tones to tell stories in Beijing dialect.

[3] Shi Kuang, a famous blind musician from the State of Jin in the Spring and Autumn period (771 – 476 BC) of ancient China.

lift a copper kettle of boiling water with his right hand and wedge six brass saucers—laden with overlapping white porcelain teacups and lids—on the palm of his left hand (if the occasion called for it, he could hold more than ten tea settings at a time). Standing before a customers' table, they'd only see a flick of his hand and the saucers would each fly spinning directly to the position before each guest. They'd only hear a "clack-clack-clack", and cups would have alighted on their saucers like birds returning to their nests. Zhou would then raise his right hand and deliver a stream of water right past each customer's ear and into their cups without splashing a single drop onto the table. And then—clink! —before the guests could get over their shock, he'd have deftly placed the lids on their cups using only the little finger of his left hand. This kind of "tea art" arose entirely out of the practical need to serve guests quickly and efficiently. It was a true skill honed over years of diligent training.

Fewer and fewer people have cultivated such skill after the founding of the P. R. C.. In the autumn of 1989, I saw such a master Wu at Heming Teahouse in Chengdu's People's Park, but nowadays this tea art has been essentially forgotten. After the Reform and Opening-up, "long-spout tea performance", as popularized by the Liao brothers, began to appear in Chengdu. This style of performance is based on the martial arts (*gongfu*), and is completely different from the traditional short-spout tea art, which developed its characteristic speed and skill through the practical demands of service.

True to his name, Fatty Si was a man of corpulence. There is no way to confirm whether his surname was truly "Si" or "Sima". He carried a bamboo basket around the teahouse, selling fried peanuts and pumpkin seeds wrapped in paper packaging. He would shout four short phrases in an endless loop: "shrimp-fried peanuts, five-spiced broad beans, savor the taste, full of flavor!" The peanuts were uniform in size, exquisite and crisp, with unbroken red skins; the pumpkin seeds were all evenly plump, perfectly shaped "crow's beaks". If you happened to chance upon one that'd gone bad, you'd be compensated immediately with two fresh packs—a hard find in the Chengdu of that day.

Today's Dongchenggen Street is an important south-north passage in central Chengdu. Home to a number of important businesses as well as party and government organizations, it sees a great deal of traffic. In the past, however, Dongchenggen Street terminated at Babao Street in the north and Xiyu Street in the south, in each case ending in a "T" form. It was extremely inconvenient for downtown traffic. Thus urban renovations in the 1990s extended Dongchenggen's reach by building Wanhe

Road—which runs north to the Fuhe River at Wuding Bridge—and Wenweng Road—which runs south to the Nanhe River at Nanhe Bridge. This greatly improves the flow of traffic. Because these three streets constitute such a major downtown corridor, and Dongchenggen is their trunk, many in the city have taken to calling Wanhe Road and Wenweng Road the north and south extensions of Dongchenggen Street, respectively.

Dongchenggenjie Primary School is where famous author and Chengdu native Ba Jin (1904 ~ 2005) began his education. Starting from May 15th, 1991, Ba Jin wrote letters or sent books to the schoolchildren on nine different occasions, encouraging them to study carefully, play wholeheartedly, speak honestly, and be good people. To commemorate this literary great, Dongchenggenjie Primary School officially changed its name to Ba Jin Primary School, and erected a bronze statue of him there.

As *Dongchenggen* means "at the east foot of the city", then rightly there should be a *Xichenggen* ("at the west foot of the city") as well. Indeed, in the Qing Dynasty, the road along the west side of the Manchu City wall was called Xichenggen. After the Xinhai Revolution, however, it was officially renamed Tongren Road, and the name "Xichenggen" disappeared.

Junping Street and Junping Alley

Located behind the People's Park, Junping Street was named to commemorate Yan Junping. Yan Junping is the earliest historical figure whose memory is preserved in one of Chengdu's street names of today.

Yan Zun (approx. 80 BC ~ 10 AD) with Junping as his courtesy name; his full name was originally Zhuang Zun, but his surname was changed to "Yan" because the name "Zhuang" was part of the name of Liu Zhuang, Emperor Ming in the Han Dynasty and thus a taboo at the time. Yan Zun was a famous reclusive thinker in the late Western Han (202 BC ~ 8 AD) and the teacher of Yang Xiong (53 BC ~ 18 AD). In his time, he had a considerable status and influence. It was precisely during the Han Dynasty that Chengdu came to be known as "literary crown of the world", even though only three famous writers left behind records of their lives and achievements there—Sima Xiangru, Yan Junping, and Yang Xiong (after the Han Dynasty, these three, along with the poet Wang Bao of Ziyang, were lauded as "The Four Gentlemen of Shu"). Throughout his life, Yan Junping made his living as a fortune teller, and had a deep understanding of Taoist philosophy. Just as Li Bai wrote in *Ode to Yan Zun*: "Observe the change of things, penetrate the primordial chaos, understand the origin of things, and educate and inspire the people." Leaving only a single and incomplete work to posterity—*The Essential Meaning of the Laozi* (*Laozi Zhigui*) —it is nevertheless one of the most important works of Taoism ever written.

Yan Junping's residence in Chengdu was most likely located on today's Zhijishi Street, where the Temple of Immortal Yan[1] was built after his death. In the early Qing Dynasty, however, Zhijishi Street was incorporated into the Manchu City in the process of its construction. As Han subjects were not permitted to be freely walked about in the city, this undermined Han literati's ability to pay respects or offer

---

[1] "Yan Zhen" Temple. Over the passage of time, Yan Junping came to be revered as a Taoist deity. [Translator's Note]

sacrifices to revere Yan Junping. Thus, the new road built south of the Manchu City wall was named Junping Street in his honor. A large household living on that road at the time happened to be surnamed "Zhuang" and thus proceeded to claim descendants from Yan Junping. They also converted the street's Zitong Palace (a hall for worshipping Lord Wenchang, the Taoist God of Culture and Literature) into the Yan Zun Temple. This was how, over time, people came to mistake Junping Street for the actual site of Yan Junping's residence in the Han Dynasty.

Junping Park, 2009. Photo by Tingdong.

Junping Alley is a small lane jutting south off of Junping Street. It was originally named Huo Xiangzi ("Fire Lane"), but was renamed because another alley on the north side of the city, near Wanfu Bridge, was also called Huo Xiangzi (the northern Huo Xiangzi was later demolished during the urban reconstruction).

In 2006, Junping Park was built on Junping Street to commemorate the great scholar. The park features a number of cultural attractions including Yanxian Pavilion (Immortal Yan Pavilion), Zhigui Corridor, and Tongxian Well (Well of Immortality).

Early records only state that Yan Junping was from Chengdu, while some later records clearly state that he was from Qionglai, a city 60 kilometers southwest of Chengdu. Among present-day Chengdu's suburban counties, Qionglai and Pengzhou each contains a Junping Village, and both Qionglai and Pixian County have Junping Tombs. The Junping Tomb at Hengshanzi in Tangchang, Pixian County, however, is the most well-preserved, with an ancestral shrine to Junping situated in front. In the Qing Dynasty, Xu Rulong wrote the poem *The Tomb of Junping* to memorize him.

Xiaonan Street

Chengdu's Xiaonan ("Small South") Street has nothing to do with its Nanda ("Big South") Street, nor are they adjacent to each other.

Xiaonan Street has the old and the new ones. The old one starts from Citang Street in the north and ends at Junping Street in the south. Because of its location in the southernmost area inside the Manchu City, it was the main road to the city from its south gate, Tongfu Gate, which stands on Xiaonan Street just north of where it intersects Junping Street today. Tongfu Gate was also called Xiaonanmen (Small South Gate) at that time, so this street was called Xiaonanmen Main Street, simplified to Xiaonan Street after the founding of the Republic of China. Construction in recent years has extended Xiaonan Street southward, essentially to make it a southern extension of Changshun Street. It stretches all the way down to the Nanhe River, and becomes a longer new Xiaonan Street.

In the early years of the Republican period, there was a bamboo-thatched cottage at Xiaonan Street's north entrance near the Jinhe River (or where where present Nulican Restaurant is located). Written on its front entrance were the two characters "*Chai Fei*". This is where the Republican heroine Du Huang once lived.

Du Huang (**1879 ~ 1929**), with her original name Huang Mingxun, from Hankou in Hubei Province. She was sociable and liked to study since her childhood. After she married Du Deyu (also called Du Guan and nicknamed Chai Fei) of Changning, Sichuan Province, she changed her name to Du Huang. They moved to Beijing in the twenty-seventh year during the reign of Emperor Guangxu (1901). There she met famous revolutionary heroine Qiu Jin; the two like-minded women became as close as sisters. From then on, Du Huang devoted herself to the democratic revolution and feminist movement. She first started the Du's Home School for Girls, then founded the Sichuan Girls' School in the Sichuan Ying Hutong, the first girls' school in Beijing. In the thirtieth year during the reign of Emperor Guangxu (1904), Qiu Jin introduced her into the Tongmenghui (United League), thus she became Beijing's first female member of the Tongmenghui. Under instructions of Tongmenghui headquarters, she started a publication for the *China Women's Association* and founded the *Guoguang News Agency in Beijing and the office of the Tongmenghui (United League) in Tianjing*, and became the first female member of the military department of the Tongmenhui. *Together with her husband, already a Tongmenghui participant, she contacted leaders in each northern province to establish the official Qianyuan* Liaison for the Gelaohui (or "Hatchet Gang") in Beijing. Du Huang was dubbed as "the female Lord Mengchang[①]" by Xiong Kewu, a senior figure in the Xinhai Revolution movement in Sichuan. She took part in a series of anti-Qing actions. There were a number of assassination plots that shocked the regime— bombings even targeted Prince-Regent Zaiyang, Qing official Yuan Shikai (unsuccessfully), and Leader of the Royalist Party General Liangbi—all of these actions were assisted by Du Huang. She provided the bombs for the assassinations, and became known as "the Tongmeng Heroine". After the Wuchang Uprising, she buried four Sichuanese martyrs of the Tongmenghui at Beijing's Wansheng Park (now the Beijing Zoo), composing an elegiac couplet for Peng Jiazhen in Chengdu. After Yuan Shikai seized control of the country[②], Du Huang and her husband Du Guan refused to cooperate, and resigned from all official posts in Beijing. They returned to Du Guan's home in Chengdu, and united all sides to fight against Yuan Shikai. At that time, however, Du Huang fell seriously ill. After several years of treatment, she did not hesitate to serve as commander of the first female troop in Sichuan in 1921, and conducted the drills herself. In 1923 she organized the Sichuan Province Women's Union, the first federation of women in Chengdu, together with another outstanding female military leader, Hu Lanqi (see "Jiangyuan Gongsuo Street"). In their later years, Du Huang and Du Guan spent their time in painting and calligraphy in their thatched cottage—upon the entrance of which hung a couplet: "Relaxing in

---

① Lord Mengchang was a highly revered and talented official of the Eastern Han Dynasty (25 – 220 AD).

② Following the Wuchang Uprising and subsequent success of the Xinhai Revolution, former Qing official (Han people) Yuan Shikai was made the leader of China as it transitioned into a republican system headed by a president. In 1916, however, Yuan used his position to reinstate a monarchy with himself as the emperor, abolishing the republic—if tenuously and quite temporarily. [Translator's note]

waterfront residence at Fanchuan; An old workhouse rattling in the wind"①. The couple passed away in the autumn of 1929, just 11 days apart, leaving behind a story that has been spread in Sichuan for a long time.

Early 20ᵗ century Jinhe Bridge on Xiaonan Street. Photo courtesy of Jacques Dumasy [France].

In 1943, the local government utilized the land of Chengdu No. 1 Primary School on Xiaonan Street to open the first Chengdu city hospital, with Peng Daozun being the president. Though small in scale, with only 50 beds, it was the first officially established and comprehensive hospital in the city, comprising departments of internal medicine, surgery, gynecology, pediatrics and ophthalmology and otorhinolaryngology. The hospital later was relocated to Zhimin Road where it evolved to become the Second Workers' Hospital (post-P. R. C. founding) and the Chengdu Seventh People's Hospital of today.

---

① These two lines are allusions to renowned poets who shared the surname "Du" —Du Mu (803 – 852) and Du Fu (712 – 770), respectively. In his later years, Du Mu contentedly retired from political service to a life of leisure in his hometown Fanchuan (Xi'An). His predecessor Du Fu resided in Chengdu, where he wrote "*The Song of the Autumn Wind Destroying My Cottage*", expressing how his poorly-built house was destroyed by an autumn wind, thus triggered his sympathy for others in that period of great unrest. [Translator's note]

Tongren Road

West of and roughly parallel to Changshun Street lies Tongren Road. Its origin also goes back to the Qing's Manchu City.

Chengdu people today are familiar with Dongchenggen Street, but few knows that there was once a correlated Xichenggen Street. While Dongchenggen ran outside the eastern wall of the Manchu City, Xichenggen ran outside its western wall. And because the Manchu City's western wall was also the western wall for the larger city at the time, Xichenggen was a major western traffic route around the entire city. This important Xichenggen (West Chenggen) Street still exists today—in the form of its descendant, Tongren Road.

The banner system of the Qing Dynasty was hereditary and mandatory; every man born into the Manchu and Mongol Eight Banners was automatically a soldier of his household's banner and a lifetime member of the Qing army. Although each received a salary for their service, they were not allowed to supplement their livelihood by engaging in any commercial activities (only when the regulation eased up in the late Qing Dynasty did some bannermen leave the Manchu City to engage in business or artistic trades in the larger city of Chengdu, but they had to renounce their citizenship of Eight Banners; this was called "leaving the banner" —for example, the famous Sichuan chef Guan Zhengxing, a solid white Mongol banner had to give up his citzenship of Eight Banners for running Zhengxing Garden Restaurant). Ordinary soldier households under Chengdu's Eight Banners were given a monthly allotment of grain in addition to their monthly wage of 2 *liang* (tael) of silver dollars and a bonus at the New Year, while the officers received their regular salaries. By the end of the Qing Dynasty, there were over 5,100 banner households and over 21,000 people in the Manchu City. Because of the embezzlement of public funds, along with the exhaustion of the Qing government's financial resources, by that time only few could maintain a privileged Eight Banners' lifestyle of eating, drinking and making merry all day long without practice of martial arts and participating in combat. However, most of the ordinary banner households had fallen into poverty; some even had to resort to dismantling their properties to get by. When the Qing regime was overthrown, the majority of bannermen had no means to support their families. The newly established military government ceased to provide them with the salaries and provisions as before, but it would cause a serious threat to the social stability if the bannermen's livelihood problem was not properly handled. After the overthrow of the Qing Dynasty, the Manchu City's bannermen were nervous. A large group of bannermen even assembled at Sanying Elementary School on Shiye Street, planning to make an all-out last-ditch assault against the new regime. Weapons not used for many years were taken out of the armory and put into the hands of the young and the middle-aged, while a unit of three battalions were stationed in the Manchu City. In light of the tense situation, a meeting was held at the General's Yamen between three parties: Deputy Tuchun Luo Lun (also vice-chairman and negotiator for the Sichuan Railway Protection League①) ; Zhao Rongan, a Manchu, also the member of Sichuan Consultative Bureau; Yu Kun, the last Qing general of Chengdu. Presided over by General Yu Kun, they agreed to have a peace settlement with the bannermen and defuse the tension between Han and Manchu. In order achieve this resolution, Luo Lun and his wife moved into the residence of Zhao Rongan's relatives on Dongmen Street within the Manchu City as a guarantee. After the former Qing Governor Zhao Erfeng was beheaded and a mutiny at Dongjiaochang (East Military Field), the representatives from each side met at East Sichuan Guild Hall on Xiyu Street to have more specific negotiations. The military government representatives were Zhou Fengxiang and Xu Jiong, a prestigious educator and the superintendent of a pedagogical college who had many bannermen students; the representatives of the bannermen were Wen Jinzhang, Guang Xingyan, Wen Diaoan, and other members of the gentry. They decided to take a number of measures to resolve the bannermen's livelihood: firstly, each bannerman would be issued six months' salary in two successive payments; secondly, all banner households would be issued property certificates, allowing them to buy and sell their residences freely; thirdly, the military government would allocate 100,000 silver dollars to make a livelihood program. 70, 000 would go to the bannermen while the remaining 30,000 would be used to set up workshops at the Guandi Temple on Zhijishi Street as well as at the junction where Xichenggen Street intersects today's Shiye Street. Over 70 bannermen were enrolled, and classes were opened to teach trades and life skills, including how to make

---

① The Sichuan Railway Protection Movement was a popular movement against the Qing government in 1911 that directly led to the outbreak of the Xinhai Revolution and overthrow of the Qing. [Translator's note]

household goods such as stocks and towels to solve the basic living needs for some bannermen's families. Meanwhile, General Yu Kun was escorted with courtesy to leave Sichuan, while the Manchu and Mongol bannermen surrendered all of their weapons. Thus, there was a peaceful transfer of power in the Manchu City. As a sign of good faith, the new regime had no prejudice against the Manchu people and treated them equally in accordance with the Republic's new ethnic principles[1]. The workshop was named Tongren Factory. (it remained in operation until 1920, but became bankrupt because of the civil wars and its mismanagement). After the Manchu City was torn down, the original Xichenggen Street gradually became a path for the public. After the renovation of the street in 1923 (overseen by Yang Baokang, the city council technical officer), it was transformed into a road of "two thousand and eight *chi* long" (approximately 670 meters long) and "one *zhang* and four *chi* wide" (approximately 4.7 meters wide).

Luo Lun

Thus, the Xichenggen Street where the Tongren Factory operated was named Tongren Road—the name it still bears until today. Considering its length, the road was divided into three sections: upper, middle, and lower sections.

There was an old archery ground of the Manchu City along the west wall of Tongren Road. Covering over 10 *mu*, many trees were planted there. In 1924 the area north of Zhijishi Street, in addition to part of the former Tongren Factory, was renovated as Chengdu's first urban forest park, where over a thousand *nanmu* (*Phoebe zhennan*) trees of more than a century old were planted. The park was called Zhijishi Park—named after the original Zhijishi Temple located at its southern end. In the early years of the Republican period, it was the third largest park in Chengdu after Shaocheng Park and Zhongshan Park, and it is an important site for the assembly. In the spring of 1928, hundreds of students from schools in Chengdu held a rally here in support of No. 1 Middle School students—which led to the "No. 1 Middle School Incident" (see "Xisheng Street"). During the War of Resistance Against Japanese Aggression, however, the Air Force Sandwich Panel Factory occupied the park, and all the *nanmu*

---

[1] The Republic of China explicitly conceptualized itself as the union of five different Chinese ethnicities—the Han, Manchus, Mongols, Hui and Tibetans. [Translator's note]

trees were cut down, and the park disappeared.

Marker of the *luo* (outer) city wall ruins on Tongren Road, 2022. Photo by Dong Qingqing.

The proximity of Tongren Road to the site of old Chengdu's western wall has been reaffirmed in recent years by successive discoveries of ruins at the former Chengdu Box Factory on Upper Tongren Road and Chengdu No. 1 Pharmaceutical Factory on Lower Tongren Road. The remnants of wall found there actually belonged to the Chengdu city wall (the outer city) in the Tang Dynasty, demonstrating that Chengdu's western wall had not significantly change its position from the Tang to the Qing dynasties. Today where Upper Tongren and Erdaoqiao Street meet, a big ficus tree stands over a ring of stones and ancient bricks, almost, resembling either a wall or a tower. This is where the ruins of *luo* city were unearthed a couple of years ago. The developer of the nearby Juxingcheng property collected all the stones and bricks excavated at the site and assembled them to form a unique structure; a place marker which designated the former site of the ancient wall. It can be considered as a place to pay tribute to the Chengdu in the Tang Dynasty. A teahouse located at the discovery site of the *luo* city ruins appropriately changed its name to Tang Cheng ("Tang City"); a couplet composed by Chengdu collector Jiang Gongju hangs on the front entrance:

Both the ancient ruins of the broken wall where Du Fu composed poems;

The Shaocheng teahouse where celebrities chat while enjoying tea.

Upper Tongren Road, 1988 Photo by Zhang Xinan

Where Tongren Road and Zhijishi Street meet, —the site of the former Zhijishi Temple, lies an exquisite and remarkably complete three-layered courtyard. This is the Chengdu Art Academy established in 1980. In its early years, the Chengdu Art Academy was temporarily located in Erxian Temple (Temple of Two Immortals) next to Qingyang Temple. Under the support of Mayor Mi Jianshu, two of three Qing courtyards at the Jing'an Hotel on Gulou Street were relocated here by the Chengdu City Housing Authority in 1984. Four years later, when another Qing courtyard in the Ye Family Ancestral Hall on Hongxing Road was set to be demolished, it was also relocated here. The reconstruction of the Chengdu Art Academy integrated the three courtyards to form the front, middle, and back courtyards of today. In 2004, the expansion of Tongren Road would affect the front section of the Academy's courtyard, however, because of the persistence and perseverance of the municipal government, the construction plan was adjusted in order to protect the integrity of the Academy (the Tongren Road we see today deviates from its otherwise straight path at Zhijishi Street; this is a specific measure which was taken to protect the Chengdu Art Academy). Thanks to the joint efforts, the site of the Chengdu Art Academy becomes the only quadrangle courtyard in Chengdu under protection of the Sichuan Provincial Cultural Relics, and is reputed as Chengdu's most complete and representative late-Qing quadrangle courtyard Aside from the building itself, two ancient gingko trees—nearly a thousand years old—stand before the Academy. They were moved from the Temple of Immortal Yan and Zhijishi Temple; for its renovation, even the bricks of the flower bed below them were taken from the ancient times. The Academy underwent a comprehensive renovation from 1987 to 1989 and a larger-scale internal renovation in 2007. Following the principles of "adhering to the original style, maintaining the original appearance, improving its functions and rational utility of its facilities", the original yards were rearranged to highlight transparent exhibition spaces. Today the Chengdu Art Academy is not only a beautiful building reflecting the character of western Sichuan folk architecture, it is also the only art gallery in the country to be housed in an old quadrangle courtyard.

At 48 Tongren Road there used to be a peaceful little courtyard named Shuangnan Hall for two *nanmu* trees standing before it (*Shuang* meaning "pair; twin"). Yet in this peaceful little courtyard, a tragedy in history of modern Chengdu culture took place—the double suicide of *guqin* (Chinese zither) master Pei Tiexia and his wife.

Pei Tiexia (1884 ~ 1950), born in Chengdu, studied in Japan in 1904 and was an early member of the Tongmenghui①. He returned to China in 1912 and held such various posts as Head of the Sichuan Provincial Department of Justice, East Sichuan Circuit Magistrate, and Editor-in-Chief of the *West City Reporter*. In 1915 he went to Beijing to serve as a consultant for the Ministry of the Interior. Seeing the political scene devolved further into chaos by the day, he withdrew from politics and returned to Chengdu, where he fully committed himself to the *guqin*②, becoming a master musician of his generation. In 1937 he founded and led the "Melodious Qin Society" —and in 1947, the "Brilliant Min Qin Society". He also collected famous *guqin* specimens, including a prize piece from the peak of *guqin* production in ancient China: a "*Lei Qin*" made by Master Lei Wei. (The Lei Family of Sichuan in the Tang Dynasty is the most famous maker of Chinese musical instruments throughout history. As many as nine members of the Lei family passed down their names to posterity. *Guqins* made by these masters are known as "*Lei Qin*", among which those from E'mei are considered the best. Writer and calligrapher Ouyang Xun dedicated the following words to the *Lei Qin*: "Solemn notes flow from the strings in a beautiful melody,

---

① The Tongmenghui ("United League") was an underground revolutionary alliance led by Sun Yat-sen in the late Qing Dynasty. [Translator's note]

② Also referred to as simply "qin" (musical instrument), the guqin ("ancient musical instrument") is a seven-stringed plucked instrument similar to a zither. [Translator's note]

resonating with tones as profound as the mountains and rivers. " Today only 18 *guqins remain that have been handed down from the Tang Dynasty*; *among these*, only 4 are " Zenith " (*Jiuxiao Huanpei*). *Lei Qins* were made by the first generation of *Lei qin*-makers. In 2008, an old specimen was discovered in the collection of late Chengdu *guqin* musician Wang Huade. On its right side was inscribed "made by Lei Wei, the second year of Xiantong in the Great Tang" — but it was proved to be a forgery made in the Northern Song Dynasty. Pei Tiexia had a second Tang *guqin* in his collection as well—the "Ancient Dragon's Call" (*Gu Long Yin*). His wife brought yet another into their household. Pei and his wife Shen Mengying met each other through musicians' clubs (Shen Mengying's father, Shen Jingqing, was a famous seal maker in Chengdu). Shen Mengying's Tang *qin* was also a genuine *Lei Qin*, made by the Lei Xiao branch of the family. The Pei-Shen household dubbed their two *Lei Qins* "Big Lei" and "Little Lei" —together, the enviable "Twin Lei". Their collection also included famous instruments of the Song, Yuan, Ming and Qing *Dynasties*—over 20 in total (the Song specimen from his collection—named *Long Ao*—can still be found in the collections of the Sichuan University Museum). During the War of Resistance Against Japanese Aggression, Pei moved to a villa in Shayan (on the western outskirts of Chengdu) to avoid the bombs of the invading Japanese forces. This is where he composed his masterpieces *Shayan Qin Collection* and *Shayan Reflections on the Qin* and printed them on woodblocks. *Shayan Qin Collection* is comprised of fourteen songs, all of them memorable and noteworthy, some even with lyrics. *Shayan Reflections on the Qin* contains sections on the rhythm, tone, quality and discussions concerning the *guqin*, and are the culmination of Pei's long years of research and personal practice. Yet the master's long-term immersion in the art of the *guqin* meant he paid little attention to the affairs of worldly life. All of his social contacts were about the *guqin*; apart from these music circles, he interacted little with others. Thus he was ignorant of the new government's policies after the founding of the P. R. C. , unable to understand or adapt to the enormous changes remade by the country. His children were also having difficulty making a living at that time. This, along with the personal pride, compelled him to free himself of the world for good—taking the Twin Lei along with him. One June night in 1950 (or in the first half of 1951, according to another source) , he and his wife smashed Big Lei and Little Lei together, then consumed poisons. They left behind a message in a large script, followed by one line of smaller script: "Big and Little *Lei Qin* are ascending to heaven together, the golden seals are left to cover funeral expenses, and the rest are burnt. —in my own handwriting of Gentleman Tie". Right at that time, Pei's friends in the music circle were looking for a suitable job for him. Zha Fuxi, the vice-chairman of the Chinese Musicians Association and head of the Traditional Instruments Department at the Central Conservatory of Music, have sent Pei Tiexia a letter especially inviting him to engage in guqin research in Beijing with his Twin Lei. But when the letter arrived, its intended invitees— both human and instrument—had perished, marking a great tragedy in Chengdu's cultural history. Famous poet and Sichuan University professor Zeng Jian composed "Twin Lei Prelude" about the suicides; the poem contains such lines as "Along the edge of Zhijishi, a deeper and deeper courtyard; ding-ding, a water clock strikes; turning-turning, the arrow ushers the dawn." This work is still circulated among poetry enthusiasts today.

Pei Tiexia with musician friends, 1937. (Pei Tiexia: front row, second from the right. *Guqin* Master Zha Fuxi: front center.)

Babao Street

Babao Street starts from Qinglong Street in the east and meets up with West Street in the west; in fact, many Chengdu people consider it as a section of West Street. In the Qing Dynasty, Babao Street was Shuncheng Hutong in the Manchu City. By the end of the Qing Dynasty and the beginning of the Republic of China, the street had already become a sort of community for the poor. Makeshift walls of thick bamboo-plaited mats were erected there, which many Chengdu people called *mieba*, so the road came to be known as "Baba Alley". However, as the name "Baba Alley" lacked a certain elegance, it was later changed to the auspicious "Babao Street" (literally "eight treasures" —in Chinese, "eight" and "bamboo fence" (*ba*) are homophones).

Throughout the Chinese history, "babao" has been widely used to refer to different good-luck items, though the term has carried slightly different connotations depending on the settings. As with the babao box (treasure chest) and babao porridge we still have today, "babao" most often denotes a general wide-ranging assortment of treasures. But in the traditional arts, it more often refers to eight specific treasures: precious pearls, *fangsheng* (a kind of jewelry with an overlapping pattern), *yuqing* (an ancient percussion instrument made of jade), rhinoceros horn, ancient coins, coral, silver ingot, and *ruyi* (a ceremonial S-shaped scepter).

West Street

Chengdu's West Street consists of a single short section. Unlike East Street, it does not reach the center of the city, but can be found not far from its northwest corner. This layout had already taken shape in the Qing Dynasty when the Manchu City occupied Chengdu's west side. The north wall of the Manchu City was located just north of today's West Street, which at that time was the Small City's northernmost *hutong*—Qingyuan Hutong. It earned this name for its position directly across from Qingyuan Gate (i. e. Chengdu's Old West Gate). Located on the west side of Changshun Street, Qingyuan Hutong had a corresponding *hutong* on the east side of Changshun Street; because it followed the wall of the Manchu City, it was named Shuncheng Hutong (*shuncheng* meaning "along the wall"). After the Manchu City wall was torn down in the Republican period, Qingyuan Hutong was renamed West Street. The name was an obvious choice, because it was the only road leading to the Old West Gate at that time. Shuncheng Hutong, meanwhile, became Babao Street. Qinglong Street (east of Babao Street) was the original street leading to the Manchu City from within Chengdu, while Xiyuecheng Street (west side of West Street) once abutted the old city gate on its other side. Thus Chengdu people heading to the Old West Gate from Luomashi would have to travel by four different streets—Qinglong

West Street in the 1970s. Photo by Feng Shuimu.

Street, Babao Street, West Street and Xiyuecheng Street. Strictly speaking, these four streets are really just one street divided into four sections, much like Chengdu's East Street, which is why so many Chengdu people simply refer to them collectively as "West Street".

After the War of ResistanceAgainst Japanese Aggression, Tan Yucheng opened a snack shop inside Anle Temple on West Shuncheng Street①. There he sold his trademark "Tan's bean curd", which would go on to be recognized by the Ministry of Domestic Trade as a "China Time-honored Brand" in 1995. It was just a stall in the beginning, but its fresh and spicy bean curd noodles were of good quality for a low price, so they naturally won people's favor. After the founding of the P. R. C. , the shop moved to Yanshikou, whence it took up the official name Tan's Bean Curd (*Tan Douhua*) and continued to primarily sell bean curd noodles. When Yanshikou underwent urban reconstruction in the reform period, Tan's Bean Curd was demolished and went out of business for a time. In recent years, however, a later generation of the Tan family recovered the business, opening a store on West Street under the name of "Little Tan's Bean Curd" (*Xiao Tan Douhua*). This restaurant specializes in bean curd noodles but sells a variety of Sichuan-style snacks, maintaining the fine tradition of affordable quality that continues to please its many customers.

"Little Tan's Bean Curd" on West Street in the 1990s. Photo courtesy of the Chengdu Construction Information Center.

The Sichuan Song and Dance Troupe (since 1984, the Sichuan Song and Dance Theater) has maintained its original location on the north side of West Street ever since its founding in 1953.

---

① West Shuncheng Street has since been incorporated into Shuncheng Street. [Translator's Note]

The General's Yamen

Chengdu people refer to the area around today's Jinhe Hotel as Jiangjun Yamen (the General's Yamen). Nearby one also finds a Jiangjun Street, but the "General" in the names of these streets is not a honorific title for senior-ranking military officers; it refers to an official title that is even more exclusive and specific.

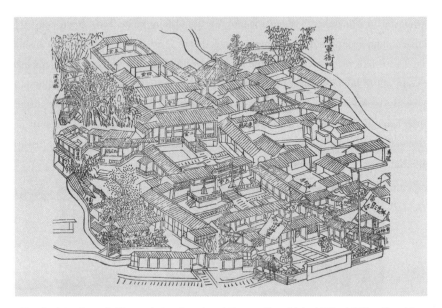

Sketch of the General's Yamen during the reign of Emperor Tongzhi (r. 1862 ~ 1875), *Chronicles of Chengdu County.*

In the early Qing Dynasty, all militarily strategic locations across the country had Eight Banners garrisons with garrison generals as their highest commanders. To take Chengdu as an example, its garrison general's full title was "Protector General of Chengdu and the Territories of Sichuan; governor of the Civil and Military Affairs of Songpan and Jianchang; commander of Han Lands, Officers and Men; leader of the Eight Banners" —but this was normally shortened to "General of Chengdu". The rank of general was only open to members of the Manchu or Mongol nobility (starting from the mid-Qing Dynasty, Han governors were allowed to act as interim generals—

but they weren't considered to hold the post, only to represent it, like a proxy. For example, Wu Tang, whose legacy of integrity is still remembered in Chengdu today, was a Han governor of Sichuan to "represent" the post of Chengdu general during the reign of Emperor Tongzhi). Other than being responsible for local military defense, the general was also in charge of all the local Manchu and Mongol Eight Banners affairs. He was also the highest representative of the imperial court and the Manchu-Mongol nobility appointed to the region, essentially "the eyes and the ears" of the emperor. Generals wielded more power than any provincial officials at that time— including governors (except for a small minority of governors who brought additional titles to their posts, such as a former imperial minister or grand secretary). Although they did not appear to manage matters of local government, in fact they had oversight of all local officials. Generals could secretly report matters directly to the Qing court, whereas the highest-ranking local officials could not act so independently. Any of the governor's or inspector-general's memorials to the Qing court had to be countersigned by the Eight Banners general to have any validity or effect. For example, in the late Qing Dynasty, Sichuan Governor Zhao Erfeng (known as "Butcher Zhao") captured leaders of the Railway Protection League (including Luo Lun and Pu Dianjun) and was fully determined to execute them, but General Yu Kun didn't agree to countersign. Thus Zhao could not even submit the memorial to the throne, let alone act upon his intentions.

Yinyue Pavilion in the General's Yamen, 1910 Courtesy of Yang Xianfeng

The Manchu and Mongol Eight Banners didn't always have generals, however. In the early Qing Dynasty, the garrison's highest officials were deputy lieutenant-generals. The first deputy lieutenant-general was Fa La (? ~ 1735), who commanded more than 5,000 bannermen and their family members. The office of general was only established in the forty-first year during the reign of Emperor Qianlong (1776), and the first to fill that post was Ming Liang (1735 ~ 1822). Henceforward, all generals of Chengdu worked and resided where Jinhe Hotel is located today. In the early Qing Dynasty, however, the buildings in this location were the garrison headquarters in name alone, and were hardly magnificent. Thus in the seventh year during the reign of Emperor Tongzhi (1868), under the direction of General Chong Shi[1], the yamen underwent large-scale expansion and renovations to form a large five-layer complex with a weeping flower gate at its central axis and multiple courtyards, containing gardens, to either side. The plaques flanking its gate read: "The Prestige of the Southwest"; "The Frontier under Control", demonstrating the authority and responsibility of the office.

After the fall of the Qing regime, as the Manchu City was dismantled, only the main gate of the General's Yamen was torn down. Most of the remaining structures continued to be used, serving as office space for the military branches of the Republican government. Sichuan Clique[2] leaders including Xiong Kewu, Liu Chengxun, Yang Sen, Liu Wenhui and Liu Xiang—as well as Chen Huan of the Beiyang Clique and Luo Peijin of the Yunnan Clique—all occupied these quarters at one point. Liu Wenhui's 24th Army command[3] was based here for a long period. At the beginning of the War of Resistance Against Japanese Aggression, Chiang Kai-shek's military strength gradually amassed in Chengdu, and established the Chongqing Field Headquarters in Chengdu[4] here on November 5th, 1935. Later, on February 13th, 1939, the Chengdu Field Headquarters for the Chairman of the National Military Commission was formally established at the same site. Thus the General's Yamen was one of the most important strongholds for Chiang Kai-shek's forces in Chengdu. From

---

[1] Chong Shi, a great lover of calligraphy, was stationed in Chengdu for many years. One can still find his inscriptions at various Chengdu locations, including Wuhou Temple.

[2] "Clique" here refers to armies or political factions among the de facto warlord states of the Republican period. [Translator's note]

[3] Liu Wenhui (1895 – 1976) was a warlord allied with the Kuomingtang and held various military command positions through the 1920s – 1940s. [Translator's Note]

[4] During the War of Resistance Against Japanese Aggression, the seat of the Republican government moved inland from Nanjing to Wuhan and finally Chongqing, which at the time was part of Sichuan. [Translator's note]

1940 until the liberation of Chengdu in late 1949, it was also the home base for Sichuan Province's largest secret service organization, the Sichuan Special Operations Committee (The committee was jointly formed by the Bureau of Investigation and Statistics of the Military Council, the Bureau of Investigation and Statistics of the Central Executive Committee, the military police, and the Nationalist Youth League[①] in Sichuan. In 1946 it was renamed the Sichuan Joint Committee of Party, Government and Military Cadres, but it continued to be referred to as "Special Operations" in accordance with custom). Many revolutionaries and CPC members were confined there in a political prison. Late at night on December 7th, 1949, a crazed massacre occurred in Chengdu. Many of the victims were revolutionaries taken from the political prison and escorted to the west side of the General's Yamen—where, at Shi'er Bridge, the tragic killings took place.

Prison established by the Kuomintang Special Operations in the General's Yamen. Photo courtesy of Yang Xianfeng.

For a long time after the founding of the P. R. C. , the General's Yamen was the Chengdu Military Area No. 3 Guest House; then after the Reform and Opening-up, the Jinhe Hotel was built over the remains of the former building, though initially, it was still the Chengdu Military Area No. 3 Guest House.

---

① Or the "Nationalist Party Three People's Principles Youth League" —the Three People's Principles being nationalism, democracy, and the livelihood of the people, as formulated by Sun Yat-sen. [Translator's note]

Banbianqiao Street

At the southeast of People's Park is a street called Banbianqiao, named after the former Banbian Bridge. Here, the city border met that of the Manchu City at the Jinhe River in the Qing Dynasty. A weir under Banbian Bridge blocked off the Manchu City from the rest of Chengdu, while atop the bridge was a simple structure that served as a guardhouse. The west half of the bridge was under Manchu City jurisdiction, while the eastern half of the bridge was part of the larger city. One Qing author expressed his discontent with the layout in a *Bamboo Branch Verse*:

> A woman gazes from the right side;
> A man looks back from the left side.
> With a fort above and a river below,
> Two lovers can not meet with a sigh.

This is why people at that time referred to it as Banbian Bridge ("Half of a Bridge") (its official name should actually have been Lingshou Bridge. In fact, literati Liu Yiming[①] once inscribed that very name onto the top of the bridge). The street running from Citang Street in the north to Shaanxi Street in the south was named Banbianqiao Street, sometimes called simply Banbian Street. In the past, it was divided into North Banbianqiao Street and South Banbianqiao Street, with Banbian Bridge marking their division near the side entrance of today's People's Park. Both sections have been torn up in recent years' urban reconstruction, their original locations now have been replaced by all markets or parts of the greenway.

As a measure of protection for the Manchu City, a weir was installed in the Jinhe River under Banbian Bridge in the Qing Dynasty. Thus Banbian Bridge was the farthest point that boats could reach after entering the Jinhe River from the Fuhe River. Banbian Bridge also came to serve as a terminal dock for any small craft being able to navigate the Jinhe River. Essentially all the Manchu City's life necessities came in through its East Gate—Shoufu Gate—where special officials inspected and

---

① Liu Yiming (1865 – 1928), a Chengdu native, calligrapher and poet.

received items. Shoufu Gate was right on the north side of Banbian Bridge. Not far west of there, inside today's People's Park, were the Manchu City's most important materials storehouses—these including the Yongji Warehouse, large grain warehouse, firewood warehouse, and hay warehouse. It was once old Chengdu's downtown district crossed by a lively commercial zone of small-scale wharves, lining both sides of the Jinhe River and stretching from Banbian to Sanqiao Bridge. As a *Bamboo Branch Verse Memories of Old Jincheng* puts it:

Half a small city inside and half a larger city outside,
Palisades straddle the river, making a dividing line.
Water meanders to the East Water Gate at other side,
While vessels sail to Sanqiao with charcoals and rice.

South Banbianqiao Street in the 1990s. Photo by Yan Yongcong.

In 1925, by the great efforts of the Qing's principle graduate[①] Luo Chengxiang (1865 ~ 1926), the Sichuan National Arts Academy was established within the side entrance of Banbianqiao Street in Shaocheng Park (in today's terms, at the dormitory area for the Sichuan Provincial Department of Culture and Tourism, 35 Banbianqiao

---

① "Principle graduate" refers specifically to *zhuangyuan*, a scholar who ranks first in the palace examination, the highest level in the imperial examination system. [Translator's note]

Street). The academy focused on martial arts, passing down techniques and keeping the tradition alive. Luo Chengxiang himself served as director, while renowned martial artist Liu Chongjun (? ~ 1938) served as deputy director. Together they played a significant role in the development of Sichuan's martial arts. In fact, the "golden badge" of the Flower Festival at Qingyang Temple in martial arts competition was organized by the Sichuan National Arts Academy. Other former directors of the academy include a number of Sichuan military and political leaders such as Liu Wenhui, Yang Sen, Liu Xiang and Wang Liaoxu.

In the Republican period, Banbianqiao Street was dominated by the leather shoe business, with shops facing the street and shoemaking workshops at the back. There was old Chengdu's famous Qianjin shoe shop, along with the likewise renowned Guangrong, Dasheng, Kexing and Yixin. During the War of Resistance Against Japanese Aggression, famous actress Bai Yang (1920 ~ 1996) specially made a trip here to buy shoes, attracting a huge crowd of onlookers. The newspapers featured it as an important story.

Several rather well-known Chengdu restaurants used to be found on Banbianqiao Street. Guo Chaohua and his wife—founders of the famous Sichuan dish *fuqi feipian* ("sliced beef and ox tongue in chili sauce") —opened a shop, which was just a storefront, there to the right side of the Shaocheng Park entrance. Another small storefront was occupied by Liao Yongtong's famous " Zhihuzi Dragon Eye Buns " (which more recently operates on South Taisheng Road). The Halal restaurant "Wang Fat Duck" was originally located at the east end of Xiyu Street, but it moved to Banbianqiao Street during the " Cultural Revolution " due to the construction of defence projects on the Jinhe River and Yuhe River. The Chengdu-style roast duck shop would marinate and oven-roast force-fed Chengdu Sheldrake duck according to methods from the Qing royal court which were originally used for roasting suckling pigs. This technology differs from later methods for the mass-processing and production of marinated duck. Still, the shop that likely left the deepest impression on old Chengdu residents was the strange, yet appealing sweets shop called Kouxuanpin, which mostly sold boiled sweet potatoes. *Xuan*, the rare middle character in the shop's name, dates back at least to the Han Dynasty, appearing in *Shuo Wen Jie Zi*, the first comprehensive Chinese dictionary. It means "everyone shouting together", as one might guess the meaning from its composition of two mouth pictograms. Since there is an alternative and more common way to write this meaning of *xuan*, most people don't recognize it any more. Therefore, people mistook the pictogram as two mouths kissing.

In Chengdu dialect, "kissing" (*qinzui*) is "*dabo'r*", so people read the character *xuan as bo'r*, changing its meaning from "everyone shouting together" to "two kissing mouths" and effectively making the name of the shop "Koubo'rpin" for decades. There was another Chengdu business that had a rare character in its name at that time—a Sichuanese restaurant located off Jiuyan Bridge. Its name was actually "Dashengchun", but, again, the vast majority of people didn't know how to read the middle character 莝. Therefore, an interesting saying came about in Chengdu: "The east has Koubo'rpin, the west has Dashengchun". Koubo'rpin had a shop on Xiyu Street for a while after the founding of the P. R. C. , and its featured products were no longer boiled sweet potatoes, but a variety of *liangfen* (bean jelly).

After entering the city from Shuiximen (West Water Gate), the Jinhe River passed through busy downtown markets, so a dense concentration of bridges was built over it to accommodate traffic. There used to be several bridges upstream of Banbian Bridge, all within the Manchu City, but today no trace of these places remains. Among all the former Jinhe River bridges, Banbian Bridge is the furthest upstream to be remembered in the form of a contemporary place name.

Baojia Alley

In the Qing Dynasty, Baojia Alley was originally Yongming Hutong, also known as "Juyuan Hutong" in Manchu City, and its most famous residents were the Mongol Bayot Hala clan. The name of Baojia Alley originated from the people who lived there. Once Bayot Hala descendants sinicized their surname to "Bao", thus neighbors would refer to this place as "Bao's home" (*Bao Jia*). The name was carried on, officially becoming Baojia Alley in the Republic of China.

In 1920, Sichuan Province's first Western medical school—the Sichuan Army Military Medical School—moved from its original location on Shaanxi Street to Baojia Alley. An army hospital was also set up nearby. The school closed in 1926 after 8 sessions and graduated over 400 students, who organized the Military Medical School Alumni Association. In 1926, through the organization and efforts of the alumni association, the Sichuan Medical Specialties College was officially established with its own hospital at the address of the former military medical school. The degree program was 7 years (2 years of preparatory courses and 5 years of college courses), but the school only remained open for 7 sessions, and was closed in 1936, at which point it was taken over by the provincial superintendent of military affairs and became the Reconstruction Supervisor's Military Medical Research Class. In 1938 after Liu Xiang[1] died of illness, his subordinates changed its name to the Fu Cheng Memorial Hospital (Fu Cheng was Liu Xiang's courtesy name). The memorial hospital was in an awkward position, however—neither publicly nor privately run—so its existence was doomed to be short-lived from the start. Before long it was recovered by the government, becoming a medical college again. It focused on training midwives and its affiliated hospital became a medical specialties hospital for obstetrics and gynecology— the first school or hospital of its kind in Chengdu. After the founding of the P. R. C. , Chengdu No. 1 OB/GYN Hospital was established at the site, but Chengdu people generally referred to it as the "Baojia Alley OB/GYN Hospital". In 2000, it merged with Chengdu No. 9 People's Hospital, after which it was known as both "Chengdu

---

[1] Liu Xiang (1890 – 1938) was the tuchun of Sichuan in the early 1920s, and remained the most influential of the Sichuanese warlords even after sole control of the province was lost. [Translator's note]

No. 9 People's Hospital" and "Chengdu OB/GYN Hospital". On November 28 th , 2008, the Chengdu Maternity Hospital celebrated its seventieth birthday. Over 70 years, a total of 400,000 Chengdu people had been delivered there. That's why many claim that half of the Chengdu's local people over 40 years old are born at Baojia Alley. On December 23 rd , 2010, the hospital moved next to Riyue Avenue in the Xinguang Area of western Chengdu, merging with the Chengdu Children's Hospital. Chengdu Maternity and Children's Medical Center was newly built on them. In July 2011, it changed its title to Chengdu Women's and Children's Central Hospital of the Chongqing Medical College.

In 1936, a famous doctor, Ye Xinqing, opened his clinic on Baojia Alley.

Ye Xinqing (1908 ~ 1967) was from Dayi County in Sichuan. In 1913, he went to Hankou (in Wuhan, Hubei) to turn to his uncle. There he met the famous doctor Wei Tinglan. After studying under Wei for 12 painstaking years, Ye finished receiving the authentic transmission of golden three-needle acupuncture (the "golden needles" are composed of ninety percent of gold and ten percent of copper casting). He became the sole master of the golden-needle school in China (all together, Wei Tinglan passed down the golden needle techniques to three apprentices, but one abandoned medicine for politics and the other died in a fire). In 1933, Ye Xinqing opened the Quintessence Chinese Medicine Hall in Chongqing. In 1936 he returned to Chengdu to practice medicine, and his reputation spread far and wide across the province. He was asked to treat such dignitaries as Yu Youren, Jiang Dingwen, Hu Zongnan, Song Xilian and Liu Wenhui. After the founding of the P. R. C. , Xinhai Revolution veteran Dan Maoxin (1886 ~ 1965) and famous industrialist Lu Zuofu (1893 ~ 1952) invited Ye Xinqing to practice medicine in Chongqing again. In his time there Ye managed to heal Marshal He Long's[1] chronically afflicted arm, which he had difficulty raising, with just 8 acupuncture sessions. In 1956, the Ministry of Health established the China Academy of Traditional Chinese Medicine in Beijing and recruited 30 outstanding doctors from around the country to practice medicine there—Ye Xinqing was among them (also invited were Pu Fuzhou and Du Ziming

---

[1] He Long (1896 – 1969), an important leader of China's early communist forces, one of the ten to be awarded the rank of marshal in the P. R. C. .

from Chengdu and Ren Yingqiu, Shen Zhonggui, and Ran Xuefeng from Chongqing). While in Beijing, Ye primarily treated foreign guests and central government leaders. His patients included Liu Shaoqi, Zhu De, Song Qingling, Dong Biwu, Deng Xiaoping, Chen Yi, Luo Ronghuan, Ye Jianying, Li Fuchun, Tan Zhenlin, and over 20 leaders of the party and state. Some of his patients gave him fine gifts in gratitude. He Xiangning[1] hand-painted plum blossoms for him; Shen Junru[2] gifted him with his calligraphy; Wu Yuzhang[3] honored him with the poem "Hua Tuo[4] Lives Again". After Ye Xinqing cured Jiang Qing's[5] severe neurosis, Chairman Mao Zedong penned a copy of his poem "Loushan Pass" for Ye in return. Ye also traveled abroad to treat over a dozen heads of states, including President Ho Chi Minh of Vietnam and King Sihanouk of Cambodia. In 1957, the Soviet foreign ministry invited Ye Xinqing to Yemen under the auspices of Chen Jiakang, the Chinese ambassador to the United Arab Emirates (as China had not yet established diplomatic relations with Yemen). The king of Yemen had been suffering from a severe chronic headache, failing to find a cure after visiting many countries, while the prince was afflicted with pustulant skin ulcers all over his body. Yemen was calling Ye Xinqing the "God of the East", giving him little choice but to accept the invitation. He spent three months treating the royal family before he could return home. Ye Xinqing was one of the most globally influential of Chengdu's Chinese medicine doctors.

In April 1913, Baojia Alley saw the Sichuan *Quanyedao*'s Zhou Shanpei[6] open the first technical school in the province's history—the Sichuan Vocational School. In August of the same year it changed its name to Sichuan Class A Industrial Vocational

---

① He Xiangning (1878 – 1972), feminist revolutionary politician and artist.

② Shen Junru (1875 – 1963), prominent lawyer, activist, and the first president of the Supreme People's Court of China.

③ Wu Yuzhang (1878 – 1966), Sichuan native, a prominent CPC leader and educator, a president of Renmin University.

④ Hua Tuo (approx. 145 – 208 AD), a medical scientist in the late Eastern Han Dynasty, renowned for his skill, especially in surgery.

⑤ Jiang Qing (1914 – 1991), communist revolutionary and wife of Mao Zedong.

⑥ Zhou Shanpei (1875 – 1958), former Qing official, participant in the Sichuan Railway Protection Movement, active in politics throughout the Republican period and early P. R. C. The Quanyedao was an administrative office of the Republic that specifically promoted industrial development.

School. (At that time, class A industrial schools were a type of provincial-level vocational school established according to the Republican government's educational system reform in 1913. They were typically referred to as *jiagong*. Graduating from a class A vocational school was equivalent to finishing middle school; meanwhile, vocational schools equivalent to a high school education were designated "class B" (sometimes "class A" is mistaken as "level A" in the sources). Chengdu only established one *jiagong*, which is located at today's 82 Baojia Alley, Courtyard 1. The teaching building, later used as dormitories for the Sichuan Chinese Medicinal Plant Company, still stands today. Back in the Republic, the school had three departments: machinery, textiles, and applied chemistry; Marshal Chen Yi (1901 – 1972) studied textiles there from 1916 to 1917. In 1937, the school relocated to Xuedao Street where it was incorporated into the Chengdu Advanced Industrial Vocational School— predecessor to the P. R. C. 's Chengdu Electromechanical College (now Chengdu Technological University). When it was still at Baojia Alley, jiagong principal Guo Yushan, having studied abroad in Japan, had the students produce imitations of Japanese rickshaws (Jinrikisha) as a manufacturing exercise. Rickshaws were the main means of transportation in the Republican-era Chengdu; at their height, they numbered about 4,000. In the early years, the vocational school was Chengdu's main source of rickshaws.

The jiagong's remains, 2011. Photo courtesy of Yang Xianfeng.

In 1935, the Chengdu Women's Vocational School in Sichuan opened on Baojia Alley. This was Chengdu's first vocational school for women. Its departments— including bookkeeping, statistics, textiles, homemaking, household chemicals and library management—offered all courses completely free of charge. Thus the school did its part to bring women of the time into the workforce.

In 1930, a famous restaurant in the history of Sichuan culinary culture was opened by Huang Jinglin on Baojia Alley. Its name was "Guguyan".

Huang Jinglin (1875 ~ 1941), with the original name Huang Xun, with courtesy name Jinglin or Jinlin. He was born and raised in Chengdu, and graduated from the Sichuan Law and Politics School. Taking to study at young age, he had a particular talent for the culinary arts. He approached cooking intellectually, pondering and exploring, trying out new ideas. As a young man, he was already renowned throughout Chengdu as a top culinary artist and master chef. For a time, he taught cooking at the Sichuan Women's Vocational School, which made him the first culinary teacher in the province, and the most famous "learned chef" as well. In the early 1920s, at the recommendation of his childhood classmate and the Sichuan Army General Chen Mingqian, Huang Jinglin took posts as magistrate for Shehong and Wushi counties in eastern Sichuan, but he soon resigned and returned to Chengdu. To support his family, he opened the "Jinlin Restaurant" on the east side of Shaocheng Park's *nanmu* forest, with help of the curator of the Chengdu Popular Education Center, Lu Zuofu. (Although this restaurant was extremely important to the development of Sichuan cuisine, there is some discrepancy over its exact name in the written records; this "Jinlin" version is according to *The Diary of Wu Yu*. In the journal, Wu Yu records eight different occasions that he dined at "Jinlin Restaurant".) Huang personally oversaw the kitchen, appointing Peng Huiting, who would end up staying with him for many years, as his head chef. Huang Jinglin's older friends, such as Chen Mingqian, continued to dissuade him from a life in the kitchens, strongly advising that he return to political service, taking office of the magistrate of Yingjing county in west-central Sichuan. Huang agreed, but resigned just over a year later and returned to Chengdu again. This time he was determined not to interrupt his culinary career, focusing all his life time on Sichuan dishes. At this point, the "Jinlin Restaurant" was hardly able to operate due to the profligacy of Huang's oldest son, so ownership was transferred to Chen Xihou from the Chengdu suburb of Wenjiang and renamed "Jingning Restaurant" (it remained open until after the War of Resistance Against Japanese Aggression). Meanwhile, Huang opened a home-style Sichuanese restaurant next to his residence on the south side of Baojia Alley's west end. Its name was "Guguyan". [Note: "Guguyan" (literally "Aunt Banquet") is a term in Sichuan dialect for "playing house" or "playing host" —i. e. when children play by imitating the adult activities of cooking and entertaining. The older generation recalled that the name of Huang Jinglin's restaurant originated from his third sister's teasing words: "Look at you with your intellectual posture, what kind of restaurant do you think you're going to open? You might as well just play house (guguyan)!"] True to his scholarly nature, Huang composed and hung a couplet on the door. In the dining room he also hung another of his compositions: "My knowledge, talent and virtue are all inferior to others', and my real skill is only sautéing a dish or boiling a soup; my relatives stop laughing at me, my friends stop laughing at me, content for me to shovel with my knife, it is a fine fate for a scholar." Huang's skill came from a combination of family inheritance and expert teachers. It was primarily Huang's sister-in-law who helped in the kitchen and waited on tables; initially the only cook he employed was Peng Huiting. Huang invented a whole batch of top-quality Sichuan dishes. He refused to use MSG (at that time known by the brand name "Ajinomoto", as it was imported from Japan). Every day they would only serve two or three tables, four at the very most (an additional table was set up for customers' attendants and drivers—it was the first place in Chengdu to do so). The menu was always personally prepared by Huang according to customers' specific situations, and he would personally bring the dishes to the table. The head table had to leave a vacant seat for him and whoever was hosting each table was required to formally invite Huang to their meal to explain the menu. Huang's special dishes and unique business model soon earned him a far-reaching reputation. Guests would have to reserve a table three days in advance—even Sichuan's military and political leaders like Liu Xiang were no exception. Due to the expansion of the military fields at Xijiaochang, some private residences toward the west end of Baojia Alley were occupied, and Guguyan had to move several times: first to North Shuwa Street, next to Baoyun Temple's Majia Garden, then to Shaanxi Street and Xinyusha Street. In 1938, Huang Jinglin was invited to open a Guguyan in Chongqing. There he hung his own couplets in the dining room just as he had in Chengdu. The most famous among them was a sarcastic commentary on the politics of the time:

Sales tax, stamp tax, banquet tax, pot donation, I have no idea if I can try to get them in order;

Steamed rooster, fried hen, stewed beef, roasted pork, refined fat and tender meat, I can get all of them in good order.

His shop was even shut down at one point just because of this couplet, whereafter he had no choice but to move from his original Chongqing location on Zhongying Street to Wangshan in Nan'an. Huang Jinglin had already fallen seriously ill when the Japanese began bombing Chongqing, which frightened him badly. He passed away in Wangshan in 1941. The Guguyan in Chongqing later moved to Minguo Road, changing its name to "Kaigegui".

Sichuanese restaurant "Guguyan". Photo courtesy of Wang Daming.

Influenced by Huang Jinglin, his third brother Huang Baolin (formerly the chief of Yibin County Tax Bureau-and member of the Sichuan Provincial Department of Finance) also quit politics to become a chef, first opening a Sichuanese restaurant called Gunücai on Dajin Street, then successively opening two more on Middle Shuwa Street and Zongfu Street called Gegechuan (Older Brother's Legacy). Huang Baolin's sons continued the family tradition; his eldest son Huang Pingbo (yet another politician-made-chef, he had been an adjutant in the Sichuan army) opened "Buzui Wugui Little Restaurant"①; his youngest son Huang Tingzhong opened a restaurant on Citang Street called Dongfeng Yizuilou. The Huang family's culinary skills were not only extremely popular in their own time; they also had a great influence on later generations. Huang Jinglin's philosophy of "the quality of a meal comes down to the soup like the quality of singing comes down to the voice" is now a classic bit of wisdom passed down from generation to generation of chefs. Famous dishes in Sichuan cooking like boiled cabbage, soft-fried pork intestine, bamboo fish, yellow catfish braised with pickled vegetables, okara pig's head, tea-smoked duck, braised beef head and *mala* beef tendon—whether inventions of Guguyan or dishes upon which Guguyan innovated substantially—remain popular to this day. Many who have passed through Guguyan's kitchens have since been recognized as masters of Sichuan dishes— such as chef Luo Guorong of the Beijing Hotel's Sichuanese Department and the Sichuan Restaurant, Chen Haiqing, head chef of Chengdu's Furong Restaurant, and Zhou Haiqing, owner of Chongqing's Yizhishi Restaurant. The "Huang school" of Sichuan cooking continues to spread. There is now one Guguyan in Japan and three in Taiwan. As for Chengdu, there's a Guguyan at the main north gate of Du Fu Cottage, as well as the Buzui Wugui Little Restaurant on Shaanxi Street.

Sources vary widely concerning Huang Jinglin's early life and deeds. Many say that he had passed either the county-level imperial exam or even the palace exam—the highest level of education in the Qing system. They also say that he had worked at Beijing's Guanglu Temple, the Qing royal family's reception establishment, where he became Empress Dowager Cixi's favored royal chef and was gifted four official titles. But after numerous investigations, I do not believe such accounts to be accurate. There are no supporting sources beyond news from recent years' local annals.

There was once a "Back Baojia Alley" running from the south side of Baojia Alley to the back entrance of the former Chengdu Military Area Clothing Factory, but it has already been demolished in the course of urban reconstruction.

---

① Buzui Wugui literally means "If you're not drunk yet, don't go home". The phrase comes from a poem in the ancient text *Book of Songs*: *Lesser Odes* (Western Zhou Dynasty, 1046 – 771 BC) expressing hope that an enjoyable dinner gathering will never end. [Translator's note]

Shuhua Street

Located west of Xiaonan Street and south of Fangchi Street, Shuhua Street used to be called Cuibai Hutong (or Yongsheng Hutong) when it was part of the Manchu City in the Qing Dynasty. In the early years of the Republican period, its name was changed to Tingzi Street. Then in 1921 during the Xinhai Revolution, Xia Zhishi, a deputy tuchun of the Chongqing Shu Military Government (see "Dongsheng Street") established the private Jinjiang Private School on this road, so its name was changed again to Jinjiang Street. A decade later in 1932, under the direction of 24th Army Deputy Commander Xiang Chuanyi and famous ethnic Hui military leader Ma Yuzhi (see Majia Huayuan Road), the Jinjiang Private School merged with the Chucai Middle School to form the Chengdu Private Shuhua Middle School. (Chucai, also a private school, was established in 1912 on West Wenmiao Street, later moved to Dongsheng Street and Yanlu Gongsuo Street before merging with Jinjiang Private School.) Although Shuhua Middle School mostly operated out of the original Jinjiang Private School campus, Jinjiang Street still changed its name, finally becoming Shuhua Street. After the founding of the P. R. C. , Shuhua Middle School was nationalized as the Chengdu No. 14 Middle School. As the campus expanded, its main gate changed locations to face the adjacent Baojia Alley. Today the school can be found there on Shuhua Street; the school grounds even retains an old "Shuhua Pavilion" inscribed with the school motto of its earlier iteration. The Most notable one among its former attendees is Zhang Luping (1921 ~ 1945), an outstanding female special agent and martyr for the communist revolution.

Shuhua Middle School in the Republican period. Photo courtesy of Peng Xiong.

Zhang Luping (1921 ~ 1945), came from Chongzhou (a city just west of Chengdu proper), was originally named Yu Jiaying. In middle school (at Jianguo Middle School), she met the father of her classmate Che Chongying, Che Yaoxian—a preeminent member of the CPC. Under his guidance, Zhang began to walk down the path of revolution. After actively participating in demonstrations against Japanese aggression, Zhang was asked to withdraw from her school, at which point she tested into Shuhua Middle School, effectively skipping a grade to begin high school. ① There she continued to engage in revolutionary activities and formally joined the Chinese National Liberation Vanguard. In November 1937, Che Yaoxin helped Zhang leave Chengdu, and the next year she arrived at the CPC headquarters in Yan'an, Shaanxi Province. There she continued her studies, first at the Counter-Japanese Military and Political University, then at the Central Military Commission School of Communications. In October 1938, Zhang Luping officially became a member of the Communist Party of China. Because her brother-in-law was a major general in the Sichuan Army, Zhang received the orders to return to Sichuan in 1939 and work for the United Front②. Upon return, the Southern Bureau of the CPC Central Committee decided to make use of her expertise in radio telegraphy for an important mission. This was when she first began to use the name "Zhang Luping." She successfully infiltrated KMT intelligence via the KMT Chongqing Bureau of Investigation and Statistics' General Telecommunication Station. Meanwhile, she served as secretary for the Chongqing Special Branch of the CPC, continuously providing the Office of the Eighth Route Army in Chongqing with core inside intelligence and communicating with Yan'an by the enemy's radio. In the winter of 1940, because of one agent's careless exposure, Zhang Luping was taken into the enemy's custody along with six other communist revolutionaries. Despite all manners of torture—including four years at Xifeng Prison in Guizhou Province—Zhang never exposed her true identity or any of the party's secrets. As one of the party's most outstanding heroines, she is

---

① A more direct translation of the middle school and high school equivalents in the Chinese education system would be "lower middle school" and "upper middle school", which cover grades 7 - 9 and 10 - 12 respectively. This is why some "high schools", or schools that offer upper middle school courses, are named "middle school". [Translator's note]

② The United Front was a provisional wartime collaboration between the KMT and the CPC to resist the Japanese Aggression. [Translator's note]

counted among the three great heroines of the communist special forces—with the other two being Chen Xiuliang (1907 ~ 1998) and Zhu Feng (1905 ~ 1950). On July 14 [th], 1945, Zhang was shot dead as a "major suspect of the Communist Party" at the Kuaihuoling execution grounds in Xifeng, Guizhou, at the age of 24.

Today one can find statues of the martyr at Chengdu No. 14 Middle School andthe Luping Square in her hometown of Chongzhou.

Members of the Chinese National Liberation Vanguard reading publications about the War of Resistance Against Japanese Aggression (Zhang Luping: far left). Photo courtesy of the Sichuan Museum of Jianchuan.

Fangchi Street

Fangchi Street runs west from Xiaonan Street, parallel and to the north of Shuhua Street. Since the founding of the P. R. C. , it has long been the home of the Sichuan Federation of Trade Unions.

In the Qing Dynasty, Fangchi Street was located within Manchu City, but its name was Zhongling Hutong. It derived its this name from a "Zhongling Archway" that used to be located at the hutong's eastern end. Later, a body of water that already existed within the *hutong* was rebuilt into a square shape, so the hutong was renamed "Fangchi Hutong" (*fangchi* meaning "square pond") and became "Fangchi Street" in the Republican period. Planted with lotus flowers, the pond was five *mu* (3,333 m^2) at its largest, making it the most expansive body of water in Manchu City. Considering the location of the street, a pond there would most likely have formed from the ancient channel of a inner river. Unfortunately, the pond has already been filled in for quite some time. Worth a mention is that locals back then would refer to the pond as *dakeng yanr* (and the nearby Xiaonan Street as "Dakeng Yanr Back Street"), which, as a term meaning "pondside" in Beijing dialect, was clearly brought to Chengdu by the Manchu and Mongol banner families. One can find the same term in certain Beijing place names like Nanheyanr and Beiheyanr.

Between 1982 and 1986, construction along Fangchi Road led to the discovery of one ancient ruin after another. A rich variety of relics were uncovered, including stone and bone tools, ceramics, oracle bones and shells. These artifacts were the first discovered within the present-day city that confirm this area as an extremely important cultural site during the late Neolithic to Warring States period. Some of the archaeological finds here that are considered the most important to the study of Shu civilization include a bound figure carved from limestone, pig dragon pottery, and three embankments of small stones and interwoven bamboo strips (indicating a water control project that predates Dujiangyan's by hundreds of years). Since then, the ruins of similar ancient Shu projects—both dykes and dams—have been successively discovered in the General's Yamen, Fuqin Community, and Zhihui Street, proving that water engineering was indeed quite common in Chengdu at that time.

Fangchi Street, 1986 Ancient Shu Water Project Ruins Photo courtesy of Zhou Ertai.

Renowned war hero and martyr Li Jiayu① had two houses in Chengdu. Both of them have been relatively well-preserved and were listed in 2001 among Chengdu's first batch of 22 cultural relics. Of the two buildings, one was Li Jiayu's personal residence, which is located at 92 Front Wenmiao Street (now under the management of the Sichuan Provincial Committee of the Communist Party of China). Located at 22 Fangchi Street, the second building was the home of Li Jiayu's brother (now under the management of the Sichuan Federation of Trade Unions).

---

① Li Jiayu (1892 – 1944) was a Xinhai revolutionary, officer in the Sichuan Army, and commander in the War of Resistance Against Japanese Aggression. Renowned for his bravery, he was tragically killed in an ambush in Henan Province and posthumously promoted to full general by the KMT. [Translator's note]

Citang Street

Citang Streetwhich lies outside the gate of the People's Park, was originally located in Shoufu Gate in the southeast of Manchu City in the Qing Dynasty, with Xiyu Street outside the gate. (Therefore, people took to calling this gate "Small East Gate on West Xiyu Street") In the early Qing Dynasty, Citang Street was called Lama Hutong or "*Menggu*" ("Mongolian") Hutong. Change came in the fifty-seventh year during the reign of Emperor Kangxi (1718) when the Eight Banners garrison residing in Lama Hutong established a temple to the powerful minister Nian Gengyao (it would have been in the northeast of today's People's Park). Henceforth, the name of the *hutong* was changed to Citang (Ancestral Hall) Street. After Nian Gengyao was sentenced to death, however, his temple was torn down. Later, a Guandi Temple was built over its remains, but the name Citang Street never changed and has continued to be used to the present day. (During the same period, a second temple was built for Nian Gengyao, located on Boji Street. After Nian's death sentence, it was torn down, too and then rebuilt as Wenchang Palace.)

Nian Gengyao (**1679 – 1726**), a famous minister during the Kangxi and Yongzheng reigns of the Qing Dynasty. In the forty-eighth year during the reign of Emperor Kangxi (1709), Nian served as the Sichuan inspector-general; in the fifty-seventh year (1718) he was promoted to Governor of Sichuan and Shaanxi. He successively pacified a number of "rebellions" at the Sichuan-Tibet frontier and became the trusted confidant of the newly ascended Emperor Yongzheng. In the early years of the Yongzheng reign, he was bestowed with the title Fuyuan General on an expedition to the Northwest, as well as Grand Guardian and Duke of the First Class. However, Nian Gengyao developed an arrogant attitude. He flaunted his nobility and was excessively proud of his merits, becoming greedy and corrupt. Ultimately Emperor Yongzheng imprisoned him; he was charged a total of 92 offences and was sentenced to commit suicide.

After Nian Gengyao's temple on Citang Street was first converted into a Guandi Temple in the forty-eighth year during the reign of Emperor Qianlong (1783), it was rebuilt again during the reign of Emperor Guangxu (r. 1875 ~ 1908) and renamed Wusheng Palace. Particularly in the early Qing Dynasty, the Manchu City was constructed according to a military encampment and the relevant regulations were stipulated accordingly. The only deities that could be worshipped within the Manchu City were the God of War (i. e. Lord Guan Yu) and Guanyin Bodhisattva (The restriction of regulation gradually eased up after the mid-Qing Dynasty, and eight temples of various size were built up across the Manchu City. In the early Qing Dynasty, other than Guandi Temple on Citang Street, there was only the Xilai Temple for Worshipping Rare Stones on Ningsha Street. The Buddhist Shuangfo Temple on Shoujing Street in the Ming Dynasty became the Taoist Zhenwu Palace; Shengshou Temple on Xisheng Street moved to Junping Street; and the Temple of Immortal Yan on Zhijishi Street was changed into another Guandi Temple. Besides, there were Wenchang Temple and Zhaozhong Temple on Citang Street, and Huanxi Temple on the side of Xilai Temple, all of which were built in the late Qing Dynasty.) The Guandi Temple on Citang Street, the largest in Manchu City included a bell tower and a lotus pond on the left and a drum tower and Taichi Pond on the right. The main structure consisted of three halls, and the Jinhe River passed by the front of its second hall as it flowed toward Banbian Bridge, making for some unique scenery. Since residents of the Manchu City were not able to come and go from the Small City (unless granted a special leave), this Guandi Temple was the bannermen's only venue for travel and entertainment for traveling and entertainment, the sole place that had a stage in the Manchu City. The pond in particular was quite renowned in its time, being the largest area planted with lotus flowers within the Small City. A *Bamboo Branch Verse* of the period calls the imagery to mind:

> Manchu City is quiet and secluded,
> Where trees and flowers are planted.
> You can hardly enjoy all the scenery in a year,
> But you may enjoy the lotus at Guandi Temple in summer.

Sichuan Governor Wu Tang established the Eight Banners Shaocheng Academy—the only such an institution within the Manchu City—at the east end of Citang Street in the tenth year during the reign of Emperor Tongzhi (1871). Specifically established for the cultivation of Eight Banners children, the results were far from excellent. In the thirtieth year during the reign of Emperor Guangxu (1904), Chengdu General

Chuohabu issued the order for its demolition.

After the Manchu City was torn down in the early years of the Republican period, Citang Street became an important east-west thoroughfare for Chengdu's urban district. It was expanded twice, first in 1936 and then in 1943. The first expansion laid down a combination pavement made from mud, grout and gravel—an advanced construction technology for Chengdu at that time—and a steamroller (bought from the UK) was used for the first time. Once the War of Resistance Against Japanese Aggression was in full swing, Chengdu gradually became the cultural center city of the rear area. And Citang Street, with its tree-lined Shaocheng Park, gurgling Jinhe River, cinemas and Sichuan opera houses, was a key site for the cultural activities. The rent there was also cheaper than that on Chunxi Road and Dongda Street, so many booksellers opened their branches on Citang Street, including the famous Shenghuo Publishing Company, Kai Ming Book Company, Commercial Press, Beixin Bookstore, Dongfang Bookstore, Dadong Book Company, Zhengzhong Bookstore, Guangyi Publishing House, and Ertong Bookstore. Chengdu's own Puyi Publishing House opened here as well (Puyi was famous throughout the city for editing and publishing of loose-leaf anthologies). Beyond selling books, many of the bookstores were engaged in publishing at the same time, and many newspapers' editorial offices were also located in the same place, earning Citang Street the moniker "New Culture Street". Revolutionary martyr Che Yaoxian (1894 ~ 1946) also opened "Our Bookstore" here, which specialized in selling progressive books. A pioneer in many respects, it was the first shop in Chengdu to use an artistic typeface and arrange its name plate horizontally to be read from left to right. Records indicate that in the twelve years from the July 7th Incident[①] to the founding of the P. R. C. , 267 different bookshops and 54 stationery shops were opened in the city, among which 183 and 34 respectively opened on Citang Street. Under the organization of the underground CPC, over a hundred bookstore clerks organized a book workers' singing group (Shenghuo, Kai Ming, Beixin, Ertong and others all had members of the CPC among their staff). Every morning they'd gather on the street and sing songs of salvation from the Japanese in loud chorus; at night they'd give speeches or put on street performances (the famous actor Zhao Dan

---

① The July 7th Incident or the Lugouqiao (Lugou Bridge) Incident, also known as the Marco Polo Bridge Incident was a battle between Chinese and Japanese troops outside of Beijing on July 7th, 1937, often used as the marker for the start of the War of Resistance Against Japanese Aggression (1937 – 1945). [Translator's note]

appeared in *Put Down Your Whip*; Bai Yang performed *All of One Mind*; Ma Yinchu and Li Gongpu were among those to deliver speeches). In Chengdu, it came to be known as the "Morning Call Squad" and the "Evening Call Squad". All bookstores at that time opened shelves to readers, meaning that customers could browse freely. Some bookstores even posted a sign of "you're welcome to read" and offered free boiled water. Many book lovers would spend all day reading and studying in the shops—as described in *Memories of Old Jincheng Bamboo Branch Verses*. Up until the "Cultural Revolution", old bookstores could still be found on Citang Street; even at the beginning of the Reform and Opening Up, the street still had some textbook and children's bookstores.

Kai Ming Bookstore on Citang Street, 1942. Photo courtesy of Yang Yongqiong.

In April 1938, the only CPC newspaper allowed to distribute openly in KMT-occupied areas was *Xinhua Daily*. Its subscription center in Chengdu was known as the "Western Sichuan North General Distribution Office" or "Chengdu Branch", or the "Xinhua Bookstore" as it sold all kinds of progressive literature, including Yan'an publications. Located at 103 Citang Street, today's 38 Citang Street, it moved to 88 Citang Street shortly after opening. Once the only public liaison office of the CPC in Chengdu, it kept up the fight for 8 years, finally was disbanded in March 1947. The place where many of *Xinhua Daily*'s revolutionary forebears worked and fought is now a widely-sought and respected red memorial. What I must point out is that, in recent years, Chengdu's media has false accounts of this office, among which the most critical error was that "such important figures as Zhou Enlai, Liu Shaoqi and Chen Yi had worked here for a time". In reality, Liu Shaoqi and Chen Yi didn't even come to Sichuan during the War of Resistance Against Japanese Aggression, let alone work for *Xihua Daily* in Chengdu. Party leaders who worked or visited here were Zhou Enlai, Dong Biwu, Peng Dehuai, Lin Boqu, Wu Yuzhang and Deng Yingchao.

The former Chengdu branch of *Xinhua Daily*, 2011. Photo by Yang Xianfeng.

During the War of Resistance Against Japanese Aggression, the leaders of the underground CPC organization printed and distributed progressive newspapers and periodicals. They are Che Yaoxian's *Dasheng* (*Shout Weekly*), Hu Jiwei and Xiong Fu's *Xingmang* ("Expanse of Stars") weekly and the peripheral "Xingmang Society" and Chengdu Students Federation's *Students in Wartime*, published every 10 days and edited by Kang Naier and Wu Derang. There was also the China Nationwide Anti-enemy Association of Literary and Art Circles Chengdu Branch's official publication *Bizhen* ("A Spate of Pens"), edited by Zhou Wen, which stood in solidarity with the

CPC, and *Jinjian* ("Golden Arrow"), a bimonthly from the Chengdu Cultural Salvation Association edited by Chen Siling. Citang Street also had the Chengdu Wartime Publishing House managed by Yang Daosheng, the Mangyuan Publishing House managed by Yao Xueyan, and the Cultural Society Qunli Publishing Group edited by Rao Mengwen. In April 1938, the Chengdu Book Industry Branch was established here with Yang Daosheng as the secretary (Yang Daosheng was a student at Tsinghua University; in 1941 he was arrested, and died on June 3nd of the following year at the Shahepu Housheng Nongchang ("Shahe Recuperation Farm") in Sichuan Province).

Taking advantage of the easy cover provided by flourishing cultural activities, Chengdu's CPC established its major underground operations here. According to data, the Southern Bureau of the CPC Central Committee, the CPC Sichuan Provincial Committee and the CPC Chengdu Municipal Committee successively established seven branches, secret points of contact or transport stations on Citang Street. During the KMT's three major anti-communism campaigns, cumulative twenty-plus party members were arrested on this street—including Luo Shiwen and Che Yaoxian—it temporarily earned the nickname "Revolution Street".

Of course, there were more than just revolutionary forces on "Revolution Street". According to the recollections of a CBIS special agent, there was a Kuomintang special operations outfit on the second floor of a teahouse just across the road from 88 Citang Street: "It's one of the largest surveillance posts in Chengdu. Bloody-handed agents came and went from that room, watching and waiting. They monitored the workers, customers, and general crowds at Xinhua Bookstore, Shenghuo Bookstore, the Wartime Publishing House, *Dasheng*, *Students in Wartime*, *Xingmang*, and the Qunli Publishing Group." The special agents "regularly exchanged intelligence there, sometimes even escorting their prisoners to sit in the teahouse, forcing them to identify persons entering or leaving the aforementioned bookstores". A gunfight even broke out in the teahouse once in 1940 when special agents mistakenly apprehended an air force officer.

In 1941, the Sichuan Fine Arts Association was founded by a merger among the "Shu Arts Society", the "Rong Society", and the "Chengdu Fine Arts Association". It was set up on Citang Street in Shaocheng Park, bringing together a multitude of the country's well-known artists engaged in propaganda for the War of Resistance Against Japanese Aggression and creative applications of the arts. It was "well-known" to the extent that the Zhang Qun, the governor of Sichuan Province served as president of the association, Luo Wenmo, the secretary of the Sichuan Provincial Party Headquarters of the KMT served as the executive director. However, the person in charge was Zhang Caiqin (1901 ~ 1984), who was a famous Sichuanese painter. In addition to six different showcases of Zhang Caiqin's works, the Sichuan Fine Arts Association hosted successive exhibits featuring such artists as Zhang Daqian, Xu Beihong, Wu Zuoren, Fu Baoshi, Pan Tianshou, Huang Junbi, Zhao Shaoang, Guan Shanyue, Wu Yifeng, and Cen Xuegong. Chengdu residents today are surely familiar with the bronze statue of Sun Yat-sen on Zhongshan Square and of the unknown heroes at the east gate of People's Park; these were created by famous sculptor Liu Kaiqu with the support and assistance of the Sichuan Fine Arts Association. This was the most active period of modern art creation in Chengdu. In 2005, the Chengdu authorities built a monument at the former site of Sichuan Fine Arts Association in the People's Park.

Monument at the former site of the Sichuan Fine Arts Association, 2010.
Photo by Yang Xianfeng.

Chengdu's widely renowned "Nulican" Sichuanese Restaurant moved from South Sanqiao Street to 137 Citang Street in 1933. It remained there until 1983, when it moved to the adjacent Jinhe Road due to the road expansion.

Citang Street also sees another major event in the history of Sichuan cuisine. In the twenty-fourth year during the reign of Emperor Guangxu in the Qing Dynasty (1898),

Li Jiuru opened Jufeng Garden Restaurant on Huaxing Street. It was one of the most important restaurants in the period of formation of modern Sichuan cuisine. Li Jiuru was a native of Hejiang in southeastern Sichuan. Before opening Jufeng Restaurant he made a living in Beijing for ten years, studying famous dishes in Jiangxi, Zhejiang, and elsewhere. His own restaurant brought together the essence of North and South Chinese cuisine with innovations as well (for example, the "three-ways chicken" that is so popular today actually originated from the "six-way chicken" of Jufeng Garden so many years ago). Guests could order individually or cater a banquet—they could even partake in a version of the "Manchu-Han Banquet" by the Qing court featuring a wealth of fine dishes from both traditions. For a while, Jufeng Garden was the talk of the whole city. In the thirty-third year during the reign of Emperor Guangxu (1907), with the support of Chengdu General Chuohabu, Sichuan's newly appointed Quanyedao, Zhou Shanpei, had Jufeng Garden moved next to Citang Street's Guandi Temple within the Manchu City. This was the first business opened in Manchu City by Han people after the implementation of the New Policy in the late Qing Dynasty. At that time Jufeng Garden not only served the most high-end Sichuan dishes, but also served Peking duck, instant-boiled meat hot pot, Western food and Shaoxing rice wine (later it would even introduce sorbet and ice cream). It was the first restaurant in Chengdu to use tablecloths, wine goblets, and Western cutlery. Servers had to go through training and stand at attention to welcome arriving guests. This created a precedent for Western-style dining in Sichuan Province and had a major effect on the development of Chengdu's restaurant industry. Famous Sichuanese scholar Liu Shiliang composed a *Bamboo Branch Verse* to describe the venue:

Jufeng Garden is where China meets the West;
All the finest fare are perfectly prepared.
Through the glass window, I try to peer;
Who is leaning on the table drunken here?

In old Chengdu, people referred to Jufeng Garden as Jufeng Nantang (in the late Qing and the early years of the Republican period, there was another modern restaurant opened by new arrivals from South China; it was named Jiangnan Restaurant but people simply called it Nantang). The famous Jufeng Garden remained open until 1944.

In 1952, the Sichuan Cinema, Chengdu's most famous theater, was built on Citang

Street. Before that, the site had been home to the Shaocheng Bookstore in the Qing Dynasty, then the West Shu Stage Theater in 1931, which changed its name to the Tianfu Daxiyuan (Tianfu Grand Theater) in 1937. In 1939, the name was officially changed again to the Xinyouxin Grand Theater, as the Sichuan opera troupe Xinyouxin had been performing there for so long that people were already referring to it as the "Xinyouxin" stage theater. After two fires and the subsequent reconstruction, it was renamed the Jinping Grand Theater in 1947. For a time when the "Xinyouxin" was one of the most famous theaters in the entire city, and it was also the first to construct a trapezoidal stage that sloped downward toward the audience. From the beginning of the War of Resistance Against Japanese Aggression until the liberation of Chengdu, its lineup of Sichuan opera stars was second to none, able to match the quality of Yuelai Tea Garden, which had been established a century earlier. More importantly, the Xinyouxin was the staging venue for the earliest and most successful modern Sichuan operas of the novel *Shizhuangxi* genre. *Shizhuangxi* was written by famous playwright Liu Huaixu (1879 ~ 1947), known as the "founder of Sichuan opera *Shizhuangxi*", and hosted by famous director and actor, Zhou Haibin. *Shizhuangxi* can be understood as "a contemporary costume drama" that used modern dress, characters and events from Sichuan's late Qing and Republican periods. In his lifetime, Liu Huaixi wrote over 140 such operas, including the hugely successful *The Mute Woman and the Pretty Wife*, *Solace of the Soul*, *Farm Girl*, *The World's Best*, *Self-harm* (an adaptation of the straight play *Thunderstorm*), the wartime play *Martyrs of Teng County* (which sold out over 50 performances), and the tragic love story *Who Hurt Her?*, which was revived by the Jianwei Sichuan Opera Troupe in 1981 to a warm reception in Chengdu. Forerunners of contemporary Sichuan opera actors, including Yang Youhe, Xiao Keqin, Wu Xiaolei, Liu Chengji, Xie Wenxin and Chen Shufang, all performed at the Xinyouxin for an extended time, Yang Youhe and Chen Shufang each successfully appearing in *Shizhuangxi*. In 1947, actor Liu Chengji was arrested there by reactionary authorities after swapping his lines for his own commentary on the bleak state of society. The Youxin Opera School established here was one of the most prolific training centers of its kind in the early years of the Republican period, training a large number of new Sichuan opera talents (in the past, the institutions for training students in the opera circle were called Keban or Keshe, i. e. Opera School, and the Youxin Opera School has developed into today's Sichuan Opera Troupe in Leshan after the founding of the P. R. C.). Many academics would say that while the Yuelai Tea Garden on Huaxin Street was the cradle and base camp of modern Sichuan Opera, the

Xinyouxin Grand Theater on Citang Street could be regarded as the largest experimental ground for successful reforms and innovations of traditional Sichuan opera. After the founding of the P. R. C. , the then-named Jinping Grand Theater was again renamed West Sichuan Playhouse, then finally became the Sichuan Cinema in 1952.

In the Republican period, Qi Luo, Chengdu's most famous professional children's clothing store, was established on this street. The owner had studied abroad in Japan, and the children's clothing her shop produced and sold was renowned throughout the city for its elegance and "foreign style".

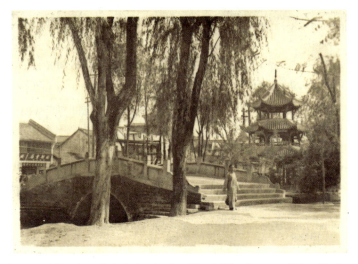

Entrance of Shaocheng Park during the Republic of China Courtesy of Yang Xianfeng

On the south side of Citang Street is central Chengdu's largest green area, which is also one of the first public parks in the province and even in the whole China—the People's Park. In the Qing Dynasty, this area was a large open space occupying the south section of the Manchu City. It mainly consisted of vegetable gardens, but also contained rice fields, military training fields, horse stables, and subsidy granaries (grain issued directly from the Qing government was stored and distributed from this location). A few *hutongs* were also found in this part of the city, including Yongqing, Yongji, and Yongshun. In the late Qing Dynasty, as government finances were stretched increasingly thin, it was felt throughout every part of the system, especially since "In the Eight Banners, all children are soldiers". That is, Manchu and Mongol officers, regular soldiers and their dependents in the Eight Banners were exclusively military, and not allowed to engage in agriculture, business, trade or other industries. They were totally dependent on a subsidy system. The Qing government regularly issued grain and silver to support each household's daily needs. After the invasion of the Eight-Nation Alliance[1], many bannermen were forced to sell their houses and land—even their sons and daughters—to stay alive. Three centuries of Qing rule have passed in the blink of an eye, the sun is setting, and the path ahead is to destitution. " The banners' plight, combined with rising nationalist sentiment, intensified calls for the Manchu-Han equality among the populace. In 1907, the Empress Dowager Cixi issued an imperial edict "to hear every view from central and local-level government offices on how to achieve complete erasure of the boundary between Han and Manchu by proper negotiation and practical means". After that, as regions nationwide set about gradually "erasing the boundary", the previously strict divisions between Manchu and Han quickly broke down. In Chengdu, Citang Street, the most important link between Manchu City and Han residential areas outside the city, has became the first place to change, and some shops were gradually opened here. In the last year of the Qing Dynasty, 1911, Chengdu General Yu Kun and Quanyedao Zhou Xiaohuai decided to open up the Manchu City and turn this stretch of land into "Shaocheng Park". The main reason for this decision lay in that, in 1907 the Qing government issued an imperial edict of cutting off banner subsidies, but it could not actually be implemented due to extreme oppositions from bannermen around the country. But if the edict was enforced, the life-long subsidy system for banners must be abolished. Thus late Qing leaders had to make every effort to find the bannermen some alternative means of livelihood. After the park was built, the bannermen could bring in a certain income with entrance tickets or by conducting business inside the park, selling food or tea. A *Bamboo Branch Verse* following the Xinhai Revolution described the matter:

The Eight Banners sit idle and eat what they own,
Raising birds happily, but they lose their throne.
Everything goes smoothly because of good luck,

---

[1] In 1900, an alliance of armed forces (sent primarily from Britain, the United States, Germany, France, Russia, Japan, Italy and Austria) fought their way into Beijing and its Forbidden City; in 1901 they forced the Qing government to sign the *Protocol of 1901*, requiring China to pay an immense indemnity. [Translator's note]

Empty – handed after their barns turned into a park.

Shaocheng Park's original gate opened to the west side of the entrance to Yongxing Street—i. e. at the location of the small gate used before, north of the Railway Protection Movement Monument.

China's first park appeared in Shanghai's concession area (i. e. the Bund) in 1868. Initially only open to foreigners, it opened to the Chinese public in 1886; its name, "Public Garden", remained the same. The popularization of parks open to city residents began with the Beijing Zoo (Wansheng Park at that time) in 1907. But research suggests that the term of public park (*gongyuan*) entered the Chinese language from Japanese, and Chengdu had the earliest park in the name of "*gongyuan*" and open to the public. At that time its official name was simply "Park" (*gongyuan*), but people began to call it "Shaocheng Park" because it was located within the Small City. Once established as a convention, this became the official name as well. In this sense, Shaocheng Park was the first public park established and operated in the whole China. In 1950, its name was changed to People's Park (Renmin Gongyuan).

The initial scope of Shaocheng Park was 50-plus mu ($33,333$ m^2) east of the Railway Protection Movement Monument, which contained the Yingxi Tower, Guanjia Tower, Songyun Tower and Huxin Pavilion and occupied about one-fifth of the area of today's People's Park. Through successive expansions over many years (with the most important one being in 1914), it gradually became the largest and most multifunctional park in the entire city. At that time it was not only the largest site for comprehensive cultural facilities, but also the largest for group activities and mass assemblies. In the Republican period, the park hosted numerous large-scale gatherings for people from all levels of society in the city and province. Among these were: May 25th, 1919 May 4th Movement meeting in solidarity with Beijing students, which was attended by over 10,000 people from all walks of life, including teachers and students from over 60 Chengdu schools; the June 8th, 1919 National Assembly that brought out more than 20,000 people from across Chengdu society to condemn the traitorous Beiyang[①] (i. e. the Republic of China) government and call for the boycott

---

① The Republican government established in 1912 was known as the "Beiyang" government after the late Qing Dynasty's (and early Republic's) dominant military force, the Beiyang Army commanded by Yuan Shikai. [Translator's note]

of Japanese goods; in 1924, the first mass meeting held in Chengdu to commemorate the May 1st labor movement and mourn Russian revolutionary Vladimir Lenin; in 1925, a mass memorial for Sun Yat-sen; in 1928, a mass memorial for 14 martyrs of the revolution including the leader of the CPC West Sichuan Special Committee, Yuan Shiyao (1897 ~ 1928); a mass send-off for the Sichuan Army on September 5th, 1937, which drew over 50,000 people (the first Sichuan Army troops which departed for battle had left four days earlier; thus September 1st was designated as the permanent anniversary of the Sichuan Army's participation in the war in the following year); a mass assembly to denounce Japanese invaders' ruthless bombing of Chengdu (including the Shaocheng Park area); and the first major Chengdu Citizens Sports Meet, held in Shaocheng Park on October 14th, 1939.

Chengdu people gathered at Shaocheng Park on July 7t, 1939 for the national salvation memorial meeting against Japanese aggression. Photo courtesy of Yang Xianfeng.

Prior to the founding of the P. R. C., the Sichuan Library was established within Shaocheng Park. Constructed in 1912, the library's first director was the eminent scholar Lin Sijin (1874 ~ 1953). Because 80 pine trees were planted around its perimeter, the library was also known as the "Eighty Pines Gallery". Shaocheng Park was also home to the predecessor of the Sichuan Museum, the Jinshi Exhibition Hall. The hall was officially converted to the provincial museum in March 1941 when it moved into the Imperial City's Mingyuan Building. In 1949 it moved back to the People's Park; then in 1965 it was relocated to Section 4 of South Renmin Road, where it remained in operation until July 2002 when it was marked for demolition. Finally, the museum reopened on May 1st, 2009 in the new building on South

Huanhua Road. Besides the libraries and museums, Shaocheng Park was also home to the Popular Education Center, a musical performance venue, amusement park, zoo, gymnasium (with facilities for soccer, basketball, volleyball, tennis, track and field), archery range (with Chengdu's famous archery club operating out of the neighboring teahouse), restaurants (including the famous Jinlin Restaurant), Shaocheng Buddhist Society and the Chengdu Office of Buddhist Scripture Circulation. [After the founding of the P. R. C. , a host of the Shaocheng Buddhist Society and Chengdu Office of Buddhist Scripture Circulation was the renowned Buddhist master Nenghai (1886 ~ 1967), who also served as vice chairman of the Chinese Buddhist Association. Master Taixu (1890 ~ 1947), another famous monk, gave a number of teachings here as well.] Shaocheng Park also had a famous theater, the Eternal Spring Tea Garden (Wanchun Chayuan), which was considered the third-ranking theater in Chengdu after the Keyuan (Elegant Garden) and Yuelai Chayuan (Yuelai Tea Garden). Chengdu's first drama troupe—the Chunliu Xiyuan (Chunliu Opera Society), established in 1912—put on Chengdu's first drama performance here in 1918. Eternal Spring also hosted performances from such groups as the Yijiu Jüyuan (One-Nine Drama Society), Meihuayuan (Meihua Society), and Sichuan Drama Association. In 1930, the Eternal Spring Tea Garden was converted into the Daguangming Cinema, which was demolished in 1941 out of safety concerns. As water from the Jinhe River was drawn into Shaocheng Park at Xiaonan Street to exit the park from Banbian Bridge, soil dug from the canal was used to form a rockery—all thanks to patriotic industrialist Lu Zuofu, who was head of the Popular Education Center in 1924.

Lu Zuofu (**1893 ~ 1952**), originally from Hechuan (in present-day Chongqing), came to Chengdu to attend school in 1908. He participated in the Tongmenghui prior to the Xinhai Revolution. After touring the country in 1914, and returning to Sichuan, he served concurrently as reporter, editor, and director/editor-in-chief of the *Masses Newspaper* (*Qunbao*) and *Sichuan Newspaper* (*Chuanbao*). During the same period, he also participated in the China Youth Association and was active in the May 4th Movement. In 1924, Sichuan Tuchun Yang Sen appointed Lu Zuofu as director of the Sichuan Provincial Department of

Lu Zuofu

Education and Chengdu Popular Education Center. In these capacities, Lu made important contributions to the construction of Shaocheng Park. In 1926 he established the Minsheng Company in Chongqing for private shipping on the Sichuan River (the portion of the Yangtze River running from Yibin, Sichuan to Yichang, Hubei), and in 1927 he took up the post of Director of Gorge Defense and constructed the famous Beibei Experimental Area (Chongqing's central district). In 1929 he served as director of Sichuan River Navigation Management. After the war broke out with Japan, he led the renowned Yichang Arms Transport and established Sichuan River Night Shipping, expediting the transport of hundreds of thousands of tons of military equipment and materials into Sichuan, and moving over 200,000 fighters and a large volume of materials from Sichuan to the frontline. Starting from 1935, he served a concurrent post as director of the Sichuan Provincial Department of Construction, making significant contributions to Sichuan's industrial and water management construction. Through many years of relentless efforts, the Minsheng Company became the country's top logistics giant, with a fleet of over 150 ships suitable for both river and sea transport. In the early years of the P. R. C. , Lu Zuofu became a member of the National Committee of the Chinese People's Political Consultative Conference (CPPCC) as well as the Southwest Military and Administrative Commission, while he continued to serve as general manager of the Minsheng Company. Sadly, he passed away in 1952 during the Five-Anti Campaign[1]. Shortly after his death, Chairman Mao Zedong declared that "there are four unforgettable individuals in China's business world," and one of them is "Lu Zuofu, who developed the transport industry. "

In those days, the most important cultural site in Shaocheng Park was the Popular Education Center established and headed by Lu Zuofu. The center consisted of eight departments—library, museum, gymnasium, music, lectures, publishing, recreation, and business—and did much to spread modern culture in Chengdu. The name Popular Education Center was not particular to or determined by Chengdu, but was the Beiyang government's uniform designation for social education institutions around the country at

---

[1] The Five-Antis Campaign was a China's political movement targeting the capitalist class in 1952; the Five "Antis" were bribery, tax evasion, theft of state property, intelligence, and cheating on government contracts. [Translator's note]

that time. In 1934, in accordance with regulations of the KMT government based in Nanjing, the Popular Education Center was renamed the People's Education Hall, and the management of the entire Shaocheng Park fell under its jurisdiction. The last director of the Chengdu People's Education Hall was renowned reporter Deng Muqing (1908 ~ 2002), who had once headed the interview department at *Xinxin News*. The Chengdu People's Education Center remained in operation into the early P. R. C. years, whereafter its many responsibilities were divided among newly established cultural institutions.

The most significant and well-known cultural artifact in the People's Park is the "Monument to the Martyrs of the Railway Protection Movement". The 31.85-meter high monument was erected in 1914 by the Sichuan-Hankou Railway Co. to memorialize the numerous martyrs whose lives were cruelly taken in the course of the Railway Protection Movement. It was designed by Wang Nan, a native of Shuangliu (a county/district in southern Chengdu) who studied civil engineering in Japan; Hu Bingsen oversaw its construction. The shape of the tower invokes Baiyun Temple in Beijing and Lingyun Temple in Shanxi Province. Its five-component design consists of a plinth, stylobate, stele base, stele body, and stele cap. Blending Chinese and Western elements to grand and solemn effect, it points straight at the blue dome above like a long sword, and shows a powerful exemplar of the traditional architectural style combining memorial tablet and tower. Each of the four faces bears the ten-character phrase meaning the "Monument to the Martyrs of the Railway Protection Movement"; each character is one square meter in size, and each side is inscribed by a different Sichuan calligrapher—namely, Wu Zhiying of Mingshan (whose clerical script appears on the east face), Yan Kai of Huayang (whose Weibei is on the south face), Zhang Kuijie of Guanxian County (whose seal script appears on the west face), and Zhao Xi of Rong County (whose Hanbei[1] is on the north face).

The monument has weathered many storms. It was first tested by the 1933 Diexi Earthquake and then by the bombs of the Japanese. Shaocheng Park was in fact one of the main targets in the brutal bombing of Chengdu that occurred on July 27th, 1941. As hundreds of people were injured or killed in the park's air raid trenches, the

---

① Hanbei is a style of stone calligraphy going back to the Han Dynasty (202 BC – 220AD), while the aforementioned Weibei stone calligraphy originates in the Northern and Southern Song Dynasties (420 – 588AD). [Translator's note]

monument's peak also took serious damage. Repairs were carried out shortly after the founding of the P. R. C. , followed by a more comprehensive restoration in 1980. In 1988, the monument was designated as a national key cultural relic protection unit.

The site initially selected for construction of the "Monument to the Martyrs of the Railway Protection Movement" was not in Shaocheng Park at all, but in the former General's Yamen on Duyuan Street, where the blood of so many Railway Protection Movement revolutionaries had been shed in the "Bloody Chengdu Incident" of 1911. At that time, as commander of the Sichuan Army's 2nd Division, Peng Guanglie lived in the General's Yamen. He was ready to move out his troops and clear the site for construction, but it was renegotiated because most people feared that demolishing the houses would cause disturbances and disputes. Ultimately, Sichuan Governor Hu Jingyi's proposal met with unanimous approval: The monument was to be built in the Shaocheng Park.

Also within the bounds of today's People's Park, there was once a statue of General Wang Mingzhang, a hero who resisted the Japanese aggression. Sculpted by Liu Kaiqu, the bronze statue depicted Wang Mingzhang seating on the horseback. It was demolished after the founding of the P. R. C.

Wang Mingzhang (1893 ~ 1938), was originally from Xindu (a county/district in northern Chengdu). In 1909 he began his studies at the Sichuan Army Primary School, and entered the Sichuan Army there. In 1925 he was promoted to division commander; in 1932 he held a concurrent post as commander of Chengdu's City Defense; in 1936 he was awarded the title of lieutenant general. Once the War of Resistance Against Japanese Aggression had broken out in full, he requested to be sent to the front of his own initiative. He once delivered a fervent speech at a troop's oath ceremony in Deyang, vowing to serve the country as a means of redemption for past sins—namely, his participation in the civil war. On September 5th, 1937, under the command of Deng Xihou, Wang Mingzhang led the 122nd Division of the 41st Army of Sichuan out of the province on foot to join in the War of Resistance Against Japanese Aggression. In late October, they fought in the bloody seven-day Battle of Niangziguan, Shanxi Province, wherein the Japanese assailed them with planes, tanks, flamethrowers and poisonous gas; finally Wang's troops helped to successfully retake Pingyao County. He then transferred to the frontline at Xuzhou (Jiangsu Province), where he served in the famous defensive Battle of Taierzhuang as frontline commander of the 41st Army, effectively blocking the enemy's southward advance into Teng County. On March 14th, 1938, the Japanese made a frantic assault under cover of plane, tank, and artillery. Wang commanded his troops, armed with rifles and machetes, to resist at all costs. At that time, Teng County's forces fell short of 3,000 men, while the enemy numbered over 30,000 and had over 20 active bombers. After four days and four nights of relentless and bloody battle, ammunition was exhausted. On March 17th, Wang Mingzhang met his end on the ground near the electric lighting factory. In his last moments, he continued to shout "Fight until the last drop of blood!" and "Long live the Chinese nation!". (Some literary and artistic works portray Wang committing suicide with his own gun, but this is inaccurate; he was in fact killed by seven bullets issued by Japanese machine guns.) General Li Zongren (1891 ~ 1969), director of the Fifth War Zone, once said: "If there was not the bitter defense of Teng County, how could there have ever been the victory of Taierzhuang? The victory at Taierzhuang belongs to the martyrs of Teng County. " Wang Mingzhang's coffin was transported to his hometown and public memorials were held for him in Hankou, Chongqing and Chengdu. The Republican government posthumously awarded Wang with the title of General, and Mao Zedong honored him with this elegiac couplet:

Fight to defend the besieged city, calmly accept the fate of death, these are the true qualities of a revolutionary soldier;

Determined to wipe out the powerful enemy, these are a will to die for the country, a drive to win glory for the Chinese people.

A cemetery was established for Wang Mingzhang in Xindu, and in 1941 the Mingzhang Middle School was built in his honor. Lin Sen, the chairman of the Nationalist government at that time, inscribed four characters on its main gate: "heroic integrity, virtuous deeds. " In 1947, the people of Chengdu had a bronze statue made for the war hero. On September 1st, 1984, the Sichuan Government posthumously confirmed Wang Mingzhang as a revolutionary martyr, built a new cemetery for him in Xindu, and had the bronze statue remade. The formerly named Mingzhang Middle School is now the Xindu No. 1 Middle School; its campus still contains a "Ming Garden" named for the hero.

The former bronze statue of Wang Mingzhang in Shaocheng Park in the 1940s. Photo courtesy of the Sichuan Museum of Jianchuan.

In today's People's Park, one can find the Heming Teahouse beneath the weeping willows and among the flowers along the lakeside. Now an icon of Chengdu's traditional teahouse culture and one of the most famous teahouses in the entire country, it was first opened by a man from Dayi (just west of Chengdu) of the surname Gong. Almost all the predecessors who lived in Chengdu in the past, including Yang Shangkun (1907 ~ 1998), Zhang Aiping (1910 ~ 2003), Wei Chuantong (1908 ~ 1996) and other proletarian revolutionaries of the older generation, would come here to drink tea and recollect old Chengdu as long as they return back. In 1943, Chen Yinke (1890 ~ 1969), a leading authority in the education world, and famous scholar Shao Zuping (1898 ~ 1969) enjoyed tea at the Green Shade Pavilion in Shaocheng Park, as recorded in the poem " *Sitting with Yinke in Early Summer at Shaocheng Park's Green Shade Pavilion* " , part of Shao Zuping's *Peifenglou Collection*:

> The early summer wind breezes the air so sultry;
> A pomegranate grows branches of two or three.
> The tea canopy is shaded over by the namu trees;
> Customers pass their time as the Buddhist retreat.

The exact timeframe of Heming Teahouse's establishment has yet to be verified. So far I have come across three possible dates: 1914, 1920, and 1923. The teahouse's former name plate was inscribed by calligrapher Wang Jiazhen in the year 1940, but was destroyed in 1952. In 1988, Wang was asked to write a new one. When it comes to old Chengdu teahouses, one might say that Heming Teahouse has all the defining characteristics, along with some of its own unique features—such as the legacy of the "Liu La War" that regularly unfolded here in the Republican period.

In the Republic of China, Shaocheng had six teahouses in total: not far from where Citang Street crossed the Jinhe River was Zhenliu; a few dozen paces beyond that laid Heming; across the canal from Heming was the Green Shade Pavilion; on the east side of the Green Shade Pavilion was Yongju; north of that and over the canal was Nongyin, and beside the Railway Protection Movement Monument laid Shedehui. Collectively, they attracted people from all levels of society and walks of life. For example, Zhenliu mostly attracted students; the Green Shade Pavilion was dominated by aristocrats; Yongju was frequented by members of the business community; the martial arts circle tended to favor Shedehui. Heming, meanwhile, was the favorite of teachers and public officials. It should be noted that at the time, teachers and public officials were all hired by contract. So, whenever summer or winter vacation rolled around, most teachers were haunted by the specter of hunger and homelessness until they could secure their next appointment. Officials were hardly better off, many faced the same dilemma at either mid or end of the year. Thus, twice a year, in June and in the twelfth lunar month, large numbers of teachers and public officials would gather in Heming Teahouse to exchange information and test their relationships for favors, doing everything they possibly could to get contracts and avoid unemployment. Various schools' principals were known to find the candidates they needed from among the teahouse crowd, some even make hires rights on the spot. Therefore, it became a highly competitive talent market. People at that time took to calling this fierce semiannual competition the "Liu La War" (*Liu* means "six", referring to June; *La* is the twelfth month in the lunar calendar). Heming Teahouse served as the main battleground for the Liu La War.

Of course, Shaocheng Park's primary function was the expansion of recreational and leisure services for tourists, as a Republican-period *Bamboo Branch Verse* recounts:

> String and woodwind instruments sound noisily;
> People play ball and laugh loudly.
> A rustic charm pervades the park there;
> Beside the short fence grow oleanders.

Another Republican-period *Bamboo Branch Verse* also describe it:

Men and women are snuggling in the park,
Drinking tea while enjoying their free love.
Playing tennis and then kicking the ball,
A lustre to stadium with a special charm.

In those days, many novelties in Chengdu, including zoos and fountains, first appeared in the Shaocheng Park. A *Bamboo Branch Verse in the* Republican period described the "water spraying machine" that one could rarely see in this way:

Relying completely on excess pressure,
the water shoots straight into the sky in a bewildering manner.
As the spray land on the lotus pond,
the Lotus Flower Fairy suspects it's the work of elves, magically relieving themselves from above.

Luo Zhongshu at Heming Teahouse, 1943. Photo by Joseph Needham [UK]. Photo courtesy of Yang Xianfeng.

Naturally, leisure and recreation includes athletic pursuits. At that time Shaocheng Park was the main athletic venue for the whole Chengdu, with the most sports facilities and competitions. It was even referred to as "Athletics Park". A number of domestic sports stars once showed off their skills in the park, including Li Huitang (soccer), Lin Baohua (tennis), Wang Yuzeng and Bao Wenpei (basketball). Two major volleyball stars also used to train at Shaocheng Park. Wang Defen, one of the founding members of the national women's volleyball team (successively as player and coach) in the P. R. C. started out playing for Chengdu's Fucheng Middle School, while Kan Yongwu, another star player on the national women's team, used to play for Chengdu Shude High School. Also, the following *Bamboo Branch Verse* is quite likely the very first Chengdu poem to describe a soccer match:

> Tinted by the setting sun is a lawn in sight;
> Crowds of people are pouring into the site.
> All trainees boast of their waists and thighs,
> Kicking the ball flying up high into the sky.

We can surmise from this poem that Shaocheng Park's soccer field at that time was covered with turf.

Aerial picture of the People's Park in the 1980s Photo by Chen Delong

The Chengdu Weiqi Society, its first *weiqi* ("encircling game") club, was established in the Nongyin Teahouse in the Shaocheng Park in 1935. The first club president was Liu Fuyi, together with club chairman Huang Muyan and vice president Xie Dekan (a few years later, the club moved to Sanyi Temple on Jiangjun Street). At that time, another Shaocheng Park teahouse—Yongju—was the *xiangqi* (Chinese chess) center of the city. Eminent players in the P. R. C. Du Junguo (*weiqi*) and Jia Titao (*xiangqi*) both rose out of the "chess culture" of Shaocheng Park.

There is one more feature of the former park that must not be forgotten. Shaocheng Park was bombed by invading Japanese forces in September 1940. A subsequent bombing on July 27th, 1941 struck Shaocheng Park and the surrounding areas on Changshun and Dongchenggen Street yet again. Not only bombs were deployed; the invaders also targeted park patrons with machine guns, resulting in immense casualties. The attack left victims' body parts hanging from the trees and caused severe damage to many buildings. The Daguangming Cinema, for example, was demolished after suffering serious damage in the raid.

Shizi Alley

Shizi Alley is an L-shaped road between Tongren Road and Jinhe Road. Initially within the Manchu City in the Qing Dynasty, it was known as Taiping Hutong. When "*hutong*" names were done away with in the early years of the Republican period, the alley was renamed for a persimmon (*shizi*) tree that grew there. Many Chengdu residents are familiar with Shizi Alley because it has been home to the Chengdu Employment Service Management Bureau in recent years.

Two of the four nationally renowned Sichuan orthopedic traditions (Du, He, Yang and Zheng) came from Shizi Alley—those are Du Family Orthopedics represented by the father-daughter team Du Ziming and Du Qiongshu, and He Family Orthopedics represented by the father-son team He Renfu and He Tianxiang. Both of their former residences were once located on Shizi Alley.

Du Ziming (**1878 ~ 1961**), born in a Manchu family of orthopedists, he studied martial arts, and learned orthopedic science from his father at a young age. In 1902 he began practicing medicine himself, gradually building his reputation as a leading authority in the field. In fact, the orthopedic techniques of Du Ziming, along with the golden needle acupuncture of Ye Xinqing, came to be known as Chengdu's two "wonder treatments". In 1931, a collapse accident occurred in the Chengdu Women's Normal University (now Chengdu University), injuring over a hundred people. After he treated the wounded, there was neither a

Site of Du Ziming's former clinic on Shizi Alley, 2001. Photo by Feng Shuimu.

disability nor a death, which became a miracle of rescuing the wounded in China. After the P. R. C. was founded in 1949, Du was hired by the Chengdu

Railway Center Hospital (now Affiliated Hospital of Chengdu University), where he brought relief to the many railroad construction workers injured at work. In 1956, at nearly 80 years old, he was invited to Beijing upon the recommendation of Vice Premier Deng Xiaoping and He Long to establish and direct the Department of Orthopedics at the Academy of Traditional Chinese Medicine. There he applied his unique skills to treat a variety of challenging orthopedic diseases. After Lieutenant General Li Shouxuan, commander of the Railway Corps, was cured of the spinal disease that haunted him for many years, he ordered each of the eight divisions of the Railway Corps to send an orthopedic doctor to Beijing to learn from Du. Many famous dancers and athletes, including Chen Ailian (dancer), Bai Shuxiang (dancer), Zheng Fengrong (high jumper) and Li Furong (table tennis player) also received his treatment in Beijing. When in Chengdu, Du Ziming was an elected municipal representative; in Beijing he was a member of the 3rd CPPCC National Committee. He also authored such works as *An Overview of Orthopedics in Chinese Medicine* and *Conventions of Treating Sprains and Contusions*.

He Renfu (1895 ~ 1969), born in a Mongolian bone-setting family, he was the fourth generation descendant of He's orthopedics. With his outstanding talents in the martial arts and self-made medicinal concoctions, he cured countless patients of painful afflictions over the course of his lifetime. In particular, he has cured many athletes and performing artists of various injuries, often with a miracle effect. He authored a number of books including *The Medical Language of Benevolent Service*, *Experiences at the Wuxiazhai Bonesetting Clinic*, and *The Orthopedic Techniques of Tehuer*. He Renfu's sons still enjoy a high reputation in Chengdu today. He Tianxiang, who is particularly well-known as the director of the Sichuan Dance Injury Research Institute, as well as He Tianzuo, director of Chengdu's Bayi Orthopedic Hospital, and He Tianqi, director of the Orthopedic Hospital of the Sichuan Traditional Chinese Medicine Research Institute.

Jiangjun Street

Jiangjunjie (Jiangjun Street) is a small street running along the edge of the General's Yamen from Upper Dongchenggen Street in the east to Upper Changshun Street in the west. Its name, though it means "General Street", has in fact no direct relationship with the abutting General's Yamen.

Once part of the Manchu City in the Qing Dynasty, this small street was originally called Yongan Hutong, but because a stone at the *hutong's* entrance resembled a tiger's head, Chengdu people took to calling it "Maomao Alley" instead ("maomao", literally "cat-cat", was a local term for tiger). In the Republican period, the Manchu City's peaceful environment and elegant architecture made it a choice location for dignitaries to settle. In 1925, another important figure in the Sichuan Army, Yang Sen, settled on Maomao Alley during his post as the military governor of Sichuan Province. Upon doing so, he ordered the street to be officially renamed "General Street" for the title "Powerful General Sen" conferred upon him by the Beiyang government. The supposed logic behind the name change was that this street neighbored the General's Yamen, but the actual reason is slightly less obvious: Yang Sen's nickname in Sichuan dialect was "The Cunning Rat" (*Haozi Jing*), so it would have been quite detestable for him to live on "Cat-cat" Alley. According to another similar account, the name change was because the governor's surname, Yang, was a homophone for "sheep", and it would not have been auspicious for the "sheep" to jump into the mouth of the "tiger".

Yang Sen (**1884 ~ 1977**), from Guang'an in East Sichuan, enrolled in the Sichuan Army Sucheng Academy in 1908. After graduation, he joined the Sichuan Army. In the warlord infighting of the early Republic, he successively joined up with various forces, becoming a representative figure among Sichuan warlords. In 1920, as Commander of the 9th Division defending Luyong Township, he made definitive contributions to the construction of Luzhou (southeastern Sichuan). Then, amid the Sichuan warlords' struggle for power, the Beiyang government appointed Yang Sen as Army General in 1924 to oversee military reconstruction and control the Chengdu region, in which capacity he advanced the city's urban construction. During the tragic Wanhsien Incident of 1926, wherein British gunboat attacks injured or killed over a thousand Chinese, Yang Sen was stationed in Chongqing and the adjacent Wanxian County (i. e. "Wanhsien") as Commander of the First Route of the Sichuan Punitive Alliance under Wu Peifu's Division of the Beiyang Clique. With the help of Zhu De and Chen Yi, Yang Sen detained and attacked British vessels, which earned him wide recognition. During the wave of Northern Expedition[1] victories that same year, Yang joined the National Revolutionary Army (NRA) as Commander of its 20th Army. In 1933, he participated in the "encirclement and suppression" campaign[2] against the Sichuan-Shaanxi Soviets, but

Yang Sen

when stationed in Yingjing (in Ya'an, Sichuan) to intercept the Central Red Army, he received a letter from its commander Zhu De. The letter compelled Yang to stand down, ordering his troops to fire into the sky and allow the Red Army to pass. In 1937, he led the 20th Army out of Sichuan to participate in the War of Resistance Against Japanese Aggression. He gained nationwide fame for inflicting heavy Japanese losses on the Songhu frontline during the Battle of Shanghai, with later military achievements in Hunan and Guizhou provinces as well. In 1939, Yang received orders from Chiang Kai-shek to carry out the "Pingkiang Massacre" targeting cadres of the New Fourth Army and their families. After that, Yang Sen served as chairman of the Guizhou Province government in 1944 and mayor of Chongqing in 1947. In the Chinese People's War of Liberation, however, his 20th Army was thoroughly annihilated by the People's Liberation Army (PLA). In December 1949, he arranged for his

---

① The Northern Expedition, led by Chiang Kai-shek, was the Kuomintang's successful 1926 − 1928 campaign to regain military control of the country from factionalist warlords, particularly the powerful Beiyang Clique. [Translator's note]

② The encirclement campaigns were a series of regional KMT military offensives intended to contain and destroy CPC forces during the early years of the Chinese Civil War. Most of these were unsuccessful, but they ultimately culminated in the CPC's retreat to the west—i. e. the Long March. [Translator's note]

nephew Yang Hanlie to lead a revolt in Jintang (a central Sichuan county now under Chengdu jurisdiction) with a newly rebuilt NRA 20th Army; Yang Sen himself, meanwhile, fled to Taiwan. Throughout his life, Yang Sen was a strong advocate of "the martial arts spirit" and "sports as national salvation". He contributed to the establishment of various athletics facilities and sports competitions. His army even established a special department specifically for sports. When serving as chairman of Guizhou in 1946, he conducted a daily morning radio program that led Guiyang city residents in physical exercises called "Revival Calisthenics". He continued to be active in the sports world after leaving the mainland, serving as long-term chairman of the "All-China Sports Federation" and as chairman of the 1968 Olympic Games of Taiwan Committee. An athlete in his right, he went mountain climbing once a week, learned to fly airplanes at age 70, and twice scaled Taiwan's Yu Shan (Jade Mountain), which is over 4,000 meters in elevation—once at 86 and once at 90 years old. Of all the Sichuan warlords, Yang Sen enjoyed the longest lifespan and had the most complex life experience.

One of the most famous artists in Chengdu's cultural history once lived at 40 Jiangjun Street—that is, Zhao Shaoxian—as well as two generations of his talented descendants.

Zhao Shaoxian (1884 ~ 1966), a native of Chengdu, was imprisoned as a young man for establishing the anti-Qing organization "Yiyou Society" along with Zhang Peijue (1876 ~ 1915) (see "Mazhen Street"). In 1918, he took a position as principal of the Sichuan No. 1 Middle School, after which he took up a series of teaching posts in schools across Chengdu and Chongqing, for a time serving as head of Department of Chinese of Sichuan University (where his students included Li Yimeng, Xu Renfu, Liu Junhui, Yin Huanxian, Zhou Fagao, Li Xiaoding, and Wang Liqi). A brilliant thinker and writer, Zhao studied tirelessly throughout his life. In China, he is well known for his expertise in writing and ancient linguistics, particularly his mastery of phonology. His yet unpublished manuscripts reach over 8 million characters in total length; among these, his works *Guangyun Shuzheng* (*" Annotations and Proofs on the Guangyun"*)① and *Jingdian Shiwen Ji Shuo Fu Jian* (*" Jingdian Shiwen: Collections, Teachings, Addendums and Commentaries"*)②, each over 3 million characters, are well known in academic circles. [along with his friend and fellow expert in ancient languages and scripts Huang Kan (1886 ~ 1935), Zhao Shaoxian held himself to a high standard of scholarship and never published works "lightly". With his self-imposed rule to "not publish a word before the age of 50", any of Zhao's known writings were only revised and completed late in his life, while Huang Kan unfortunately passed away just before reaching the 50-year milestone, leaving behind piles of unorganized manuscripts on ancient texts.] Of Zhao Shaoxian, the renowned scholar Cheng Qianfan (1913 ~ 2000) once said: "In the more than three hundred years that have passed since the reign of Emperor Qianlong and Emperor Jiaqing, there has only been one true master of ancient linguistics." Most regrettably, before several of his works could be published, they perished in the ravages of the "Cultural Revolution". In the autumn of 1966, Red Guards confiscated more than 150 boxes containing his life's writings and an enormous personal library (as well as the personal library of his son-in-law, Yin Menglun). For the already grieved man nearly 80 years old, this proved too heavy a blow. He passed away in anger on December 21st of that year. Most of his manuscripts were destroyed in the ensuing catastrophe; of the original 32-volume *Guangyun Shuzheng* and 30-volume *Jingdian Shiwen Ji Shuo Fu Jian*, we are now left with only 8 volumes each. In recent years, Zhao's students have revised and released *Guangyun Shuzheng* and *Collected Works of Zhao Shaoxian*.

---

① The *Guangyun* is a Chinese rime dictionary from the early 11th century. [Translator's note]

② *Jingdian Shiwen* (*"Explanations of the Classics"*) is a commentary on the Confucian canon written by Lu Deming (550 − 630). [Translator's note]

Three generations of Zhao family: Zhao Shaoxian (front center) , Zhao Youwen (front left) and Zhao Zhenduo (back right)

Zhao Shaoxian and his descendants are iconic as a contemporary Chengdu family engaged in the research of traditional Chinese culture. Many of his family members followed in his intellectual footsteps: One of his sons, Zhao Youwen, was an expert in Three Kingdoms[1] history at the Chinese Academy of Social Sciences Institute of History; another son, Zhao Lüfu, was a professor of history at Nanchong Normal Institute (now China West Normal University); his son-in-law Yin Menglun was a renowned scholar of ancient linguistics and professor at Shandong University; likewise, Zhao Shaoxian's grandson Zhao Zhenduo is a well-known scholar of ancient linguistics and professor at Sichuan University.

Where the Chengdu Children's Hospital now stands at the east end of Jiangjun Street was once the residence of an extraordinary young woman Dong Zhujun.

---

[1]　The Three Kingdoms period (200 – 280) that followed the Han Dynasty divided China into three major states (Wei, Shu, and Wu). [Translator's note]

Jinhe Road

Naturally, *Jinhelu* (Jinhe Road) derives its name from the Jinhe River, which has not existed now. It runs from Upper Changshun Street in the east to Lower Tongren Road in the west.

Jinhe Road's original name was Jinhe Street, which was the first road to connect the traffic between Citang Street and the newly opened Tonghuimen (Tonghui Gate) when Manchu City was first dismantled in the early years of the Republican period. As it neighbored the Jinhe River, its eastern section at that time was also known as "*Shunhe* ("Along the River") Street". Despite the destruction of the Jinhe River during the "Cultural Revolution" —for conversion into an air raid shelter—the name "Jinhe Street" remained unchanged. After Shudu Avenue was constructed in 1987, Jinhe Street became a section thereof, and its name changed to "Jinhe Road" accordingly.

Kindergarten of Logistics Department of Chengdu Military Region on Jinhe Road, 1990. Photo by Tang Yuewu.

The former Kindergarten of Logistics Department of Chengdu Military Region on the Jinhe Road offers a rare sight for central Chengdu western-style architecture. It was first built as a mansion for Yang Minsheng, brigade commander in the Sichuan Army. In 1918, it was leased to the Japanese Consulate in Chongqing as a workspace. At that time, Chengdu was not a port of trade, so regulations did not permit it to establish consulates. Nevertheless, the Japanese used the house on Jinhe Road as a base to forcibly establish a new *de facto* consulate. Chengdu citizens acted out in opposition to the Japanese imperialists, attacking the premises in 1926. After the September 18th Incident[①] in 1931, a wave of protests in Chengdu forced the unofficial consulate to finally close. The building served as a private residence once again, occupied by Wang Zejun (1903 ~ 1974), former lieutenant general commander of the 44th Division of the KMT Army and son of Sichuan warlord Wang Zanxu (in November 1948, Wang Zejun was captured by the PLA during the Huaihai Campaign; during the re-education through labor campaign period, he later died of illness as a war criminal in Beijing's Qincheng Prison). The mansion was remodeled and rebuilt in 1931 to become the distinctive building we see standing there today.

Located at the intersection of Jinhe Road and Xiaonan Street, Nulican Restaurant is not only a famous place for Sichuan dishes, but also a key Chengdu Cultural Relics Protection Unit. On May 30th, 1929 (or in 1931, according to another source), Nulican Restaurant was first established at the south entrance of South Sanqiao Street (opposite of the Sichuan People's Art Theater on today's South Renmin Road). Then in May 1933, it moved to 137 Citang Street. It was forced to move again in 1983 when Shudu Avenue was expanded, but was rebuilt according to the same design at its current location on Jinhe Road. It was Che Yaoxian, then leader of the CPC West Sichuan Special Committee, who first opened Nulican. The name (*Nuli* literally meaning "work hard") was an homage to the Last Will and Testament of Sun Yat-sen (1866 ~ 1925), which contained the famous phrase "The revolution isn't over yet, comrades, keep up the fight!" Aptly enough, Nulican was an important base of covert CPC operations, providing cover for various revolutionary activities in Chengdu. It drew progressives from all circles of society and even functioned as the editorial and

---

① The September 18th Incident refers to the opportunistic Japanese seizure of Mukden in Manchuria (now the city of Shenyang in Northeast China). This event prompted Japan's full military occupation of Manchuria and establishment of the Manchukuo puppet state in February 1932. [Translator's note]

distribution office of the weekly publication *Dasheng*. Many revolutionary and salvation organizations[1] held meetings at the restaurant—including the Chengdu Cultural Circles Salvation Association, the Chengdu branch of the Sino-Soviet Cultural Association, and the Chengdu Constitutional Forum.

Nulican also distinguished itself by its business practices. Instead of an upper-upper-class clientele, it served the public, offering low prices and good quality. This couplet was hung in the dining room.

> To ensure one's subsistence, *Nuli*! *Nuli*! (One only needs to work hard);
> to bring about democracy, *Shuji*! *Shuji*! (one only needs to wish it were so)

On the door it also reads: "Feasts by the table, Nulican; mixed stew pots, famous in Sichuan; a great taste, at a great price." Every year during the flower festival, Nulican would set up a temporary restaurant on the festival grounds. Upon such occasions they'd post an advertisement on the city wall: "the flower festival, at Erxian Temple; in the middle of the road, next to the woods; the machine-made noodles, a delicious taste; It is food for the revolution, Nulican." For the head chef, Che Yaoxian hired the famous He Jin'ao, who used to serve as Zhu De's chef in the Yunnan Army. His specialty (which in turn became Nulican's specialty dish), *shengshao shijin* (instant stew pot assortment), was directed at the masses, offering top quality at an affordable price. Meanwhile, his special meat dumplings were exclusive property, only sold to the rickshaw drivers. Besides these, the restaurant sold highly economical "revolutionary meals" —bowls of steamed rice with morsels of meat, bamboo shoots, and beans added in, which were well-received among the city's poor (one might regard these bowls as the first successful Sichuanese "fast food"). One of Nulican's advertising slogans was so popular that various versions of it have since been used by countless restaurants and adapted to other service industries as well: "If my food isn't good, please tell me; if my food is good, please tell your friends."

---

[1] China's national salvation movement was a response to Japanese aggression in the 1930s. Salvation organizations published propaganda to raise public awareness and patriotic sentiment while putting pressure on the Republican government to act. [Translator's note]

Nulican Restaurant, 2021 Photo by Chen Ke

Che Yaoxian (**1894 ~ 1946**), a native of Dayi County in Sichuan. He joined the Sichuan Army in 1912 and participated in revolutionary activities while serving as regiment commander. He joined the Communist Party amid the White Terror[1] of 1929 and undertook military work for the party for an extended period, contributing, for example, to planning for the 1930 Guanghan Uprising[2]. He returned to civilian life in 1933, teaching at Sichuan Teachers College (a forerunner of Chengdu University). In 1937 when the War of Resistance Against Japanese Aggression broke out in full, Che was chosen to head the "Chengdu Huabei Resistance Support Association". Making use of the former Dayi Division of the Sichuan Army and his status as former adjutant general of the 24th Army, he contributed significantly

Che Yaoxian

---

① "White" denoting anti-communism, "White Terror" refers to the Kuomintang's persecution of communists and other political dissidents beginning in 1927, or the resulting atmosphere of heightened fear. The term originates from an essay by Lu Xun (1881 – 1936). [Translator's note]

② The "Guanghan Uprising" (at Guanghan in Deyang, just northeast of Chengdu) was a mutiny that broke out on October 25th, 1930 within the National Revolutionary Army instigated by the underground CPC. It became a major military achievement for the CPC and established the Guanghan Soviet and independent CPC army units. [Translator's note]

to party objectives, especially engaging in United Front work for a long time. He was highly respected in society, his fellow comrades at that time referring to him as "line leader". A new branch of the Communist Party of China was established from within the *Dasheng* weekly that he managed, hailed as the party's "United Front Work Department". *Dasheng* (*Shout Weekly*) was first established on January 17 th, 1937. Circulation of its weekly issues quickly 5,000 copies; at its height, it circulated over 7,000 copies. The publication's influence spread beyond the pages themselves. Drawing largely upon its reader base, it organized a number of *Dasheng* readers' forums as well as the "Dasheng National Salvation Propaganda Society for the War of Resistance Against Japanese Aggression" (known as the "Dasheng Society" for short, this organization established a new party branch of nearly a thousand members distributed across more than ten Sichuan counties). After *Dasheng* was shut down by authorities, Che Yaoxian simply moved its offices to Yimin Bookstore on Upper Changshun Street and began publishing a different "Dasheng" (using a homophone of the original publication's name). When the authorities shut it down a second time, Che moved his office to 45 Zhongxin Street and started a weekly publication under the name *Tucun* (*Try to Survive*). After authorities shut down *Tucun*, Che resumed the publication of *Dasheng* (*Shout Weekly*). From that point, *Dasheng* remained in operation until being forced to stop yet again in August 1938. All told, it went through three name changes and four closures, released 61 issues and 7 supplements, and printed 5 essays or speeches of Chairman Mao Zedong. A rhythmic chant that circulated in Chengdu at that time illustrates just how widely Che's leadership was recognized: "When you think of Yan'an, look for Che Yaoxian." Unfortunately, Che was arrested on March 18 th, 1940 at Nulican Restaurant. The enemy then detained him for six years. He refused to cooperate with them even under the temptation of incentives; at one point they offered him the post of Director of Civil Affairs of Sichuan Government, but Che held steadfast to his values and cause. On August 18 th, 1946, Che Yaoxian was executed at Songlinpo within Chongqing Baigongguan Prison.

Following the arrest of Che Yaoxian, Nulican Restaurant continued operations under the management of his wife and her brother Huang Yixin. [Che Yaoxian married his wife in 1918. At that time, girls in rural areas were not given names, so during her youth she was known only as "Huang San" —Huang being her family name, "San" meaning "there". Che Yaoxian chose a real name for his wife, (Huang) Tixian—*ti* as in *shenti* ("body"), *xian* as in *xianfeng* ("vanguard"). The name embodied what Che Yaoxian encouraged her to become: a pioneer of women's liberation, unbinding her feet, achieving literacy, and entering society.] A decade later, in 1950, Nulican was handed over to the Chengdu Municipal People's Government. Today there is a small gallery at the west end of the first floor dedicated to the life and deeds of Che Yaoxian, martyr of the revolution. One of the martyr's poems titled "Zishi" ("Self Oath") is particularly worthy of our continued reciting: "I am delighted to see auspicious signs growing in the East; I ask not about the harvest but about the plowing and tending of the fields. I am willing to give my blood to water the earth of tomorrow, in exchange for everlasting peace across the Chinese nation."

Dongsheng Street and Xisheng Street

There were two *hutongs* on each side of the south section of Changshun Street's in the Manchu City during the Qing Dynasty. The two major subordinate offices of the Chengdu generals were stationed there, respectively the Yousi Yamen (" Right Bureau") —responsible for personnel, revenue, and rites, and the Zuosi Yamen ("Left Bureau") —responsible for war, justice, and works. [In ancient China, starting from the Sui (581 ~ 617) and Tang (618 ~ 908) dynasties, the central government had Six Ministries of Personnel, Revenue, Rites, War, Justice and Works to comprehensively manage the affairs of the state. In the Qing Dynasty, were the highest representatives of the emperor and Manchu and Mongolian nobles stationed in several important military and political areas across the country. However, they did not actually manage specific local affairs. The Yamen set up in imitation of the Six Ministries is mainly to deal with the internal affairs of Manchu and Mongolian compatriots and supervise the local government]. Thus, the eastern *hutong* was called Zuosi Hutong and the western one Yousi Hutong. In the Republican period, all " *hutong*" names were abolished and renamed. To signify the new age ushered in by the victorious Xinhai Revolution and based on their position on either side of the General's Yamen, Zuosi and Yousi were respectively changed into " Dongsheng Street" ("East Victory Street") and " Xisheng Street" ("West Victory Street").

In the Republican period, the north side of Dongsheng Street's east end (the former Zuosi Yamen) was used for private residences. Later on, the Sichuan warlord Tang Shizun (1883 ~ 1950) built the Sullivan Hotel there (Tang Shizun's mansion was also located on Dongsheng Street, where the Sichuan Provincial Department of Culture and Tourism stands today). During that period, the Sullivan Hotel was the premier Western-style hotel in Chengdu. Most of the " new style" weddings for the children of the city's rich were hosted here. When the War of Resistance Against Japanese Aggression broke out, in the upsurge of nationwide fund-raising for the front line, Tang Shizun donated the property rights of the Sullivan Hotel to the municipal government for its public use. For a time, the Chengdu branch of the Northeast National Salvation Association (led by the underground CPC organization) established itself at the hotel. Later, a US military liaison office was set up there. When Song

Zheyuan (1885 ~ 1940), a famous War of Resistance general left the army, he settled there as well when he arrived in Chengdu (as his wife was from nearby Mianyang, General Song spent his later years in Sichuan and was finally laid to rest in his wife's hometown). In 1948, the Sichuan Provincial Council also moved into the hotel. Shortly after Chengdu's liberation, the newly arrived leaders of Chinese People's Liberation Army and the underground party in Sichuan met at the Sullivan Hotel to officially join forces. On March 16th, 1950, the first session of the regional Chinese People's Political Consultative Conference (CPPCC) was held here as well. Ever since then, the site has been always occupied by the Chengdu CPPCC.

Meeting room of the original Sullivan Hotel where the first Chengdu meeting of the Chinese People's Political Consultative Conference took place in March 1950. Photo courtesy of Yang Xianfeng.

There was also a "Sullivan Arts Center" within the Sullivan Hotel. Established in 1938, it put on straight plays, crosstalk, Jingyun Drum and all kinds of dance performances. In the Republican period, it was the most diverse venue for the performing arts in Chengdu.

Dong Zhujun, an extraordinary young woman in modern Chinese history, once lived in Chengdu. Among her two former residences in the city, one was located on Jiangjun Streetwhile the other was on Dongsheng Street.

Dong Zhujun (**1900 ~ 1997**), born in an impoverished family in Haimen, Jiangsu Province. At 13 years old she was sold to a brothel as a "pure girl" (a girl who primarily sang rather than engaging in sex work), studying opera and selling songs to customers. There she became familiar with Xia Zhishi (1887 ~ 1950), the former deputy tuchun of the Shu Military Government and Xinhai Revolution Shu Army commander. At that time, Xia was wanted by Yuan Shikai. Dong became devoted to him, escaped from the brothel, wed Xia in secret, and went with him to Japan for study when she was only 15 years old. In 1917, she returned to Xia Zhishi's hometown in Hejiang, southeastern Sichuan Province. In 1919 they moved to Chengdu. There, Dong first lived on Dongsheng Street, then moved to the east end of Jiangjun Street, where the Chengdu Children's Hospital is found today. (The Xia residence implemented the Western dining practice of individual portioning and it was the first to do so in Chengdu.) Dong Zhujun was an active woman; she founded Chengdu's first rickshaw company, " Flying Eagle" , and opened the Fuyang Hosiery Factory, which specifically employed female workers. However, Dong was dissatisfied with her marriage because of the oppressive shackles of the large and feudalistic Xia family and Xia Zhishi's increasingly negative state of mind. She gave up a comfortable life, separated from Xia (their divorce was announced in 1934), and returned to Shanghai in 1929 with her parents and four daughters. Though she went through incredibly tough times, Dong Zhujun relied on her intelligence and talent and joined the ranks of China's first-generation female entrepreneurs. In Shanghai, she established the Qunyi Spool Factory and then the Jinjiang Sichuanese Restaurant and Jinjiang Tea Room, which would become particularly well known over the country. (Dong named these after Chengdu's Jinjiang River, simultaneously expressing nostalgia for her decade spent in the city and the similar feeling and experiences with Xue Tao, a female poet who once lived along the Jinjiang.) She also founded the magazine *Shanghai Women*. At the same time, she kept up with revolutionary activities. (Dong Zhujun applied to join the CPC in 1930. After a comprehensive consideration, the party organization advised her to continue to focus on running her business without official party affiliation, and assist the revolution by various means. She accepted the arrangement.) With her social connections and economic power, Dong was able to do significant work for the CPC. After the founding of the P. R. C. , Premier Zhou Enlai held a banquet specifically to thank Dong Zhujun for her great contributions to the revolutionary cause. In the early years of the P. R. C. , Dong donated all her properties (worth 3,000 taels of gold) to the state. According to the arrangements of the central government and the local governmet of Shanghai, she established the Jinjiang

Hotel on the basis of the Jinjiang Sichuanese Restaurant and Jinjiang Tea Room, which was the first hotel in Shanghai qualified to receive guests of the state (now it is China's most world-famous hotel). Dong Zhujun served as both chairman and general manager of the Jinjiang Hotel, receiving more than 500 heads of state and government from 134 countries in her lifetime. She was also a long-time member of the National Committee of the Chinese People's Political Consultative Conference. In her later years, she wrote an autobiography titled *My Century*. After her passing, the Dong Zhujun Memorial Hall was established in her ancestral city of Haimen, Jiangsu Province. Her life saga was also adapted into a 31-episode television series titled *Century Life: Legend of Dong Zhujun* and a Sichuan opera, *Dong Zhujun, the Tuchun's Wife*.

Dong Zhujun (third from the right) and Xia Zhishi (fourth from the right) with family members in the central garden of their home on Dongsheng Street, 1919. Photo courtesy of Xia Damin.

The Sichuan TV (SCTV) station was located on Dongsheng Street for many years. Formerly at that same site was a mansion built by Chengdu's most renowned local tyrant and spy ringleader, Leng Kaitai (1889 ~ 1950) in the Republican period.

In the Ming Dynasty, there was the Shixi (" Stone Rhinoceros ") Temple on Xisheng Street. According to a legend, Shixi Temple's predecessor was Longyuan Temple, and it was established with the donation of Wang Yu who sold his private residence in the Jin Dynasty. Longyuan Temple (later renamed Konghui Temple) was most likely the first Buddhist temple in all of Chengdu. After renovations in the Tang Dynasty, it was again renamed Shengshou Temple. In its time, Shengshou was the second-largest Buddhist temple in Chengdu as well as one of the seven largest Buddhist temples in the entire country. Shengshou Temple in the west and Daci Temple in the east were equally renowned in Chengdu at that time. Like Daci Temple, Shengshou Temple had a number of exquisite clay sculptures and wall paintings— among the latter category, the most famous works were *Chuxiatu* ("Leaving the Gorge") and *Wuzhongshantu* ("Mountains in Fog"), both painted by Li Sheng (known as "General Li Junior"). Xuanzang[①] not only resided in this temple when he was studying Buddhism in Chengdu; and was ordained there, too (but some articles say that Xuanzang was ordained at Daci Temple, so there is a dispute about it). Shengshou Temple had a stone rhino within it, said to be a relic during the time of Li Bing[②], an considerable historical interest in Chengdu. For this reason, people began to call Shengshou the "Stone Rhinoceros Temple" (*Shixi Si* or *Shiniu Si*). Du Fu (712 ~ 770), Cen Shen (715 ~ 770) and Lu You (1125 ~ 1210) were among the poets to write heartfelt poems devoted to the relic. [Before the two rivers in Chengdu changed their courses in the Tang Dynasty, an inner river most likely flowed past the site of the temple, and the stone rhinoceros was placed along its bank, and that's why Lu You sighed in his poem *Ye Shixi Miao* ("Paying a Visit to Shixi Temple"): "The river returns while the landscape differs; The stele is broken while the city has changed."] When the Manchu City was constructed in the early Qing Dynasty, Shixi Temple moved next to Nanjiaochang (South Military Field) and Yousi Yamen was built over the original site. Thus "Inscription on the Stone Rhinoceros on Xisheng Street" by Li Zhesheng describes: "Only one ancient rhinoceros can be found in Chengdu now; at the foot of the western city wall is the Yousi Hutong."

In the final years during the reign of Emperor Guangxu (r. 1875 ~ 1908), No. 2 Primary School was opened at the former site of the Yousi Yamen. In 1913, Sichuan No. 1 Middle School originally established on Yuhuangguan Street moved here as well.

---

① Xuanzang (602－664), a Buddhist scholar and monk during the Tang Dynasty, is one of the most important and well-known figures in the history of Chinese Buddhism. As a young man, he traveled throughout China in search of sacred texts, then embarked on a long journey to India, where he spent years translating scriptures and observing interactions between Chinese and Indian Buddhism. He returned to China with hundreds of texts and continued his translation work until his death. The records of his journey to India inspired the classic novel *Journey to the West*. [Translator's note]

② Warring States-era politician and engineer Li Bing (c. 3 rd century BC) is credited for the Dujiangyan water project.

This was Sichuan's first government-established provincial middle school, and Chengdu people generally called it "Provincial No. 1 Middle School". Once the May 4th Movement[①] kicked off in 1919, Provincial No. 1 Middle School was known as one of the most revolutionary middle schools in Chengdu, with one-fifth of its students joining the Communist Youth League. A saying at that time went: "To join the revolution, go to Shixi." Both Li Shuoxun and Yang Hansheng were once student leaders at the school (their names were Li Kaizhuo and Ouyang Benyi at that time). In 1928, the ongoing struggle between reactionary authorities and both teachers and students at the school escalated into a major wave of student demonstrations. Opportunistic KMT party member Yang Tingquan took up the post of school principal (much against the will of teachers and students at the school) and was beaten to death in an altercation with students on February 14th—an event which was known as the "No. 1 Middle School Incident". Two days later, the authorities used the incident of Yang's death as rationale to arrest over 100 progressive teachers and students across the city. In the afternoon of the same day, 14 people were taken to Xialian Pond and executed for their alleged crimes—among them was CPC member Yuan Shirao. This incident also came to be known as the "February 16th Incident". On February 22nd, authorities announced the closure of Provincial No. 1 Middle School. Years later, in 1933, several influential figures in the province jointly established the Xiejin ("Cooperative Progress") Middle School (the chairman of the board was Chen Li; other executives included Zhang Zhihe, Wu Jingbo, and Chen Shunong). Upon its founding, the school was temporarily located at Yanlu Hall; it then relocated to the former site of Provincial No. 1 Middle School in 1934. Beyond sharing its address, Xiejin Middle School also carried on the strong revolutionary spirit: all in all, more than 20 underground CPC members taught at Xiejin. New party branches were established among its teachers and students—one of the student branches had almost 80 members at its height. To avoid bombings during the War of Resistance Against Japanese Aggression, the school moved to a more remote area of the city, holding classes in Xinfan Town's Longcang Temple from 1939 to 1943. Particularly during this

---

① The May 4th Movement (1919) began with student protests against the Qing government, specifically in response to the Qing's weak negotiations for the Treaty of Versailles, which was to give Japan the right to former German concessions in Shandong Province. Protests spread throughout the country, many becoming violent, and the movement continued as a push for modernization reforms and national strengthening. [Translator's note]

period, progressives in Sichuan referred to the school as "Sichuan's Shanbei School" (i. e. the Northern Shaanxi School of Politics and Law①) , and those in Chengdu would recite this rhythmic chant:

To join the revolution, study at Xiejin; to save the nation, go to Shanbei.

Loncang Temple, meanwhile, became known as " Little Yan'an ". According to records, more than 100 students from Xiejin Middle School went on to Yan'an or engaged in other revolutionary work.) After the founding of the P. R. C. , Xiejin Middle School merged with the original Qinghua Middle School to form the Qingxie Union Middle School, which was later renamed Chengdu No. 28 Middle School and then Jinhejie Middle School before the Xiejin Middle School name was reinstated in 1993. Finally, in 2009, the name was amended to "Chengdu Shude Xiejin Middle School".

Li Shuoxun and his wife Zhao Juntao

Li Shuoxun (**1903 ~ 1931**) , from Gao County, enrolled at Sichuan Provincial No. 1 Middle School in 1921. On June 11th , 1922, Wang Youmu (Sichuan's first Marxist) helped Li and others (including his classmate and fellow

---

① The Northern Shaanxi School of Politics and Law was a cadre high school established in 1937 by the Communist Party of China at their headquarters in Yan'an, Shaanxi Province. [Translator's Note]

countyman Gao County native Yang Hansheng, as well as Sichuan Higher Normal School student Tong Yongsheng) publish their "Manifesto of the Establishment of the Sichuan Socialist Youth League" in Chengdu's *National Gazette* (the Sichuan Socialist Youth League was the earliest communist party organization in Sichuan, in place before the CPC had officially established itself in the province). Wanted for alleged crimes by Sichuan warlord Liu Chengxun, Li Shuoxun left Chengdu in November 1922 and went to study at Shanghai University. There he continued to be active in revolutionary activities, officially joining the Communist Party of China in 1924. Li was a bridge between parties in those years, engaging in CPC-KMT cooperation, once elected as president of the National Union of Students, and once serving as secretary-general of the Shanghai Municipal Party Department of the Kuomintang. In 1926 he was minister of the Wuchang Prefectural Party Organization of the CPC, and the following year he participated in the Nanchang Uprising[1] as party representative and director of the political department of the 25th Division of the 11th Volunteer Army. After the uprising was defeated in Guangdong Province, Li Shuoxun, Zhu De and Zhou Shidi formed the Front Committee, leading insurgents to continue their struggle in southern Hunan Province. In October of that year, Li was ordered to report back to the Party Central Committee in Shanghai, whereafter he was dispatched to various locations to engage in underground work. He once held posts as a member of the Central Military Commission, secretary of the Military Commission of the Zhejiang Provincial Party Committee, secretary of the Military Commission of the Jiangnan (incorporating Jiangsu, Anhui, Zhejiang Provinces and the city of Shanghai) Provincial Party Committee, secretary of the Military Commission of the Guangdong Provincial Party Committee, and political commissar of the Seventh Red Army. Arrested by the Kuomintang in Haikou, Hainan Province in July of 1931, Li Shuoxun died a hero's death on September 5th at Haikou's East Military Fields. The martyr's wife, Zhao Juntao (1903 – 1985), was the younger sister of Zhao Shiyan, a famed early leader in the CPC. Zhao Juntao joined the CPC in 1926 and was propaganda minister for the Hubei Women's Association and head of the Women's Work Department of the Communist Party of China. After the

---

[1] The Nanchang Uprising was an armed revolt against KMT forces that broke out on August 1, 1927 in Nanchang, Jiangxi Province. This date has since been recognized as the founding date of the Chinese Workers' and Peasants' Red Army. [Translator's note]

failure of the Great Revolution①, she worked as a teacher—in Chengdu and elsewhere—as a cover for her underground revolutionary work. With guidance from the Southern Bureau of the CPC Central Committee, she opened a nursery school that cared for many children in need during the War of Resistance Against Japanese Aggression. She continued to work in education after the war's victorious conclusion. Zhao Juntao finally passed away in Beijing in 1985. Comrade Li Peng② is the son of Li Shuoxun and Zhao Juntao.

Yang Hansheng (**1902 ~ 1992**), was from Gao County, Sichuan Province. In 1920 he went to study at the Sichuan Provincial No. 1 Middle School, where he was the founder of the Sichuan Socialist Youth League along with Li Shuoxun. Like Li, Yang was wanted by warlords in Sichuan and consequently left Chengdu to study at Shanghai University. He joined the Socialist Youth League of China in 1924; the following year he became an official member of the Communist Party of China. He taught politics at the Whampoa Military Academy in Guangzhou for a time,

Yang Hansheng

then participated in the Nanchang Uprising as secretary-general of the Uprising Army's Central Political Department. After the Nanchang Uprising failed, Yang continued to work for the party, but on the cultural front. In 1928 he served as secretary for both the League of the Left-Wing Writers and the Cultural Work Committee of the Communist Party of China. During the War of Resistance Against Japanese Aggression, he took up the posts of chief secretary of the third office of the KMT political department in the second CPC-KMT United Front and deputy director of the Cultural Work Committee. After the founding of the P. R. C. , he served as deputy secretary-general of the Culture and Education

---

① In the spring and summer of 1927, after the success of the Northern Expedition, Chiang Kai-shek and other Kuomintang leaders betrayed their alliance with communists and revolutionary forces, carrying out a violent purge of all communists in areas under their military control. This is the failure of the Great Revolution that was to be realized through KMT-CPC cooperation [Translator's note]

② Li Peng (1928 ~ 2019) was an illustrious PRC politician, serving as Premier of the P. R. C. from 1987 to 1998. [Translator's note]

Committee of the State Council, deputy director of the State Council General Office, vice chairman and party secretary of the China Federation of Literary and Art Circles, and chairman of the China Film Association. Yang Hansheng also achieved renown as a scriptwriter and novelist. His representative works are the films *Myriad of Lights* and *Jiangnan in the North* and the straight plays *Chronicle of the Heavenly Kingdom* and *Greenwood Heroes*.

Outstanding Chinese geologist Huang Jiqing also studied at the Sichuan No. 1 Middle School from 1917 to 1921.

Huang Jiqing (1904 ~ 1995), was from Renshou County in Meishan, Sichuan. His long career in geology began when he was admitted to the Geology Department of Peking University in 1924. From 1929 to 1930 he conducted a large-scale geological survey from Shaanxi Province to Guizhou Province via Sichuan, which provided the basis for his masterpiece *The Permian Formations of Southern China*, as well as

Huang Jiqing

other great works highly acclaimed by the international geological community. Many of his colleagues called him "Huang Erdie" (literally "Huang Permian"). In 1932 he left China to study abroad in Switzerland, where he obtained his doctoral degree. He returned in 1936 and joined the Central Geological Survey, for which he successively served as director of the geology division, deputy director, and director. He organized a 1937 expedition to search for petroleum in Northwest China, which successfully discovered Yumen oil field in Gansu Province—it was the first known oil field in the country. In 1938, Huang Jiqing conducted a survey in Sichuan, discovered natural gas and had it mined at Shengdeng Mountain in Longchang County, southeastern Sichuan. This marked the first natural gas field which was established in Sichuan (prior to that, Sichuan Tuchun Liu Xiang had specifically hired a geologist and petroleum expert from Germany to search for oil and gas in the province, but after two years of surveying and drilling wells, it was determined that "Sichuan has no oil or gas of economic value"). After that, Huang conducted studies on Sichuan's well-known Weiyuan gas field and Xinjiang's Dushanzi oil field. The findings led to his highly significant theories of terrestrial petroleum generation and of multi-layer, multi-stage petroleum generation and storage; he was the first in the world to propose these ideas. Huang Jiqing did not only completely overturn European geologists' erroneous conclusion that China lacked oil and natural gas. He laid a solid foundation for the gradual development of oil and gas extraction in China, thus honored as "the father of Chinese petroleum" and "the geology master of a generation". He is also the pioneer and father of historical geotectonics in China. In 1945 he completed *On Major Tectonic Forms of China*, which is regarded as a classic in the international geology community. The book proposed a number of important new theories, including the theory of polycyclic tectonic movement and a foundational theory of Chinese geotectonics. In 1946, Huang was selected as an Academician of the Academica Sinica (later the Chinese Academy of Sciences). In 1948, he oversaw the completion of a 1 : 3,000,000 scale geological map of China, which provided crucial guidance for subsequent geological work in the country.

In 1949, Huang Jiqing went to Europe and North America for a scientific visit. At that time the KMT did everything it could to compel him to go to Taiwan, but Huang was resolute. He returned to the China Geological Survey in Chongqing's Beibei district to await the liberation of Southwest China. After the founding of the P. R. C. , when he was chief engineer at the China Bureau of Petroleum Geology, Huang and fellow geologist Xie Jiarong led a team of scientists and technicians into the field. Their expedition found a number of large-scale oil fields—including Karamay, Daqing, Dagang and Shengli oil fields and other natural gas fields in Sichuan. Huang also supervised the surveys that discovered the famous Zhongliangshan coal field (in Chongqing) and Dongchuan copper deposit (in Sichuan and Yunnan). He served as president of the Geological Society of China and was an Honorary President of the Chinese Academy of Geological Sciences, Honorary Professor of the University of Zurich, honorary member of the Geological Society of America, and a Foreign Academician of the Academy of Sciences of the Soviet Union. In his later years, Huang dropped a bombshell on China's sci-tech community, stating at the Congress of the China Association for Science and Technology on November 14th, 1978: "It may be concluded that the discovery of the Daqing, Dagang, and Shengli oil fields has been of complete irrelevance to the field of geomechanics. " However, the most famous sentence he left to future generations was " I would rather just hammer away at the rocks in the world than seek for the fame and fortune. " This sentence had been engraved onto his personal rock hammer.

Shaocheng Primary School at the east entrance of Xisheng Street is another school with a long history. Its predecessor was the Eight Banners Advanced Primary School, itself built using materials from the Shaocheng Academy that was torn down in the Manchu City in the thirtieth year during the reign ofEmperor Guangxu (1904). In 1912, it was renamed the Shaocheng Advanced Primary School. According to the recollections of elder residents, the stone foundation of the school flagpole was made from the broken ruins of the ancient stone rhino.

In January 1949, leaders of Chengdu's underground CPC Pu Huafu and Hua Jian were arrested, while Ma Shitu and Wang Yuguang were dispatched to Hong Kong on the orders of their superiors. In October of that year, west Sichuan's underground party organization established a temporary working committee with Li Weijia as secretary, primarily to lead the "Chuan-Kang[1] People's Guerrilla Column" (based out of Ya'an, it consisted of eight detachments and two directly-subordinate brigades). According to the decision of the temporary working committee, the underground CPC organization in Chengdu established the "West Sichuan Temporary Working Department of the Underground Party in Chengdu" ("Temporary Work Department" for short) on November 5th with Wang Yiping as secretary. The "Temporary Work Department" served as headquarters for the last underground CPC organization to operate in old Chengdu. Before long, the group had successfully recruited members for the guerilla column, gathered weapons, ammunition and medicine, protected national property and archives, incited defection within enemy forces, and made preparations for the Pengxian County Uprising and the liberation of Chengdu. This "Temporary Work Department" was established in the dormitories of Jincheng Bank on Xisheng Street—specifically, in the residence of progressive figure Wang Hongshi.

---

[1]　Kang refers to "Xikang", a Chinese province in existence from 1939 to 1955, comprised of modern-day western Sichuan and eastern Tibet. [Translator's note]

Jing Alley

East of Lower Tongren Road and south of Zhai Alley curves a small lane. In the early years of the Qing Dynasty, it was known as Ruyi Hutong; later it was called Mingde Hutong for the "Mingde Lane" in its north. During the name changes of the newly established Republic of China, it was finally named "*Jingxiang* (Jing Alley)" for the well within its bounds (*jing* meaning "well").

The water well in Jing Alley (Well Alley) was quite famous within the Manchu City in the Qing Dynasty, for a legend was passed downabout its origin: When the Qing army invaded Chengdu, the chaos and fires of war inadvertently contaminated or filled in many of the city's wells. The Qing forces were facing a serious shortage of drinkable water. At that time, several of their war horses gathered in that precise spot and were licking the ground. When urged to move on, the horses refused to budge. When army officers took a closer look, they discovered that the ground there was particularly moist, then they began to dig. Very soon they had uncovered clear, clean water, the dangers of thirst and starvation thus averted. They dug a well in this very spot and specially fashioned a well cover out of stone. The well became famous throughout the city for its ample reservoir and high-quality water.

The Jingzi Alley well, dug in the period of Emperor Kangxi
(r. 1654 ~ 1722), 1994. Photo by Zhou Mengqi.

Water from the well continued to be drawn up until—and even after—the founding of the P. R. C. , even though the well was located right in the middle of the lane. But as the water supply began to lessen year by year, it ceased to be used. In order to protect the famous well and prevent traffic obstructions, the municipal administration moved the mouth of the well to the sidewalk on the north side of the street. In 1990 the Xicheng District People's Government erected a stone tablet to its side. It reads: "This well was first dug during the reign of Emperor Kangxi by the Manchu and Mongol Eight Banner Army when they were stationed in Chengdu. It was within Mingde Hutong in front of the Qing army barracks in the former Shaocheng. Following the Xinhai Revolution, Jing Alley was given its current name based on the presence of this well. "

Jing Alley, 2021 Photo by Zhang Xinan

Jing Alley and neighboring Kuan and Zhai Alleys underwent a comprehensive transformation to become central Chengdu's folk art district. Now they constitute a famous cultural and tourist attraction. Sculptor Zhu Cheng used an old wall from the former Xiejin Middle School on the south side of Jing Alley as the base for his original design, creating an old-style brick wall which was used for modern Chengdu folk art exhibitions. It has become the most representative feature of the cultural landscape of Kuan and Zhai Alleys.

Binsheng Street

Binsheng Street lies west of Dongchenggen Street, east of Upper Changshun Street, south of Guihua Alley, and north of Dongsheng Street. In the Qing Dynasty, its name was Binsheng Hutong. After the founding of the Republic of China, the name was amended to "Binsheng Street". *Binsheng* is an auspicious two-character phrase in Chinese; the first character *bin* itself is made by combining the characters for *wen* (writing) and *wu* (military), invoking the old idiom *wen wu shuang quan* ("master both pen and sword"); the second character *sheng* means to get a promotion; thus *binsheng* expresses residents' desire to have a bright future in both literary and martial arts.

Urban mural art on Binsheng Street, 2021 Photo by Chen Ke

During the infrastructure construction in theP. R. C., a rather thick deposit of cultural materials in the Tang Dynasty was discovered underground at Binsheng Street. Notable finds included Kaiyuan Tongbao coins, Qianyuan Tongbao coins, and even amber. Experts have hypothesized that here was Chengdu's southern commercial district during the Tang Dynasty.

Teachers and students of the German School on Chengdu's Binsheng Street. This was the first foreign-run German language school in Sichuan Province. 1914. Photo by Fritz Weiss [Germany].

Under the trend of late-Qing modernization reforms, in the twenty-ninth year during the reign of Emperor Guangxu (1903), the No. 3 Primary School was established at the east entrance of Binsheng Street; it was one of Chengdu's first "new-style" schools.

In May 1935, the famous writer Li Jieren (1891 ~ 1962) resigned from his post as manager of the Minsheng Machinery Plant in Chongqing and returned to his hometown Chengdu, where he rented the courtyard at 13 Binsheng Street. In a bout of intensive writing that summer, he penned his entire novel *Sishui Weilan* (*Ripples Across Stagnant Water*). That winter, he wrote the first part of *Baofengyu Qian* (*Before the Tempest*). In early 1936, Li moved to neighboring Guihua Lane (at No. 64, specifically), finished writing *Baofengyu Qian*, and continued with his next installment in the series, *Da Bo* (*The Great Wave*). Thus were Li Jieren's masterpieces—the entire *Dahe Trilogy*—created right here in these two small Shaocheng courtyards.

The renowned scholar and poet Pang Shizhou also resided at 5 Binsheng Street for a long period of his life.

Pang Shizhou (**1894 ~ 1964**), a native of Chengdu and disciple of the renowned scholar Zhao Xi (1867 ~ 1948). His poems were no less admired than those of Lin Sijin or Xiang Chu. Throughout his career he served as head of the Chinese departments in three different schools: Chengdu Normal University, West China Union College, and Kwang Hua University (now the Southwestern University of Finance and Economics). After the founding of the P. R. C. , he was a professor of Department of Chinese, Sichuan University and headed the Classical Literature Teaching and Research Section. Among his students are a number of famous contemporary scholars, including Yang Mingzhao and Qu Shouyuan. Pang is also the author of *Guogu Lunheng Shuzheng* (*Annotations on the Guogu Lunheng*)[1], *Yangjingshi Biji*, *Yangjingshi Shilu*, and *Yangjingshi Cilu*. He also has a fascinating connection to the *baijiu* industry[2]. The *baijiu* brand Jian Nan Chun is known far and wide today, but few people appreciate the rich historical and cultural connotations of its name (which was translated to "Jiannan Spring" — spring is the season; Jiannan is a place name once used in Sichuan). The phrase was once used to mean "a fine spirit" (particularly in the Tang Dynasty), when "*chun*" *hunijiu* brand Jian Nan Chun is known far and wide today, but few people appreciate the rich historical and cultural *codaqujiu*[3] from the Mianzhu Distillery (in Deyang county, Sichuan). He based the phrase on a line in *Tangguo Shibu* (*Supplement to the History of the Tang Dynasty*), written by Li Zhao in the Tang Dynasty: "*Jiannan zhi shao chun*" (the spring is burning in Jiannan)[4].

---

① *Guogu Lunheng* (*"Discussion and Evaluation of China's Intrinsic Culture"*) was written by Zhang Taiyan in the early 1900s.

② *Baijiu* ("white alcohol") is a traditional hard liquor most often distilled from sorghum.

③ *Daqujiu* is a Sichuan regional *baijiu* variety made with sorghum and wheat.

④ Here, *chun* ("spring") refers to the alcohol from Jiannan, while *shao* ("burn") may refer either to the strength of the liquor, or its improvement upon heating. [Translator's note]

Guihua Alley

Guihua Alley was another former *hutong* in the Manchu City during the Qing Dynasty. It was named "Guihua Hutong" (literally "Osmanthus Flower Hutong") for orange osmanthus that grew there at the time. Its name was changed to "Guihua Street" in the early period of the Republic of China, but because there was another street of the same name on the south side of Chengdu, it was reverted back to "Guihua Alley", the name it bears to this day. Guihua Street is a rather short stretch of road which is located to south of Zhihui Street, bound by Yandao Street in the middle with Donggui Street at its west. It was ultimately torn up for the construction of the Minshan Hotel.

In December 1935, a famous writer Li Jieren moved from Binsheng Street to "Juyuan" at 64 Guihua Alley. Having already completed *Sishui Weilan* (*Ripples Across Stagnant Water*), he completed the second and third books in the trilogy— *Baofengyu Qian* (*Before the Tempest*) and *Da Bo* (*The Great Wave*) —here at Guihua Alley, in less than two years' time.

Guihua Alley, 2021 Photo by Chen Ke

Kuan and Zhai Alleys

At the southwest corner of the Manchu City in the Qing Dynasty were two adjoining *hutongs*—Xingren Hutong and Taiping Hutong, where the homes of bordered red banner were located. One of the alleys was rather wide (*kuan*), while the other was rather narrow (*zhai*), so people took to calling them "Kuan Alley" (Wide Alley) and "Zhai Alley" (Narrow Alley). When all *hutongs* were renamed at the beginning of the Republic of China, these colloquial names became their official names.

Within the former Manchu City, the Kuan Alley and Zhai Alley[①] *hutongs* were hardly important. Likewise, throughout the Republican period, they seldom housed high-ranking officials or other tenants of great importance. During the early years of the P. R. C., no government agencies demolished the bungalows to have multi-storied buildings built here. According to longtime residents of the former 45 Kuan Alley, at that time the residential compound had an 8 *mu* (5,333 m^2) vegetable garden with a large well for watering—a rarity in the city by that time. The garden was tended by several households. When the gymnasium was built, more than 30 families relocated from Donghuamen to build their homes in the vegetable garden, turning the spacious compound into a crowded tenement. It was precisely because of this long-term commonness that the alleys have not experienced major demolition and reform. After the Reform and Opening-up, they still commendably retained the old style of streets and alleys in Old Chengdu and a number of small quadrangles with local characteristics. Not a single tall building among them, the alleys had fully maintained the architectural style of the Qing Dynasty, thus they became downtown Chengdu's most valuable area in terms of concentrated historic architecture and folk custom preservation. As early as the 1980s, Chengdu's relevant municipal departments had decided to designate and protect the two alleys as a characteristic cultural district, which might provide a window to the past of Chengdu for researchers and sightseers alike. In downtown Chengdu, there are a total of four "old Chengdu" characteristic cultural districts under protection (Kuan and Zhai Alleys, Daci Temple, Wenshu

---

① Technically two alleys, popular culture and official tourism materials so often refer to them collectively; hence the title here was translated as "Kuan and Zhai Alleys". [Translator's note]

Monastery, and Jinguanyi Post), among which Kuan and Zhai Alleys are the best preserved and protected. Over the past decades, countless visitors have walked the alleys and countless films or television series have been shot here. Kuan Alley and Zhai Alley have become living symbols of old Chengdu. In 2005, a comprehensive renovation began under the direction of relevant municipal departments. It targeted most of the buildings in the historic district (including the neighboring Jing Alley). The neighborhood was fully remodeled with modernized infrastructure, including various pipe networks and underground parking lots. The upgraded Kuan and Zhai Alleys officially reopened in June 2008, not long after the Wenchuan Earthquake on May 12th. It has become an exhibition area for old Chengdu culture and a distinctive cultural tourism district.

Kuan Alley, 1994 Photo by Chen Xianmin

Kuan Alley before reconstruction, Photo by Qi Yanan

Zhai Alley, 1995 Photo by Zhang Xinan

Zhai Alley reconstructed in 2003 Photo by Chen Xianmin

New‐built brick gate in Kuanzhai Alley, 2021 Photo by Chen Ke

Though I did say that in the past Kuan Alley and Zhai Alley were seldom homed to officials or other figures of great importance, I did not mean to imply that there were no such persons who resided here. The famous scholars Zhang Shengzang, Li Zhi, and Xu Renfu, the major figure in the Democratic Movement Han Wenqi, Sichuan Normal University Professor Guo Chengyong, and Chengdu's most famous Republican-era gangster, Shi Zhaowu, all lived here at one time.

Zhang Shengzang (**1903 ~ 1992**) from Jingzhou, Hubei Province, was the thirteenth-generation descendant of Zhang Juzheng[①]. He was brought up by his uncle Zhang Guocheng, an eminent scholar and cabinet minister of education in the Beiyang government. When studying at Tianjin Nankai High School, he had classmated with Zhou Enlai[②] for four years. In 1918, when Zhang Shengzang was just 15 years old, he was admitted to the Department of History of Peking University, where he studied under Li Dazhao[③], befriended Mao Zedong, and became one of the

Zhang Shengzang

seven founders of the Marxism Research Association. When in Shanghai in 1922, Zhang was recognized by Sun Yat-sen for his extensive knowledge and skills in calligraphy. Sun Yat-sen even specifically requested that Zhang write a copy of his famous *Strategic Plan for Building the Nation*. After that, Zhang Shengzang studied abroad in the UK, Germany, and the USA, becoming proficient in English, French, German, Russian, Spanish, Portuguese, Japanese, and even Sanskrit. He obtained five doctoral degrees in succession—in literature, medicine, law, economics, and history. (Among these, his Ph. D. in economics was from America's Ohio State University, for which his thesis topic was "A Comparative Study of the Planned and Market Economy"; his Ph. D. in literature was from Oxford, for which his thesis topic was "A Comparison of Du

---

① Zhang Juzheng (1525 – 1582) was a prominent official in the late Ming Dynasty who espoused a kind of legalist political philosophy. [Translator's note]

② Zhou Enlai (1898 – 1976) was a principal leader of the Communist Party under Chairman Mao and the first Premier of the P. R. C.. [Translator's note]

③ Li Dazhao (1889 – 1927) was active in modernization reforms and a co-founder of the Communist Party of China in 1921. [Translator's note]

Fu and Shakespeare".) During his years in Europe, Zhang kept up friendships with Zhou Enlai and Deng Xiaoping①. He was once received by the Queen of England; at one point, he was even in contact with Mussolini and Hitler (before they came into power). Zhang translated the *I-Ching* (*Book of Changes*) into English and organized the "Chinese I-Ching Association" in the U. K.. All together he wrote five books on the I-Ching, including *Yi Jing Xin Jian* ("*New Notes on the I-Ching*") and *Yi Jing Bianzhengfa* ("*Dialectics on the I-Ching*"). Zhang returned to China in 1929, whereupon he held successive teaching positions at Northeastern University (during which time he wrote his famous book *An Outline of Uighur History* in classical Chinese), Fudan University, Jiaotong University, Chongqing University, and the National Central University. (Because of Zhang's talent in calligraphy and painting—especially painting horses—he became close friends with master painter Xu Beihong (1895 ~ 1953) when teaching at the National Central University. The divorce ceremony of Xu Beihong and Jiang Biwei was even held in Zhang Shengzang's home.) National Central University President Luo Jialun referred to Zhang as "the all-knowing professor", as he was proficient in 9 languages and had opened 28 different courses. At that time, Zhang was an appointed professor of the Ministry of Education, and Chiang Kai-shek once invited him for private lessons, in which Zhang instructed him on the I-Ching. Zhang was one of the founders of Chongqing University and the primary founder of Shuzhong University, established in Neijiang, Sichuan in 1946 (this university was jointly funded by the three great salt merchant families of Zigong—Wang, Li, and Yan; it had 11 colleges under the 3 departments of literature, business, and engineering). From 1933 to 1936, he also managed the *New Sichuan Reporter* in Chengdu. When the construction began on the Chengdu-Chongqing Railway in 1950, Zhang's old friend Deng Xiaoping appointed him as the leader of cultural relics survey and collection team, in which capacity Zhang made an important discovery—the fossilized skull of "Ziyang Man", indicating a previously unknown Paleolithic *Homo sapiens* group. In 1953, after an academic seminar was held in Beijing on the discovery of Ziyang Man, Chairman Mao and Premier Zhou invited Zhang

---

① Deng Xiaoping (1904 – 1997), originally from Sichuan, was a prominent early figure in the CPC and served as paramount leader of China following Chairman Mao's death in 1976. [Translator's note]

Shengzang to dinner at Chairman Mao's home, where the three could reminisce about their deep-rooted friendship. The next year, Zhang was appointed committee director of the Sichuan Provincial Office of Cultural Relics Management, specifically to oversee the P. R. C. 's first comprehensive study of cave art in Sichuan. Based on the results, Zhang published the important essay "Cave Art of Dazu and Anyue" as well as "Suggestions for Compiling an Encyclopedia of China". In 1962, he served as researcher for the Sichuan Library, then in 1986, as special librarian for the Sichuan Literature and History Institute. That year he also served as counselor in the Counsellors' Office of Sichuan Provincial People's Government. Throughout his life, he had a great fondness for Chairman Mao's poetry. He once created five *changhe* poems each for 37 different Chairman Mao's poems—a total of 185—which he then carefully set into scrolls[1]. When Zhang Shengzang's home was ransacked during the "Cultural Revolution", the poetry scrolls came into the hands of Chairman Mao, who was quite delighted, and penciled in his remarks. In 1972, they were passed on to Zhang Shizhao[2] for his appreciation. After reading through them, Zhang Shizhao entrusted the scrolls to his daughter Zhang Hanzhi, who was to visit Chengdu on business; thus they finally returned to their creator's hands. In 1991, Zhang Shengzang, already ill, wrote his final article: "I discovered the skull of Ziyang Man." It was in his later years, up until his death on January 7th, 1992, that he resided in the Deng Zesheng Courtyard at 24 Kuan Alley.

Li Zhi (1885 ~ 1975), courtesy name Peifu, was from Dianjiang County (now part of Chongqing). He was an early member of the Tongmenghui (United League), a senior figure in the Xinhai Revolution, and once the long-term resident of 19 Kuan Alley—though in his later years, he resided at Jiaojia Alley. After the Wuchang Uprising, he held a mass meeting (at the scale of 10,000 people) at Nanjiaochang (South Military Fields), hoisting the banner of "United League President Sun Yat-sen" and delivering a revolutionary speech. This effectively made Sun Yat-sen a familiar name in Sichuan. Li Zhi once served as

---

① *Changhe* refers to a poetic exchange maintaining the same rhythm and rhyme. In this case, Zhang imitated and elaborated on Mao's original poems. [Translator's note]

② Zhang Shizhao (1881 – 1973) was a prominent journalist who advocated for a combination of modernization reforms and adherence to Confucian ideals.

counselor for the Great Han Sichuan Military Government
and adviser of the Sichuan Pacification Army Command, but
he quickly retired from the world of politics. He spent time
in Japan, studying Chinese civilization under the renowned
Chinese revolutionary and scholar Zhang Taiyan (1869 ~
1936). Li himself became well-known in Sichuan for his
academic achievements in phonology—especially his truly
unique insights on the study of archaic Chinese initials
(*guniu*). Upon reaching middle age, he held a series of

Li Zhi

teaching posts at various Chengdu universities, serving as Chinese department
director at the National Chengdu Higher Normal School, Sichuan University, and
Chenghua University respectively. He retired in 1952. On September 27th,
1936, the people of Chengdu held a memorial service for Zhang Taiyan, who had
passed away on June 14th. The elegiac couplet composed by Li Zhi for that
occasion has been praised as one of the best in contemporary times:

> Not corrupted by wealth or honors, never deterred by destitution, unable to be
> subdued by force. Mount Taishan has collapsed! The pillars have buckled! The
> great sage has passed away!

Xu Renfu (1901 ~ 1988) was from Dazhu County in Dazhou, Sichuan Province.
Following his graduation from National Chengdu Higher Normal School, he
devoted his life to teaching and the study of ancient Chinese. In Sichuan, Xu
Renfu is a representative scholar of the late-period (the late Qing Dynasty and
onward) school of "New Text Confucianism". Throughout his life, Xu was a
prolific writer. In the first decade of the Reform and Opening-up, he published a
number of outstanding and highly influential academic works, including *Dushi
Zhujie Shangque* (*"Further Discussion on the Annotations of Du Fu's Poems"*),
Guang Shi Ci (*"Spreading the Words of the Buddha"*), *Gushi Biejie* (*"New
Interpretations of Classical Poetry"*), and *Guang Gushu Yiyi Juli* (*"Points of
Doubt in the Classic Texts"*). During my time working for a publishing house, I
was the chief editor for Xu's important book *Zuo Zhuan Shuzheng* (*"Annotations
on the Commentary of Zuo"*).

Han Wenqi (1901 ~ 1983), a respected scholar (particularly of Buddhism) and calligrapher, he was a native of Neijiang in southeastern Sichuan Province. Prior to the founding of the P. R. C. , was the minister of education for Xikang Province and director of the Xikang Province History Compilation Bureau. During the War of Resistance Against Japanese Aggression, he founded the monthly periodical *Chongguang* ("Seeing the Light") in Chengdu. Its editor was Tang Junyi, who later became one of China's major representatives of modern Neo-Confucianism. In 1946, Han joined the China Democratic League (CDL) and served as chairman of its Chengdu chapter. He did a lot of work to welcome the birth of the the P. R. C. , Several memoirs of that period say that Han Weiqi was the one to draft the open telegram for the Pengxian Uprising waged by Liu Wenhui and others in 1949. After the founding of the P. R. C. , Han served successive posts as deputy director of the West Sichuan Department of Agriculture and Forestry, deputy commissioner of Mianyang Prefecture[1], standing member of the CPPCC Sichuan Provincial Committee, standing member of the CDL Sichuan Provincial Committee, and counselor of the Sichuan Provincial People's Government. In 1957 he was wronged in the Anti-Rightist Campaign[2] and sent to prison. He was released on medical parole much later and lived out the rest of his life in his daughter's home on Zhai Alley.

Shi Zhaowu (? ~ 1933), originally from Pingshan County in Yibin, Sichuan Province. He claimed to be a descendant of Shi Dakai (1831 ~ 1863), Wing King of the Taiping Heavenly Kingdom[3]. (According to some local tales in Sichuan, Shi Dakai spent his last years in seclusion. The "Shi Dakai" who died a hero's death in Chengdu was not the real person but a substitute with similar appearance.) Shi Zhaowu went from a life of crime to serve in the Sichuan Army under the watchful eye of his adoptive father Liu Wenhui. In ten years, Shi had

---

① At that time I (the author) was attending Mianyang High School, and personally heard him deliver a report to the teachers and students of the school. [Author's note]

② The Anti-Rightist Campaign was a massive political movement against the "rightist" intellectuals from 1957 to roughly 1959 in China. [Translator's note]

③ The Taiping Heavenly Kingdom was a short-lived breakaway state established by the Taiping Rebellion, an armed religious uprising that lasted from 1850 to 1864 and was only defeated at tremendous cost to the Qing Empire. [Translator's note]

risen to the rank of guard brigade commander. His first estate in Chengdu (around the year 1926) was located on Kuan Alley. In 1931 he moved to a new home on South Gulou Street, which became well-known as the "Zhao Mansion" (though it was confiscated from him two years later). Chengdu people during the Republican years utterly detested Shi Zhaowu. Totally lacking morality, there was no bottom limit to the crimes he would commit. He was a rapist and tyrant, robber and kidnapper. Thus it comes as no surprise that after he was defeated and captured by Li Jiayu during a battle between warlords (specifically the "Battle of the Two Lius" in 1933), Liu Xiang ordered that Shi was immediately executed. A cage containing Shi Zhaowu's severed head was hung in the People's Park for public display. Even today, there is a saying among the community of old Chengdu residents: "Is that Shi Zhaowu's head? Off with it!"

Renhou Street

Renhou Street, so named after the founding of the Republic of China, was originally the "Renhou Hutong" in the Manchu City. It was founded between Changshun Street and Upper Dongchenggen Street, south of Duozi Alley and north of Guihua Alley.

In 1933, during the fighting among warlords, a battle took place in the alleys of Chengdu. This stone fortification was built at the entrance of Renhou Street. Photo courtesy of Yang Xianfeng.

"Renhou" (meaning "honest and kind") is not only an auspicious phrase, but also a moral imperative. It was taken from a phrase in *Fuguo* (*Enriching a State*), a chapter in the *Xunzi* (a Confucianist text attributed to Master Xun Kuang of the 3rd century BC): "Honesty and kindness are all sufficient to stabilize the world."

Famous Chinese painter Chen Zizhuang resided at 11 Renhou Street in his later years. (Prior to that, he successively lived in Kangzhuang Street, Ningxia Street, and Jianghan Road.)

Chen Zizhuang (1913 ~ 1976), styled himself as "Shi Hu", was from Rongchang County (now in Chongqing). His father was a folk artist who painted pottery and made paper fans, so Chen Zizhuang felt the influence of the arts from a young age. At 16 he came to Chengdu, where he studied martial arts and painted, and gradually became well-known in both regards. He was also an active member of Chengdu society. In 1949, he helped plan the successful revolt of Wang Zanxu's division within the Sichuan Army, and then he himself revolted as a major general in the Kuomintang Army. After the founding of the P. R. C., Chen was hired as librarian at the Sichuan Museum of Literature and History and moved to Chengdu in 1955. In 1963, he became a member of the Sichuan CPPCC. For many years he painted and taught Chinese painting for a living. Because he had little contact with the outside world, his skills were little-known during his lifetime, but after Chen Zizhuang passed away—especially with the Reform and Opening-up—his works were met with high praise both within China and beyond. When his paintings were showcased in a Beijing exhibition in 1988, they were acclaimed as "a sensation in Beijing and a shock to the world." The Ministry of Culture publication *Fifty Years of Chinese Art* only lists four painters from Sichuan, and Chen is among them (the other three are Zhang Daqian, Shi Lu, and Jiang Zhaohe). Many researchers believe that Chen is the finest painter after Zhang Daqian in Sichuan Province. In particular, it is the innocent natural world brought to life by his freehand brushwork—with its strange abruptness, vigorous strokes, and vivid elegance—that has won him many researchers' hearts. He has even been named "the Van Gogh of China". In Chen's hometown there is now an exhibition hall dedicated to his art.

Chen Zizhuang painting in his home, July 3rd, 1976.

Zhijishi Street

There are several streets named after stones in Chengdu. Actually, except the pebbles in the rivers, there are no huge stones on this alluvial plain. Those stones used for architecture and gardens are all carried from other places. That is to say, huge stones used to be scarce in Chengdu, but the history and culture of Chengdu has a very close relationship with these huge stones.

Beside the pool in Chengdu Cultural Park, an irregular square-shaped stone, about two meters high is protected by a railing, with the big Chinese characters "*Zhi Ji Shi*" (Zhi Ji Stone) engraved on it. This old stone has a long history.

Zhiji Stone placed in Chengdu Cultural Park Photo by Yang Xianfeng

Early in the Sui Dynasty, Yu Mao said, "the loom was supported on huge stones, and the ship looks like a raft crossing the sea." This is the earliest record of Zhiji Stone in Chengdu in reliable historical materials, which has obvious mythological characteristics. a Tang Dynasty poet spent his last years in Chengdu, and left one of the poems in Chengdu titled "The Store Which Sells Oracles": "Jun Ping used to sell oracles here, but the shop has been deserted for a long time. I still have some money to buy wine, but I don't know whether the Zhiji Stone remains in the world". The man who sold oracles is just Yan Zun whose courtesy name is Jun Ping. Zhao Lin who lived later than Cen Shen also depicted the stone in Yin Hua Lu, one of his novel collections, "there is a stone in the Temple of Immortal Yan in Chengdu, commonly known as Zhiji Stone. Witnesses all said that the stone was left by Jun Ping. " The legend about the huge stones was recorded in many versions after the Tang Dynasty, and the most acceptable one is recorded in The History of Sichuan · Biography Yan Zun written by Cao Xuequan, a scholar in the Ming Dynasty. According to this book, Zhang Qian traveled as far as the source of the Yellow River on his diplomatic mission to Daxia (Tochari). Zhang is a famous general during the Han Dynasty, and opened up the route to the Western Regions. After he returned in a boat with a stone in it, he asked Yan Junping, who was good at astronomy and geography if he could tell where the stone came from. Yan Junping looked at the stone for a long time and then said, "Last August I observed the sky and saw a guest star enter the area of Altair and Vega. Now I think it is a reflection of your whereabouts. This stone is used by the woman weaver in heaven to support her loom, but you have brought it back to earth". Zhang Qian replied, "Just as you said, I saw a woman weaving cloth and a man pasturing cattle when I arrived at the source of the Yellow River. I asked them where I was now. The weaver said I was not on the earth but in the heaven. Putting the big stone into my boat, she told me to look for Yan Junping in Chengdu when I returned, and Yan would tell me something about the stone". Since then, the stone in the Vega has been left in Chengdu.

This myth tells us that this is an unusual stone sent by the goddess in heaven. According to the records in the Tang Dynasty or even earlier, the stone, known as the one hidden among the sea clouds and between Altair and Vega, has been enshrined in the Temple of Immortal Yan in honor of Yan Junping. Inscribed with three characters "Zhi Ji Shi" in seal script, it has a height of more than two meters. After the Temple of Immortal Yan collapsed, this stone still stood on the vacant lot of the original site. During the Ming and Qing dynasties, a street was built there. In the Ming Dynasty, the name of the street was unknown. When it came to the Qing Dynasty, it was named Renli'er Hutong within Menchu City, which was a typical street name in the north of China. However, it was also called Junping Hutong because the Temple of Immortal Yan was located there. In the Republican period, it was renamed Zhijishi Street. In the Qing Dynasty, the original site of the Temple on Zhijishi Street was reconstructed as Guandi Temple (according to the regulations, only Guanyin Bodhisattva and Lord Guan Yu were allowed to be worshiped in Manchu City. This regulation had been strictly observed in the early Qing, but eased in later period of Qing Dynasty). This Guandi Temple was also called Zhijishi Temple by Chengdu residents since Zhiji Stone stood inside. By the end of the Qing Dynasty, the temple was destroyed and the Zhiji Stone was left in the open air. In 1924, Mr. Lu Zuofu, a famous industrialist who was also the director of the Chengdu Popular Education Museum, planned to build a Zhiji Stone Park, but failed in the years when the warlords were fighting with each other. In 1985, the stone was finally moved into the Culture Park, with a measured height of 2. 05 meters. The three characters "Zhi Ji Shi" engraved on the stone in ancient times were not obvious. When moved into the park, the three characters were re – inscribed by the famous calligrapher Wu Shoumei.

According to the consensus of academic circles, people in ancient Shu Dynasty had a belief of worshiping huge stones, often setting up a stone specially brought from the mountain area in front of the cemetery or other important buildings. The main ancestors of the ancient Shu were the Qiang people. This worship can still be seen not only in the sarcophagus, but also in the customs of white stone worship still maintained by the present Qiang people in Maoxian and Wenchuan counties. There remain ancient huge stones in some places of Chengdu, and the streets or places are named after these stones, which are the relics of stone worship of the Shu ancestors. Because the stones selected by ancestors and transported to the plains were to be erected as some kind of sign, they were mostly in the shape of stele or bamboo. As for the purpose of erecting huge stones, the ancients had their own valuable opinions about them. For example, the famous Qing Dynasty poet Wu Weiye said: "Emperor Yu Fu built his state in a dangerous environment. The huge stone was used as the Men Guan (gate view). " What he said about "Men Guan" is basically consistent with the one regarded by today's historians as the sign erected before the large buildings (Sichuan is famous for Han Que in China, a landmark erected before large buildings in the Han Dynasty).

In order to keep the memory of the ancient huge stone culture, Chengdu Government has done a lot of work in urban construction in recent years. For example, during the comprehensive renovation of Fuhe River and Nanhe River, a number of large stones were placed in the greenbelts on both sides of the river. During the renovation project of Qintai Road, a number of tall stone tablets were specially designed on the southern end of the road. On the side of Huanhua Stream and its downstream Nan River, a new long street extending westward from Binjiang Road was specially named East Dashi (Huge Stone) Road and West Dashi (Huge Stone) Road. All these above are the special measures to review the ancient history of this city.

Although Zhiji Stone has been moved into the Culture Park, Zhijishi Street still exists in the old Manchu City, with changshun street in the east and tongren road in the west. It is said that the west section of this street used to be the place where Yan Junping read books and sold oracles in the Han Dynasty. Later in the Tang Dynasty, the Temple of Immortal Yan was established. In the Song Dynasty, Lü Gongbi described it in his poem *Temple of Immortal Yan*: "The oracle shop remains open with the falling curtain, and the old Zhiji Stone is left there with moss growing on its surface". Judging from this, Zhiji Stone was just inside the Temple of Immortal Yan at that time.

In 2006, a small amusement park was built at the intersection of Zhijishi Street and Tongren Road. A replica of Zhiji Stone according to the shape of Zhiji Stone in the current cultural park was established as the symbol of Zhijishi Street.

It should be noted that in numerous books, maps and public signs, including the authoritative *Annals of Chengdu, Sichuan Province*, Zhiji (机) Stone is written as Zhiji (砍) Stone, which is incorrect. On one hand, Zhiji (机) has already been recorded in all ancient literature. On the other hand, the Chinese character *Ji* (机) just refers to the loom machine. *A Study of Historic Relics in Chengdu* (1987 version) adopted the character *Ji* (机). In 1992, *An Overview of Street Names of Chengdu Blocks* clearly pointed out that *Ji* (砍) was the misuse of Ji (机). In this book, the author strictly follows the authoritative *Annals of Chengdu, Sichuan Province* in terms of street names.

In the Republican period, the Jigu Medical Society founded by the famous doctor Zhang Xianshi in Chengdu was located on Zhijishi Street.

The former residence of Li Huang, a famous political figure in the Republican period is located on Zhijishi Street.

Li Huang (1895 ~ 1991), born in Chengdu, was admitted into the Anglo-French Civil Servant School of Chengdu Westernization Bureau when he was 13 and later studied in Shanghai Aurora College. In 1918, he founded the Young China Association in Beijing with celebrities such as Wang Guangqi and Li Dazhao. In 1919, he went to study in France. In 1923, he founded the Youth Party of China with Zeng Qi and others to advocate nationalism and oppose communism. After returning to China in 1924, he served successively as a professor at Peking University, Chengdu University and other universities. His works include *History of French Literature*, *History of Ancient European Culture*, and *Education of Nationalism*. Meanwhile, he founded the weekly newspaper *Sober Lion* to propagandize the standpoint of anti-Communism and anti-Soviet Union, and became a representative of the Sober Lion Sect. During the War of Resistance Against Japanese Aggression, he followed KMT

Li Huang

and served as a member of the Supreme National Defense Commission, a member of the National Political Consultative Council and chairman of the Presidium of the National Political Consultative Council. In 1945, he became a member of the Chinese delegation of the United Nations Constitutional Assembly. The KMT government had appointed him as the economic minister, but he did not take office because of illness. In 1949, he went to Hong Kong and then Taiwan, and nominally assumed the position of national policy advisor in the "Presidential Office" of Taiwan. In fact, he did not take part in political activities, but was engaged in the research of the history of the Republic of China.

Duozi Alley

Between today's Upper Dongchenggen Street and Upper Changshun Street was the Duozi Alley, at the eastern end of which lay the office of the Sichuan Provincial Committee of the Communist Youth League.

As one of the many *hutongs* in the Manchu City, Duozi Alley was originally named Taiping Hutong, in which there were some workshops that made knives, guns and weapons for the Eight Banners of Manchu and Mongolia. In the Republican period, it was renamed Daozi Alley. The residence of Liu Xiang (for the introduction to Liu Xiang, see "Tiyuan Road"), the general of Sichuan Army, was located in the alley. In the year of 1935, Liu Xiang followed the advice of the famous scholar Zhang Shengzang and changed the name of Daozi Alley into Duozi Alley [Liu Xiang invited Zhang Shengzang to Chengdu to start *the New Sichuan Newspaper* and he was living in Liu's mansion at that time (for the introduction to Zhang Shengzang, see "Kuan Alley")]. Change of the street name was based on the following reasons: First, the name Daozi (Knife) Alley implied murder and was not auspicious. Second, both Liu Xiang's eldest son and his second son died at a very early age. At that time, he had only one son and one daughter. In order to have more children and more happiness, Liu Xiang changed the name of the alley into Duozi (Many Children) Alley.

There used to be another Daozi Alley in Chengdu, which was today's Xiangyang Street located between Daye Road and Qingshiqiao Road. This street was renamed Xiangyang Street in the Republican period because its original name was the same as Daozi Alley in the Manchu City.

Liuxiang's Mansion in Duozi Alley, Photo courtesy of Yang Xianfeng.

The former residence of Yu Zhongying, the famous calligrapher and seal engraver, was located at the eastern end of Duozi Alley (He lived in the residence of his friend on Zhijishi Street).

Yu Zhongying (**1899 ~ 1983**), born in Pixian County of Chengdu, styled himself as Xinggong. After graduation from Chengdu Army Primary School, he worked in Sichuan Army, but was addicted to calligraphy and painting. After resigning from the army, he went to Beijing to learn from Master Qi Baishi and became one of the first batches of Baishi's disciples. He had a deep attainment in the art of calligraphy, and was the most accomplished calligrapher in modern Chengdu. Since the beginning of the War of Resistance Against Japanese Aggression, he served as

Yu Zhongying

deputy chief of staff with the rank of lieutenant general in the Seventh Warzone, deputy chief of staff of Sichuan Field Headquarters, mayor of Chengdu, etc. During his tenure as mayor of Chengdu from 1940 to 1944, he had made many achievements in municipal construction, such as setting up the first municipal public hospital and the first municipal public middle school, constructing the waterwork, and opening the private bus route from the Entrance of the Bull Market to the Tea Shop. After the founding of the P. R. C. , he was appointed as a staff member of the Sichuan Institute of Culture and History, a member of the Sichuan CPPCC, and vice chairman of the Sichuan Branch of the Chinese Calligraphers Association.

Paotongshu Street

Paotongshu Street lies between the Shiye Street and Zhijishi Street. It was within the area of the former Renli Hutong in the Manchu City. In the early years of the Republican period, the name of this *hutong* was abolished and was renamed Paotongshu Street after the big paulownia tree on the street.

Founded in the year of 1961, the Paotongshu Primary School was the National Modern Educational Technology Experimental School authorized by the Ministry of Education. It was located at the east end of this street and was one of the most famous primary schools in Chengdu and even in Sichuan Province.

Paotongshu Primary School, 2021 Photo by Chen Ke

The first road in Sichuan Province is the Chengdu-Guanxian Road. The head office of its construction and administration unit was located on Paotongshu Street. As far as I know, the first road that China prepared to construct is not in the coastal regions, but is the Chengdu-Guanxian Road in Chengdu. In 1912, Hu Jingyi, the governor who was responsible for the safety of Sichuan Province, adopted the suggestions proposed by some reformers and decided to build a road on which automobiles could run (at that time the road was called "Malu" which means the road where horses can run). He appointed Dai Hongchou, the chief inspector of patrolmen, as the chief director and employed Liu Xisong as the chief engineer. The route they measured out was today's old Chengdu-Guanxian Road in a total length of 55 kilometers. The project started from Guanxian County but met some fierce opposition from some people along the way, for they believed that the road may break the geomancy and disturb the environment of the tombs, and was especially rejected by all the Gelaohui (or "Hatchet Gang") in the four counties (Chengdu County, Pixian County, Chongning County and Guanxian County) along the way. So after the one-kilometer-long demonstration roadbed was built, and reached Zhaojiayuan, this project had to be halted thoroughly and the completed one-kilometer-long section was later restored to the farmland. However, next year, the Changsha-Xiangtan Road in Hunan Province was completed, so this "first road in Chengdu" was found only in the documents. After the halt of Chengdu-Guanxian Road, the Anti-Yuan Shikai War broke out, followed by the endless fighting among the warlords in Sichuan. In 1924 Yang Sen ruled over Sichuan Province. He decided to change the government-run project into a joint one between government and businessmen, and recruited commercial shares. The largest shareholder was Zhang Luqiu from Jiangjin. So Zhang Luqiu was appointed as the vice inspector of the General Office of Chengdu-Guanxian Road and the office moved from Guanxian to Zhang Luqiu's house at Paotongshu Street in Chengdu. At the same time the merchant-operated Coach Company for Chengdu-Guanxian Road was established with a total number of nine coaches.

The former residence of Zhang Weijiong, a famous patriotic and democratic figure in Sichuan Province, was located on Paotongshu Street.

Zhang Weijiong (**1888 ~ 1972**), born in Dechang, Sichuan, joined the Chinese Revolutionary League while he was studying in Xi'an Army Middle School. Because he was a native of Dechang and Liu Wenhui's classmate in Baoding Military Academy, he had been serving as Liu Wenhui's important assistant for a long time. After the founding of the government of Xikang, he served as the secretary general in the provincial government. So long as Liu Wenhui was not in Xikang, he would act as the chairman of the provincial government, so he had been called "acting chairman" for a long time. He was a lifelong Buddhist and a man of high reputation in Xikang for his incorruptibility and self-discipline. On December 12th, 1949, he announced the Xikang uprising in Ya'an and accepted the leadership of the Central People's Government in Beijing according to the decision that Liu Wenhui had discussed with him (at that time Liu was not in Xikang, for he was holding the uprising in Pengxian County of Chengdu). The uprising was in a critical condition. On one hand, the armed force under his command was in a small number while the People's Liberation Army could not reach them in a short period of time. On the other hand, the KMT troops under the command of Tian Zhongtian were attacking Ya'an while Tang Ying, the former division commander under Liu Wenhui, also intended to defect. In this emergency moment, Zhang Weijiong, with a firm stand and calm perseverance, led the provincial personnel to retreat around Lingguan Village (today's Lingguan Township) to hold down the fort until the People's Liberation Army came into Ya'an. His action was highly praised by the Party and the people, so he was elected as the vice chairman of the People's Government of Xikang Province. After the merger of Xikang and Sichuan, he served as the vice mayor of Chengdu, the vice governor of Sichuan Province and the chairman of the Sichuan Branch of the Revolutionary Committee of the Chinese Kuomintang.

Shangye Street and Shiye Street

Located in the former imperial city, the original name of the Shangye Street is Vice-general Hutong because the vice-general government was set up there in the Qing Dynasty. Under the Eight Banners Systems of the Qing Dynasty, the supreme office of each banner is called "general" which is usually taken by a prince concurrently, and the vice officer is called "vice-general". In fact, among the officers and soldiers of the Eight Banners garrisons throughout the country, the vice-general is the highest officer of local officers and soldiers, and his position is subordinate to the garrison general. It was during the reign of Emperor Qianlong that the government of the garrison general began to be set up in Chengdu. Therefore, this government ranked first in the local government system of Manchu City in the early Qing Dynasty, and ranked second later in Manchu City of Chengdu in the mid-Qing Dynasty. In the Republican era, a special business school was set up in the place where the former vice-general government was located. Therefore, this *hutong* was called Shangye Street in that period.

The special business school did not open for a long time. According to predecessors' recollections, a brigadier in the Sichuan army forcibly married a maid as his concubine, but the maid had always loved Jin Can, a student in the school, and they still kept contact after marriage. Then, the brigadier arrested Jin Can on charges of rape and tortured him. Jin Can refused to admit the crime and accused the brigadier of forcibly occupying maid with the help of his alumni, which shocked the public at that time. The military flagrantly shot Jin Can on the Xijiaochang, causing the teachers and students to protest in all kinds of ways, but the school was then closed by the military, and all the teachers and students were driven out. Since then, the school has not been reopened. In 1931, Chengdu Branch of Inspirational Community was established on the site of the older school. Founded by Chiang Kai-shek in Nanjing in 1929, this community aimed to strengthen the internal ties among the top military and political personnel of Chiang Kai-shek's clique through cultural activities, and later has established branches in all major cities. Actually, it was a liaison office and a high-class guest house for senior members of the KMT's military, government, police and spy circles. In the period of the War of Resistance Against Japanese Aggression, a building designed by the renowned architect Yang Tingbao was built here. It was the only palace-style building in Chengdu in the Republican period, (today's Jinshan Hotel on East Zhongshan Road in Nanjing is the headquarters building of Nanjing Inspiration Community in the Republican period, which was also designed by Yang Tingbao. Therefore, the building of Chengdu Inspiration Community designed by him later is very similar to that of Nanjing Inspiration Club in architectural style except for the smaller scale.) and was used as the base for the U. S. China Relief Military Advisory Group as well as the guest house for USA troops stationed in Chengdu. Members of the famous Flying Tigers (i. e the American Volunteer Group established by Chen Nade) used to live here when they had holidays by turns, and the vice president Wallace once met with them in this building. In June 1941, the famous American writer and Nobel Prize winner Ernest Hemingway came to Chengdu with his wife as a reporter to learn about the situation of American aid to China. He also lived in this building and wrote down his impressions of Chengdu (the most interesting record is the camel caravan walking on the streets of Chengdu). The building still stands today. It has been in existence ever since and has served as the office of the Sichuan Provincial Committee of the CPC since the founding of the P. R. C.. Sichuan revolutionary predecessor Zhang Xiushu once summed up the history of the commercial street: "This street was established in the early Republic of China. Neighbors gave the name Shangye Street. It was once a mansion to welcome guests from afar during the War of Resistance Against Japanese Aggression, but is now used as the command post of the provincial party committee."

The Mansion of Inspirational Community. Photo by Yang Xianfeng.

In the period of the War of Resistance Against Japanese Aggression, the Chengdu branch of the Press Office of the American embassy in China was set up in the Youth Club on Shangye Street for a long period (initially inside the youth association on Chunxi Road, but later moved to Xiyu Street). Forster, director of the office, was an underground member of the Communist Party of America, so all the staff he employed such as Wang Jun were underground members of the CPC or progressive youth who took advantage of their position in the Press Office of the American embassy in China to do a lot of useful work in boosting the anti-fascist war and in promoting the ideas of the Communist Party of China. For example, Mao Zedong's book *On Coalition Government* was spread throughout Chengdu by them.

Opposite the provincial party committee office on Shangye Street, there was an excavation site of the Chengdu boat-coffin complex of the Warring States period, which was surrounded by a greenbelt and once shocked the archeological circle of the whole country.

The boat coffin is a special burial form in the ancient Bashu area, which carves the whole huge wood into a hollow boat, and places the dead and its funeral articles inside the boat. Since the founding of P. R. C. , boat-coffin burials have been found in many places of Sichuan Province and since the Reform and Opening-up, boat coffins, which belong to the middle and later periods of the ancient Shu state (equivalent to the Spring and Autumn and Warring States period of the Central Plain), have been found in the construction sites of the areas such as Qingyang Community, Fuqin Community, Baiguolin Community, and Shirenba when Chengdu was engaged in developing residence communities. On July 29th, 2000, the provincial party committee tried to rebuild its canteen and planned to build a basement for food storage. In the process of digging down, the site of the unprecedented oversize boat-coffin burial was discovered. In a 30-meter-long and 20-meter-wide giant shaft grave, there are 17 boat coffins all made of giant nanmu, the largest of which is 18. 8 meters long and 1. 7 meters in diameter, with many sleepers under it, thus is the king of the boat coffins in our country and all around the world. Inside the coffin, exquisite lacquer ware, pottery, bronze ware, the wooden frame used to display chime bells and the mallet used to strike chime bells were also found. Unfortunately, the bronze chime bells had been stolen by tomb robbers as early as the Han Dynasty. Relics of a large wooden structure have also been found above the grave. According to the preliminary study, this site is probably the royal cemetery of King Kaiming in the ancient Shu state. This site, together with Sanxingdui Site and Jinsha Site in the ancient Shu state, is regarded as one of the three most important discoveries in the ancient Shu civilization so far as well as the most important archaeological discoveries in downtown Chengdu (According to the detection, there must be hidden underground treasure around the giant grave, which remains to be excavated in the future). The Chengdu boat-coffin burial complex on Shangye Street has already been listed among the important heritage sites under state protection and the largest boat coffin museum of our country will be built to protect the original site according to the decision of the department concerned.

The excavation site of the boat-coffin burial on Shangye Street, 2000. Photo by Li Xucheng.

The Shiye Hutong adjacent to Shangye Street was the former Gantang Hutong in Manchu City. The term Gantang originates from *The Book of Songs · The Revered Shao Gong's Inspection to the South · Gantang* in which the famous scholar Zhuxi explained as follows: "The Revered Shao Gong went to the south to propagate the policy of King Wen of the Zhou Dynasty (1046 – 256 BC) and took a rest under Gantang, a birchleaf-pear tree. His descendants loved Shao Gong and thus also loved this type of tree." Therefore, later generations used the term "Gantang" to refer to the policy of benevolence implemented by local officials in favor of the people. In the Qing Dynasty, there was an official school of Eight Banners, which was a place to train the children of Eight Banners, so this street was named after the very exquisite term Gantang. In the sixteenth year during the reign of Emperor Qianlong (1751), the first official school in the imperial city called "Chengdu Official School for Eight Banners" was set up on this street (Before long, the second Official School for Eight Banners was opened in Baojia Alley, and in 1871 the two schools merged, just leaving the one on Shiye Street). In the early years of the Republic of China, a women's industrial institute was opened on the original site of the Official School for Eight Banners, so this street was renamed Shiye Street then.

In 1917, Xu Zixiu, a celebrity in the cultural circle of Chengdu and one of the Five Old Seniors and Seven Sages, initiated and raised money to rebuild the Temple of Six Scholars, also known as the Liugong Temple, on the north side of Shiye Street (it was originally built on West Wenmiao Street) to sacrifice the six famous scholars of the Song Dynasty in Sichuan: Fan Zhen, Fan Zuyu, Zhang Shi, Li Daochuan, Wei Liaoweng and Qiao Ding. Liugong Temple was originally built next to Jiangdu Temple and its initial construction date is unknown. (the six scholars of sacrifice before were Li Bing, Wen Weng, Lian Fan, Zhang Yong, Zhao Bian and Cui Yuzhi.) Due to various reasons, it was difficult to maintain the temple and soon it was abandoned. However, this is the largest temple built for Sichuan cultural sages with the centralized resources in modern cultural history of Chengdu (In the school of the late Qing Dynasty and the early Republic of China, the Temple of Four Scholars was once built to sacrifice four scholars such as Fan Zhen, Fan Zuyu, Zhang Shi and Wei Liaoweng). The brief introduction to the six Sichuan sages enshrined in the Temple of Six Scholars is as follows:

Fan Zhen (1008 ~ 1089), born in Chengdu, the famous politician and historian in the Song Dynasty, participated in the revision of the *New Book of Tang* and *Archives of Emperor Renzong of the Song Dynasty*. He once became a member of the Imperial Hanlin Academy as well as the Duanming Hall and was recognized as the duke of Prefecture Shu.

Fan Zuyu (1041 ~ 1098), born in Chengdu, the famous historian in the Song Dynasty, wrote the *Mirror for Tang History* and the *Research on Emperor System*. He was one of the major assistants who helped Sima Guang revise the *History as a Mirror*. He served as the assistant minister of the Ministry of Rituals and the governor of Shanzhou.

Zhang Shi (113 ~ 1180), born in Mianzhu, the famous scholar of the Southern Song Dynasty (1127 − 1279 AD), is known as one of the "Three Sages in the Southeast of China" together with Zhu Xi and Lü Zuqian. Known as Mr. Nanxuan, he had lectured in Yuelu Academy for many years and was the main founder of Huxiang School. He also served as the assistant minister of the Ministry of Personnel, the governor of Jiangling, and the Editor of the Right

Literary Hall.

Li Daochuan (1170 ~ 1217), born in Jingyan, the famous scholar of the Southern Song Dynasty, took the research on later school of Zhu Xi as his duty. He also severed as the governor of Zhenzhou, the tea-salt affairs managing officer of Jiangdong Province.

Wei Liaoweng (1178 ~ 1234), born in Pujiang, the famous scholar of the Southern Song Dynasty, the founder the chief teacher of Heshan Academy. Known as Mr. Heshan, he was the main representative of Sichuan academic in the Southern Song Dynasty. He also severed as the director of the Ministry of Rituals, the acting director of Privy Council, and the grand secretary of Zizheng Hall.

Qiao Ding (the birth and death date is unknown), born in Fuling, the famous scholar of the Southern Song Dynasty, once followed Cheng Yi to study *The Book of Changes*, and later lived in seclusion on Mount Qingcheng to give lectures and teach students, and was called "Master Qiao" by the people of Sichuan. The saying "Yi learning in Shu", which is still in circulation today, is closely related to his impartation of Yi learning in Bashu.

The forerunner of the Shiyejie Primary School (now the Campus of Paotongshu Primary School on Shiye Street) is No. 3 Public Primary School, which was founded in 1904 on Zhijishi Street and moved to Binsheng Street in 1905 at first, then to Shiye Street in 1906, and was renamed Sanying Primary School in 1909. Sanying Primary School was so famous because it was the place where the representatives of Sichuan Military Government and Manchu and Mongolia held an important negotiation which realized the peaceful transfer of government to solve the issue of Manchu without violence (for relevant situation, see "Tongren Road") and greatly reduce damages that may arise. What calls for special attention is that Sanying in the school name does not mean "three heroes" but is the counterpart Mandarin transliteration of Manchu words "shan" (kindness) and "mei" (beauty). To interpret the meaning of the school name, the Manchu scholar Wu Si'an once erected a monument which was set up in Shiyejie Primary School but was ruined in the year 1960.

In April 1926, the Communist Party of China founded its first local association, and

Chengdu Special Branch which was set up in the home of Zhong Shanfu opposite the Shiye Hotel. The periodical *Spark* of this branch was also edited there. Zhong Shanfu was the earliest member of the youth league and the communist party in Chengdu and took charge of the labor movements of the whole city at that time.

On January 28th, 1926, the first bus company in Chengdu history, Huada Bus Company, was set up on Shiye Street. This company was actually founded by He Jiamo, an overseas student who returned from France. He persuaded his father He Yuyi and a friend of his father's Hu Youxin to jointly raise funds to establish Huada Bus Company, and invited Deng Xihou, the famous general of Sichuan Army who was a fellow of He Yuyi, to serve as the nominal chairman of the board. He Jiamo bought the complete set of fittings from Shanghai, shipped them back to Chengdu and assembled them into seven 1. 5-ton Ford cars, which had 20 seats in wooden compartments (people in Chengdu at that time called the cars "walking foreign-style houses" because the wooden compartments looked like small houses and this metaphor had been popular in Chengdu for a long time). Huada Bus Company designed the following bus routes: from the old East Gate to the Old West Gate, from the North Gate to the South Gate, from the Front Gate of Commercial Area to Shiye Street, and from the Back Gate of Commercial Area to East Intersection of Huaishu Street. After training drivers, the company officially opened on January 28th, 1926. Since the streets at that time were too narrow and the cars could not move easily, it was easy to cause traffic accidents. Some conservatives applied to Liu Xiang, the ruler of Chengdu at that time for the prohibition order against cars, claiming that cars were too noisy, too fast and would affect the appearance of the city and frighten the old people. Thus, Liu Xiang prohibited all the cars on the ground that cars may hurt people like tigers. At that time, a man named Hou Youpo wrote a *Bamboo Branch Verse* titled "*Cars*", which reflected Chengdu citizens' disgust and resistance against this new thing "City Tiger":

> Myriads of hibiscuses grow over the wall,
> Out with an old idea, in with a new thought.
> Living in a city just like living in a mountain,
> You can hear the "tigers" ceaselessly roar.

A scholar wrote in a letter to the authorities: "The city is only ten square *li*, what urgent things need to be done so hastily? Besides, those who ride in such cars are curious about the car itself. Once they start driving the car at a high speed, they will kill and injure many people just because of their pleasure. Pedestrians feel frightened when they walk, as if they face an abyss..." Pullers of rickshaws all over the city also blocked the cars, throwing stones and tiles at the sight of them. Confronted with this situation, the municipal authorities banned buses from running in the city, leaving only one route from Chunxi Road to Qingyang Temple via the South Gate, and charging each passenger one mint-made copper. So, another *Bamboo Branch Verse* reads:

> The easy transportation has been talked about years,
> Now, cars running in Sichuan is a sight to behold.
> With only one copper coin that you offer,
> It takes you to Qingyang Temple from Chunxi Road.

Even so, it was not tolerated by the old guard; someone continued to complain to the government. Huada Company had to change this route into a completely out-of-town route, from Liuyin Street to Qingyang Temple, specifically for the flower festival. After the end of the flower festival, the company was forced to stop operation, and had to be changed to operate the long-distance route from Chengdu to Xinjin. Due to poor roads and few passengers, Chengdu's first car company only lasted until 1927 when it had to close down because of heavy losses. Until the War of Resistance Against Japanese Aggression, the Chengdu Bus Company, a joint venture between government and business, was established at the end of 1942 due to the increasing population of Chengdu, with 12 cars using wood charcoal and two bus routes was set up: one from Shahe Store to Chadianzi; and another from Hongpai Tower to Sima Bridge. But less than a year later, the company had to be closed due to the losses caused by the harassment of soldiers and rogues. In 1947, the company once restored its business with seven cars and only one operation route from Shahe Store to Chadianzi. Unfortunately, the company went out of business completely just more than a year later. It was not until July 1st, 1952, several years after the founding of the P. R. C. that Chengdu started to develop more and more perfect public transportation.

At the west end of Shiye Street, Chen Zhiqian, a famous Chinese public health expert (who was then the director of the Sichuan Health and Experiment Office), established the Sichuan Infectious Diseases Hospital during the War of Resistance Against Japanese Aggression, with Dr. Du Shunde, who had studied in the United

States, as the director. This was the first professional infectious disease hospital in Chengdu and was later moved out of the city. Its original site was converted into a maternal and child health hospital, and in 1950 it was again converted into the second maternal and child hospital in Chengdu. After many times of expansion, the hospital on the original site has become one of the largest maternal and child health care hospitals in Chengdu up to now.

Niangniangmiao Street

Located to the north of today's Dacisi Road and the east of West Shuyuan Road, East Shuyuan Road used to be called Niangniangmiao Street which originated from the Guangsheng Hall on this street, and the hall also had the name of Niangniang Temple.

The deity enshrined in Guangsheng Hall was the Goddess of Fertility who blessed women to have more children and wished them to give birth to sons and daughters smoothly, so she was very much respected in ancient China. In Sichuan, she was also called Songzi Goddess. Just as the *Bamboo Branch Verse* in the Qing Dynasty reads:

> Behind Daci Temple stands the Guangsheng Hall,
>
> Where deities bless you to conceive the best of all.
>
> You may tell your love affairs and make a wish,
>
> For the deity herself is a woman caring for the all.

In ancient times, the Goddess of Fertility was a folk deity with various forms of personification such as the Queen Mother, the Heavenly Princess (i. e. Mazu), the Empyrean Profound Woman, the Goddess Mount Taishan (also known as Goddess Bixiayuanjun) as well as the famous Songzi Goddess, etc. There were also many temples which enshrined the Goddess of Fertility. Many of these temples and even some Guandi Temples house the Goddess Hall inside. Since the Guangsheng Hall no longer existed, it was not clear how many Goddesses of Fertility used to be enshrined in Guangsheng Hall at Niangniangmiao Street.

There used to be another saying among people in Chengdu: The deity enshrined in Niangniang Temple was not the Goddess of Fertility but the Goddess of Emperor, who was the wife of the Prince Liu Chen of the North Land of Shu Han.

The regime of Shu Han in the Three Kingdoms period began to decline after the death of Zhuge Liang. One of the main reasons was that the young emperor Liu Shan had done nothing positive for the country. Liu Shan was Liu Bei's unworthy son, "a black sheep of his family" called by later generations. When the country was besieged by Wei Army, Liu Shan opened the gate to surrender to the enemy. He not only went to Luoyang to beg for the enemy's mercy, but also enjoyed food and amusement there, leaving the long-lasting notorious reputation of "being too delighted to be homesick". Liu Shan had seven sons in total and five, of whom Liu Cong died young and only six grew up. When the Wei army attacked, five of the sons raised their hands and surrendered with Liu Shan. Only Liu Chen, who was granted the title of the Prince of the North Land, resolutely refused to surrender. According to *The Spring and Autumn Annals of Han and Jin Dynasty* cited by the *History of the Three Kingdoms · the History of Shu · the Biography of the King*, when Liu Shan decided to surrender, "the Prince Liu Chen was so angry that he said, 'If we are weak and unjustified, we will fail and suffer, but we are not, so, all of us have to fight to win or die for our country to repay the late emperor.' But Liu Shan did not listen to him. Finally he sent the imperial jade seal to the enemy (i. e. the seal stands for the sovereignty of the country). On the same day, Liu Chen burst into tears, killed his wife and sons and then committed suicide in the Zhaolie Temple (the predecessor of Wuhou Temple which was built to enshrine Liu Bei, the founding emperor of Shu). At this, all people at present cried bitterly." In ancient times, the a man who decided to commit suicide must kill his wife first, which was regarded as an action that "all the family members commit suicide" to protect them from being humiliated by the enemy. As a result, this heroic action of Liu Chen as well as his martyred wife have long been respected by later generations.

As for the Niangniang Temple, we have to refer to another Niangniang Temple and Niangniangmiao Street in Chengdu history.

On the back of today's Wenshu Monastery there is the Ximadao Street. At No. 50 of this street stands a common folk warren which used to be a Niangniang Temple and was also called Guangsheng Hall at that time. Sun Zhixing, a female Taoist of Quanzhen School, became a nun here at the age of seven until her death in 2006 at the age of 86. Today, her disciple Chen Liqing still guards the seven-star lamp in a small room (once the Sanguan Hall of the Niangniang Temple) and continues to burn incense of the Niangniang Temple. Beating bells and drums with her Taoist friends, they worship the statue of the Prince Liu Chen and his wife Cui. After the restoration of the Niangniang Temple on September 16th, 2008, a memorial tablet in front of Cui was put up wrote that "the Goddess with Her Family Name Cui, the Princess of the North Land".

The Niangniang Temple at 50 Ximadao Street, 2009. Photo by Lin Li.

On the basis of my survey on the Goddesses in two Niangniang Temples above, I regard them as the Goddesses of Fertility rather than the empresses. Sun Zhixing recalled that there used to be 29 halls in the Niangniang Temple on Ximadao Street, such as Sanqing Hall, Zhenwu Hall, the Guanyin Hall, Doulao Hall and Huangjing Hall. The Niangniang Hall was just one of them at that time. At the annual "Goddess of Happiness Fair", two statues made of ginkgo wood were brought down from the shrine, washed, dressed in beautiful clothes, and carried along the streets in sedan chairs, which was called "the honor guard for goddess's outing". *The General Survey on Chengdu* in the late Qing Dynasty said that "according to the local custom, both Yanqing Temple and Niangniang Temple in the provincial capital should perform plays to to pay tribute to the goddess [this is what Chengdu people call "the Goddess of Happiness Fair", which used to be held every year until the founding of the P. R. C.. In recent years, the parade of "You Xi Shen Fang" (going to the location of the God of Happiness to pray for peace and good luck) is held in Wuhou Temple on the first day of the first month of the first month. Zhuge Liang is regarded as the God of Happiness, and this was quite different from the previous "Goddess of Happiness Fair". Everyone scrambled to touch the "God of Happiness Monument" in Sanyi Temple to pray for more happy events that year]. At the beginning of the fair, people enjoy their banquet. Wood statues of young boys and girls were then thrown into the crowd of people. The person who has grabbed the statue would play drums, hold colorful flags and umbrellas, light candles and fire crackers, and then place the statue inside the decorated pavilion. This scene is more bustling than that when one witnesses the birth of his own son". Judging from this, we can make sure that these two Niangniang Temples above must be the ones which enshrined the Songzi Goddess. However, Chengdu people respected the Prince Liu Chen so much that they regarded the Niangniang Temple as the one dedicated to Liu Chen's wife. This was a noteworthy folk phenomenon and a manifestation of the popular will of Chengdu people to respect loyals and martyrs. On the third day of the third lunar month in 2010, the traditional "Boy Fair" was resumed in the Niangniang Temple on Ximadao Street, where the statues to be snagged are replaced by the "boy statues" made of cloth about the size of red dates or peanuts.

In today's Liubei Hall inside the Wuhou Temple reconstructed during the Qing Dynasty, apart from the statue of Liu Bei, only the statue of the Liu's royal family members was enshrined. Although Liu Shan has been emperor of Shu for many years, he was not among them in the hall. It is said that the statue of Liu Shan was enshrined once a time, but was spit on and damned so that it was finally dismantled.

It is also worth mentioning that Comrade Deng Xiaoping has been to the Wuhou Temple for five times. He came the third time in 1963 the third time with other central leaders. He said to all the escorts that "Liu Bei's son is not good, but his grandson is good and the three generations of the descendants of Zhuge Liang are all good." The good grandson mentioned by Deng Xiaoping just refers to Liu Chen.

There was no Shangye Back Street in the past. It was established after the demolition of a small street on Niangniangmiao Street, as well as most part of the former Huangwa Street and a small part of Changfa Street during the urban renewal after the founding of the P. R. C.. This Niangnaing Street was originally called Jishan Hutong or Yuying Hutong on the east entrance, of which a Niangniang Temple was built to enshrine the famous Songzi Goddess.

Yang Angong, the main leader of Sichuan Province in the early developing stages of the CPC, had been living at 24 Niangniangmiao Street from 1921 to 1924. On January 12th, 1924, he and Wu Yuzhang initiated the "Youth Communist Party of China", and announced its establishment here. He also founded the official newspaper *Chi Xin Review* and carried out a lot of revolutionary activities. The Youth Communist Party of China was not a real party organization of the CPC, but a local revolutionary group taking Marxism as its guiding ideology to seek the road of Chinese revolution. Yang Angong and Wu Yuzhang did not know that the CPC had been established in

Shanghai, but they believed that there should be a Marxist political party in Sichuan. As Wu Yuzhang was too old to join the established China Communist Youth League in Chengdu, they decided to found the Youth Communist Party of China. However, when Yang and Wu soon got in touch with the CPC in Shanghai and Beijing respectively, they disbanded it immediately.

Yang Angong (1898 ~ 1927), born in Tongnan, studied Marxism and took part in the patriotic movement during his overseas study in Japan at an early age. Being arrested and sentenced by the Japanese police for supporting the May 4th Movement, he returned to Chengdu to carry out revolutionary activities with Wu Yuzhang, Liu Bocheng and others after he was set free. In September 1924, he joined the CPC and served as the secretary of Chongqing Prefectural Committee of the Communist Youth League. In 1926, he became the secretary of Chongqing Prefectural Committee of the CPC. Together with Liu Bocheng, he planned and led the Luzhou Uprising and Shunqing Uprising. On April 6th, 1927, he died heroically at Futu Pass in Chongqing.

Yang Angong (first from right), Liao Huaping (second from right), Tong Yongsheng (second from left) and Wu Yuzhang in Chengdu, 1922. Photo by Party History Research Office of Chengdu Municipal Party Committee of CPC.

Yang Angong, with the original name Yang Shangshu, was the fourth brother as well as the revolution guider of Comrade Yang Shangkun. (Under Yang Angong's guidance, six members of his family joined the CPC.) Comrade Yang Shangkun came to Chengdu in 1921 when he was 14 years old. He first studied in the primary school affiliated to Chengdu Higher Normal College and was admitted to the attached high school of the same college in 1922, where he participated in revolutionary activities. After graduating in 1925, he went to Chongqing. During his stay in Chengdu, he stayed at his fourth brother's home at Niangniangmiao Street.

After the end of the War of Resistance Against Japanese Aggression, the KMT's largest spy organization, Chengdu Branch of the Secrecy Bureau of the Ministry of National Defense, was located at 38 Niangniangmiao Street. The decision and deployment of the "Shi'er Bridge Massacre" by KMT spies was made here on December 3rd, 1949 under the instruction of Mao Renfeng, the director of the Secrecy Bureau.

Zhazi Street

Located between Middle Changshun Street and Middle Tongren Road, Zhazi Street and West Zhazi Street used to be the same street which was cut off into two sections because of the expansion of the third guest house of the Sichuan Provincial Committee of CPC (now the Shiye Hotel).

Shuangzhazi Street lies on the west of the second section of Hongxing Road and the north of Buhou Street. The Zhongxin Street which has been mentioned before used to be Zhongzhazi Street.

In the Qing Dynasty, Zhazi Street used to be one of the *hutongs* in the Manchu City and was called Liren Hutong at that time because of the Liren Lane inside this *hutong*. After the founding of the P. R. C. , Liren Hutong was renamed Zhazi Street since the term "Hutong" was no longer used while the fence gate was reserved. Shuangzhazi Street was named after the two fence gates on the southern end of this street. This street was near the Fanku Street where the grain and money storehouse of the provincial government was located and both the fence gate of the government and the fence gate of the street were established there at the same time. So, the name of the street was given.

"Zhazi" is a word in Sichuan dialect and refers to the fence gate made of wood. In the Qing Dynasty, each street in Chengdu had a fence gate with a shed for night watchmen on its side. In the middle of the night, all the gates were closed and locked and the keys were kept by night watchmen so that residents who needed to enter or exit the gate in an emergency had to ask the watchman to open the lock. This was, in effect, a city-wide curfew, which had a positive effect on the stability of the social security. Since 1905, the police had been in charge of the social order of Chengdu, and the gates were no longer locked, so the gates gradually lost their function. In 1924, when Yang Sen was in charge of Sichuan Province, he adopted some "new policies" for municipal construction in Chengdu, one of which was to announce the abolishment of all gates in streets and lanes. But after that, whenever unrest and disorder took place in the city, the gates were rebuilt at both ends of the streets and alleys.

The last large-scale wave of fence gate construction in Chengdu took place in mid-

November 1949, close to the liberation of Chengdu. At this time, as the KMT army was losing its ground, the number of stragglers and disbanded soldiers as well as ruffians entering Chengdu was increasing. The commander of the Third Army of the KMY army, Shengwen, who had just come into Chengdu to serve as the commander of the Chengdu Defense General Command with a shaky foothold, only knew how to protect the safety of a few important figures of the KMT who had just arrived in Chengdu such as Chiang Kai-shek and was unable to control an increasingly chaotic social order. Under such circumstances, in order to protect the life and property safety of the people in the city, with the support of the underground organization of the CPC in Chengdu, Qiao Zengxi, the deputy commander of the "Chengdu People's Self-Defense Corps", who had participated in the peripheral organization of the Communist Party of China with the name of "New Democracy Practice Society", mobilized the city's citizens to contribute money and efforts (note: the "Chengdu People's Self-Defense Corps" was a local people's armed force composed of people who were not away from their work. Its main responsibility was to maintain local public security. With a total of more than 30,000 members and more than 4,000 long and short guns, this force was divided into 14 regions with 147 households and was led by Mayor Leng Yindong, who also received the guidance from the CPC's underground organization in Chengdu). As a result, wooden fence gates were erected at all the entrances of the streets, alleys and gaps of the city walls within a dozen of days. Strangers who did not live on their own streets were questioned when entering or exiting the gate. At the entrance of important streets, wooden barricades with three legs and sandbags were placed. This measure played an important role in increasing the sense of security of the citizens and preventing stragglers and disbanded soldiers as well as ruffians from entering Chengdu. The KMT leaders, including Chiang Kai-shek, Gu Zhutong, and Sheng Wen, believed that this measure would lead to the separation of military and political forces in the city, which would thus affect the deployment of troops, so they ordered the demolition of the gates three times. However, as a result of the covert resistance of Leng Yindong, Qiao Zengxi and others, together with the apparent and secret resistance of the people in the whole city against this order, the barricades in the streets and alleys of Chengdu remained in place until December 27th, 1949, when the spearhead of People's Liberation Army entered the city. From then on, the people of Chengdu could no longer see the fence gates.

Wu Yu, a famous modern scholar in China, lived in Chengdu for the longest time in the former residence at 50 Zhazi Street, and named it "Wisdom House". Wu Yu and his wife Zeng Lan also died here (Wu Yu's another former residence in Chengdu is located on the back street of Back Wenmiao Street).

Wu Yu (**1872 ~ 1949**) , born in Xinfan, was admitted into the Zunjing Academy in 1891 but was more interested in the new learning from the West and was known as " the first person who advocated new learning in Chengdu ". After studying in Japan in 1905 and returning to Chengdu in 1907 , he published a series of commentaries and articles opposing Confucius and Confucianism, attacking the despotism, and openly suing his father over family problems, therefore, he was called "the sinner against Confucianism" and "the scum among the scholars" by conservatives. He was expelled from the education

Young WuYu

circles by the Sichuan Education General Association, and an arrest warrant was issued by Wang Renwen, the governor whose responsibility was to secure Sichuan. So, he had to take refuge in the country. After the Xinhai Revolution, he was very active in the press and education circles in Chengdu, and published a large number of articles that struggled against feudal ethics in the magazine of *New Youth* and other publications and shocked the whole country. These articles shone well in the south with those of Chen Duxiu in the north, and Hu Shi praised him as "the old hero who attacked the Confucian Store in Sichuan with only one hand" (note: In many articles which introduced Wu Yu, this sentence, which could be found in the preface written by Hu Shi for the *Selections of WuYu*, was often miswritten as "the person who beat the Confucian Store" and the word "beat" was quite different from the word "attack"). The most influential one was the article "Man-eating Ethics" published in *New Youth*, Volume 6, No. 6 in 1919, which had an unprecedented influence on the whole country together with Lu Xun's *Diary of a Madman*. In 1921, he went to Beijing and taught at universities such as Peking University and China University. In 1925, he returned to Chengdu and taught in Chengdu University, Sichuan University and other universities. He still persisted in his academic views against Confucius and Confucianism, and opposed the KMT authorities' educational policy of worshiping Confucius and advocating the reading of Confucian classics. As a result, he was threatened by a spy who sent him a revolver bullet. In his later years, Wu Yu retired and lived in his home for most of the time and became depressed. After the outbreak of the "Southern Anhui Incident" in 1941, he wrote a poem titled "*Reading Lian Po's Biography*", which accused the KMT's reactionaries of their crimes. He died of illness on April 27th, 1949 and was buried with his wife Zeng Lan in Gongjianian, Xinfang.

Zeng Lan

Zeng Lan (**1875 ~ 1917**), the wife of Wu Yu, was also a memorable figure in modern cultural history of Chengdu. As a famous poetess, novelist and calligrapher and painter, she was born in Front Wenmiao Street and lived next to Wu Yu. She was the childhood sweetheart of Wu Yu, was married to him at the age of 15 to become the supporter of WuYu who advocated new learning and rebelled against the old ethical codes in his life. In 1912, she served as the chief writer of the first women's newspaper *Women's Circle* sponsored by Sun Shaojing in Chengdu, and wrote a series of articles advocating women's rights, some of which were published in the famous magazine *New Youth* (Her family was one of the only five subscribers of *New Youth* in Chengdu). She was an important promoter who led Sichuan women's circle to step on the social stage. For example, thanks to the appeal of *Women's Circle*, the Provisional Council of Sichuan Province set up a conference room especially for female journalists and awarded the first admission ticket to Zeng Lan. Her vernacular novel *An Unrightful Couple*, which was one of the earliest modern novels in China (three years earlier than *Diary of a Madman*), first published in the *Book of Leisure and Entertainment* in Chengdu, was then reprinted in the following year by the famous *Novel Monthly* in Shanghai. The couple and their two daughters, Wu Kai and Wu Huan, all could compose poems, and all the four members of the family joined the famous literary association "Southern Association", and were entrusted by Liu Yazi, the leader of the "Southern Association", as the liaisons of "Southern Association" in Sichuan, which became an interesting story on everybody's lips in the cultural history of Chengdu (at that time, there were about 20 people who participated in the Southern Association in Sichuan). Many researchers believed that Wu Yu's depression and even decadence in his later years should be related to Zeng Lan's premature death and the lack of support. Zeng Lan wrote two preserved volumes of *Posthumous Manuscripts for the Room with Wisdom Arising from Peace* in her lifetime.

Wu Yu's former residence in Chengdu no longer exists, but the property "Wisdom House" he bought in 1938 on North Xinfanzheng Street in his hometown is still there and becomes the protected historic site of Xindu District.

After the end of the War of Resistance Against Japanese Aggression, the KMT's largest spy organization, the Bureau of Investigation and Statistics of the Military Council, changed its name into the Defense Ministry's Secret Service. The "Chengdu Branch in Chuan-Kang District" of the former Bureau of Investigation and Statistics of the Military Council was subsequently changed into Chengdu Branch of the Secret Service. It was the most important secret service in Chengdu area, and many criminal activities occurred in Chengdu before the founding of the P. R. C. were carried out by this branch at 44 Zhazi Street. On the night of January 13th, 1949, it was in the interrogation room of this branch that Pu Huafu, the main leader in charge of the underground Communist Party in western Sichuan, turned traitor and went over to the enemy.

In the Republican period, the private residence of Zhu Liangfu, who was known as the "God of Wealth with the Family Name Zhu", was located at Shuangzhazi Street. Inside the residence there was the largest private chrysanthemum garden in Chengdu. Known as the garden of Zhu Family, it had thousands of basins of chrysanthemum People who were not the relatives of Zhu Liangfu or scholars were not allowed to enter this garden. According to legends, the main method of breeding and fertilizing chrysanthemums in this garden was to bury an egg at the root of each chrysanthemum plant as the base fertilizer.

Xiaotong Alley

The half-section alley in Shaocheng was located to the south of Kuixinglou Street and to the east of Tongren Middle Road. This alley was called Renfeng Hutong in the Qing Dynasty and then renamed Xiaotong Alley. In the early years of the Republic of China, when the *hutongs* were renamed, this *hutong* was named Xiaotong Alley because it was as narrow as a corridor.

Xiaotong Alley, 1992. Photo by Chen Jin.

Zeng Xiaogu, the predecessor in China's modern cultural history, who was almost forgotten by today's people, once lived in Xiaotong Alley.

Zeng Xiaogu (**1873 ~ 1937**), born in Chengdu. He studied in Shandong and Beijing with his father at early age. In 1906, he won an official's scholarship and went to Japan to study abroad. Together with the famous scholar and artist Li Shutong (namely later the Master Hongyi), he was enrolled into the Tokyo Arts College and majored in Western painting. Together with Li Shutong, Tang Ken and others, he founded the Spring Willow Society, the first drama society in China. In February 1907, Zeng Xiaogu translated the famous play *The Lady of the Camellias* and played the role of Ya Meng's father in the public performance, which was the first modern drama performed in China. In June 1907, he wrote the play called *Black Slaves Appeal to Heaven*, based on the famous novel *Uncle Tom's Cabin* by Mrs. Stowe, and played the role of the slave's wife in the public performance. As China's first drama play, *Black Slaves Appeal to Heaven* was widely regarded as a symbol of the birth of modern drama in China. The famous dramatist Tian Han once said that Zeng Xiaogu's composition "opened the first page of the Chinese drama movement". In 2007, in order to commemorate the 100th anniversary of the birth of Chinese modern drama, Beijing People's Art Theatre and China National Theatre specially compiled and staged the drama "Searching for Spring Willow

The photo of Zeng Xiaogu (the right) in costume taken in 1906 when Zeng Xiaogu was organizing the Spring Willow Society in Japan together with Li Shutong.

Society". After graduating from the Tokyo Arts College in 1911 with the major in Western painting, Zeng Xiaogu spent one year studying Western painting as a postgraduate student (so he was also China's first postgraduate student studying Western painting), then he dropped out and returned to China. After living in Shanghai for a short time, he returned to Chengdu and served as a drawing professor in Chengdu Higher Normal School in 1915. He was the first teacher imparting Western painting in Chengdu as well as the first oil painter in Chengdu. He also established the "Spring Willow Drama Society" in Chengdu, which was the first drama society in Chengdu and even one of the first batches of drama societies in China. In 1918, he organized a group of middle school students from Chengdu County Middle School to perform the first modern drama play in Chengdu history (commonly known as the "improvisation drama" at that time), still based on the play *Black Slaves Appeal to Heaven*. From then on, he once served as the second curator of the General Knowledge Education Museum in Shaocheng Park (the first curator was Lu Zuofu, the founder of the museum) and made great contributions to cultural popularization. Zeng Xiaogu later worked as a middle school teacher and lived a poor life in his later years. He even rented out most parts of the single house at Xiaotong Alley called "the Mansion beside Mengming Lake", which has its own entrance and courtyard, to support the life of the whole family. His funeral expenses were even collected by some of his students, including Qu Yilin, a famous contemporary painter in Chengdu. The famous scholar once wrote an elegiac couplet which read: "Du Fu lived in troubled times while few appreciated Zheng Qian's three wonders". (Note: Zheng Qian, the famous painter in the Tang Dynasty, was good at poems, books and paintings, which were called "three wonders" by people at that time.) Zeng Xiaogu's poems were collected in the book *Poems of the Mansion beside Mengming Lake*, which was prefaced by his old friend Xie Wuliang and were spread up to now.

Huangwa Street

Located at the back of the today's Shangye Street, Huangwa Street used to be the Pine Hutong in the Manchu City. Two impoverished aristocrats once built their enclosure into the red wall with yellow tiles, which was rare at that time so that the street was called Huangwa Steet in the Republican period.

Huangwa Street, 2021 Photo by Zhang Xinan

Liu Yuan'an, an early and important leader of the Communist Party of China in Sichuan, once lived at Huangwa Street, and the office of the Chengdu Committee of the China's Socialist Youth League (also called Special League Branch) was set up in Liu Yuan'an's house before April, 1926.

Liu Yuan'an (1895 ~ 1930), born in Shanxi Province, grew up in Chengdu with his father since childhood. During the Xinhai Revolution, he joined the army. He was upright and sympathetic to the poor. In 1922, when he served as the magistrate of Fengdu County, he was dismissed by his warlord leader for punishing corrupt officials and abolishing exorbitant taxes and levies. However, the common people set a monument for him in

Liu Yuan'an

honor of his moral governance. After returning to Chengdu, he got acquainted with the forerunners of Sichuan proletarian revolution such as Wang Youmu, Yun Daiying, Wu Yuzhang, and began to study and propagandize Marxism on one hand and joined the revolutionary movement with the open identity of the secretary general of Sichuan Parliament on the other hand. He joined the Communist Party of China in 1925 and was appointed as the secretary of the Chengdu Committee of the China's Socialist Youth League at the end of the year, and the secretary of CPC Chengdu Special Branch in the following year. In 1927, he was transferred to Chongqing and served as the Secretary General of Sichuan Provincial Party Committee of CPC. In March 1928, after the sacrifice of Fu Lie, the secretary of the provincial committee, he was appointed as the acting secretary. Soon he went to Shanghai to report his work to the Central Committee and then to the Soviet Union to attend the Sixth National Congress of CPC, where he was elected as an alternate member of the Central Committee. At the end of 1928, he returned to Chengdu and served as a member of the standing committee and director of the Propaganda and Agitation Department in the new Provincial Party Committee. In June 1929, he was appointed as the Secretary of the Provincial Party Committee. On May 5th, 1930, he was arrested in Chongqing because of a traitor's informant. Warlord Liu Xiang sent Liu Yuan'an's relatives to persuade him to surrender, promising that he would be appointed as " dean" " director" and other senior officials. Confronted with such temptations, Liu Yuan'an remained unshaken. On May 7th, Liu Yuan'an died a heroic death.

In the summer of 1938, the secret office of Chengdu Municipal Party Committee of CPC once moved from Zhongxiao Alley to the second floor of a building on Huangwa Street, which was the temporary residence rented by Zhang Xuan, the director of the Propaganda Department of the Municipal Party Committee.

Hongqiang Alley

Similar to Huangwa Street, Hongqiang Alley also used to be a *hutong* in the Manchu City in the Qing Dynasty. It is located to the east of Upper Changshun Street and to the north of East Mapeng Street with the former name Puan Hutong or Jixiang Hutong. There used to be the Guandi Temple on this street with a red enclosure around, which became the special scenery of this street. Although the Guandi Temple no longer existed in the Republican period, the street was still renamed Hongqiang Alley.

Dandan noodles, the famous Sichuan snack, could be found almost everywhere today, but the most famous Dandan noodles in old Chengdu used to be found on the north side of the east end of Hongqiang Alley, which was moved from this alley to Tidu Street in 1956.

Hongqiang Alley, 1995 Photo by Chen Xianmin

Kuixinglou Street and Kuzi Street

The *hutong* in the Manchu City of the old Chengdu was called Guangming Hutong at first. It was also known as Kuixinglou Hutong in the Qing Dynasty because at the west end of this *hutong* there used to be the Guandi Temple inside where the Kuixing Pavilion was built later. When it came to the Republican period, this *hutong* was renamed Kuixinglou Street.

Kui (奎) Star was also called *Kui* (魁) *Star*. According to the official name of ancient Chinese astronomy, it should be named as Kui Constellation, which was one of the twenty-eight lunar mansions, comprising sixteen stars. These sixteen stars formed the shape which was similar to the strokes of a character such as bending, turning and hook, and were thus believed to be the god in charge of literary fortune in the eyes of ancient people. The imperial examinations in Tang and Song dynasties selected scholars depending on the results of the examinations about Five Classics (i. e. *the Book of Poetry*, *the Book of History*, *the Book of Ceremony*, *the Book of Changes* and *the Spring and Autumn Annals*). The person took the first place of each of the five examinations was called *Kuishou* (this is the origin of "Five Kuishou" that people shout in the drinking order when they drink and do Finger Guessing Game today.) The Chinese character "*Kui*" just came from the ancient people's worship of the Kui-star God in charge of literary fortune. Later, there were more myths about those who pass the imperial examinations are lucky ones because Kui-star God has ticked the name of the candidate using his red-inked writing brush. Therefore, there used to be Kui (奎) -star Pavilion, Kui (奎) -star Tower [sometimes called Kui (魁) -star Pavilion and "Kui (魁) -star Tower"] all over over country. These structures were dedicated to Kui-star God, the god of literary fortune, who would decide the fate of the people who took part in the imperial examination (the statue of Kui-star God is not a common sitting statue but a dynamical one who stands on the ground with a huge writing brush in hand ready to nominate the lucky person who would pass the examination.) Scholars of the past often went to these places to worship Kui-star God.

In the Qing Dynasty, a memorable archway called Liren Archway was built on Kuixinglou Street, with eight Chinese characters "*Liyou Renfeng*, *Tanhua Jidi* (里有仁风，探花及第)" (which means that there was an atmosphere of benevolence, so the scholar lived here could rank the third in the imperial examination). It was supposedly inscribed to honor the Tanhua (the scholar who ranked third in the imperial examination) from this *hutong*. However, there was no record of the Tanhua in documents, which remained a mystery in the local history of Chengdu.

In the past, Kuixinglou Street was also called Kuzi Street for the reason that the east end of Kuixinglou Street in the early Qing Dynasty was divided into two exits, just like the two legs of a trouser. (If you look carefully at a few maps leftover from the Qing Dynasty, you will find that there used to be more than one *hutong* with two exits like this, an unexplainable phenomenon.) In the Republican period, more and more houses were built on this street, so these two exits in the shape of two legs of a trouser were no longer seen.

Kuixinglou Street, 2021 Photo by Chen Ke

Wei Shizhen, a famous mathematician, had lived for a long time in the apartment he designed and built at 13 Kuixinglou Street.

Wei Shizhen (1895 ~ 1992), born in Peng'an, was admitted to the High School Affiliated to Sichuan Higher College in 1908 and thus became the classmate of Guo Moruo, Wang Guangqi, Zhou Taixuan, Li Jieren, Meng Wentong, etc. He was admitted into Shanghai Tongji Medical and Engineering College (the forerunner of Tongji University) in 1913 and joined the Young China Association in 1918. Later, he introduced people such as Zhang Wentian, Shen Zemin and Zong Baihua to join the Young China Association. (According to the materials I have studied, Wei Shizhen was the last member of the Young China Association to pass away). He studied abroad in Germany together with Wang Guangqi in 1920 and was the first Chinese student in the University of Gottingen known as the "Kingdom of Mathematics and Physics" at that time. After communicating with the leading scientist Einstein and getting his support, Wei Shizhen set up "*the Special Column for Relativity Theory*" in the monthly magazine *Young China* in 1923. Wei also published his two articles together with Einstein's reply to him, which played an important role in the

Wei Shizhen

earliest dissemination of relativity theory in China. In 1925, he got a doctoral degree from the University of Gottingen and became the first doctor in mathematics in Sichuan Province. During his study in the University of Gottingen, Wei Shizhen had also taught newly-arrived Zhu De and Sun Bingwen to learn German for nearly two years. The textbook he used was *the Communist Manifesto* (archived in the National Museum of China now) and Bukharin's *the ABC of Communism*. When Zhu De came to Chengdu in 1955, he met and entertained his old friend twice. After returning to China in 1925, Wei Shizhen had been teaching in various universities in Sichuan for a long time. He served as the dean of the College of Science of Chengdu University and the College of Science of Sichuan University. He was the founder of the subject of partial differential equations and theoretical mechanics in China, and a pioneer advocating that the arts and sciences should not be separated from each other. He also insisted that students should eat multivitamins. In Chengdu Institute of Science he founded in 1946 (The forerunner of this institute was the Chuankang College of Agriculture and Engineering he founded in 1939. Peng Yunsheng was appointed as a lecturer on classical literature, while Wu Tianxi lectured mainly on the general history of China. Later the Chengdu Institute of Science was merged into Sichuan University after the founding of the P. R. C. In 1949, he refused the invitation from the KMT authorities to go to Taiwan and chose to stay in Chengdu. He was not only one of the earliest mathematicians in modern China as well as the author of the first book of *Partial Differential Equations*, but also a scholar who had been studying philosophy for a long time. In 1937, he published an essay titled "*the Dialogue between Kant and Marx*". In 1958, he became the chief editor of the philosophy magazine "*Relativity Theory*", and in 1980 he wrote the book *"Discussion on Confucius"*. In 1984, the University of Gottingen awarded the "Special Commemorative Certificate for Millennium Jubilee Doctorate" to Wei Shizhen, in honor of his great contributions to the education and scientific research and the promotion of cultural exchanges between China and Germany, as he was the first Chinese to receive a doctoral degree from this university 60 years ago.

Changfa Street

This was a *hutong* in the Manchu City in the Qing Dynasty with the former name of Changfa Hutong and was renamed Changfa Street in the Republican period. Today, it is located to the east of Middle Changshun Street and to the south of Dongmen Street.

The name of Changfa Hutong came from a local legend. There used to be a nunnery where a long-haired Buddhist nun could not only foretell the harvest and failure of crops, but also ward off diseases and avoid evil spirits with each strand of her long hair. This was, of course, a legend expressing good wishes. On different versions of maps in the Qing Dynasty, we could see three different names of this *hutong*: Changfa (发) Hutong, Changfa (法) Hutong and Changling (陵) Hutong. As for the origin of the name of Changfa (发) Hutong, there were also two sayings: One saying was that there used to be a memorable archway named Fayu Archway. The other was that the name came from a line: "May auspicious and prosperous things often appear", which was used as an auspicious greeting in *The Book of Songs ·the Ode in Memory of Shang Dynasty ·Frequent Appearance of Auspicious and Prosperous Things*.

In May 1940, through the arrangement of the underground party organization of CPC, Zhou Enlai held a very important meeting with Pan Wenhua, the general of the Sichuan Army and the successor leader of the Liu Xiang's faction after Liu Xiang's death. It was at Qiao Yifu's private residence at 32 Changfa Street that the two sides reached a long-term united front relationship with the same voice and spirit. Since then, the Communist Party of China has sent Tang Wuyuan and other people to Pan's faction as liaisons. Nearly 20 underground party members of CPC had been sent to Pan's faction to hold various posts including Wang Daoyu and Su Aiwu as the consultants and Tian Yiping as the chief staff officer. All these works done by CPC in KMT controlled areas played a very important role during the later liberation of Chengdu.

Jixiang Street

Jixiang Street is the first small street south of Huaishu Street, between Tongren Road and Changshun Street. It used to be one of *hutongs* in the Manchu City in the Qing Dynasty with its original name of Tongshun Hutong as well as Jixiang Hutong. In the early years of the Republic of China, it was renamed New Alley and was later renamed Jixiang Street.

Jixiang Street, 1995 Photo by Yan Yongcong

In July 1919, the weekly newspaper *Sunday* presided over by Li Jieren was founded at 8 Jixiang Street by the Chengdu Branch of the Young China Association. Sun Shaojing was the manager and Li Jieren was the editor. *Sunday* was the first weekly newspaper in Chengdu whose main purpose was to propagate new ideas and criticize the old system. It advocated that "labor is sacred" and declared that socialism was "the lucky star of human beings". This newspaper had published important articles of Mao Zedong, Li Dazhao, Chen Duxiu, etc. It was one of the four major periodicals during the May 4th Movement along with *Weekly Review*, *Week Review* and *Xiangjiang Review*.

In 1946, the first accounting professional college in Sichuan Province was opened on this street, named Sichuan Accounting Vocational College, which was based on the original Accounting Special Course of Sichuan Education Institute. The college was founded in 1943 with Wang Yinchu as its first president and took the site of the Chengdu County Middle School on Qinglong Street as its own school site (at that time Chengdu County Middle School was dissolved and moved to the suburb). In 1946, this college was taken over by Yang Youzhi and moved to the special site on Jixiang Street.

Yang Youzhi (**1893 ~ 1971**), born in Nanjing. When studying business at Peking University, he became the excellent student of Ma Yinchu, the leading authority in the field of economy in our country. Yang came to Chengdu in 1938 and had been teaching in Sichuan University, West China University, Sichuan Institute of Finance and Economics and other universities until he passed away. He was the first professor teaching the Advanced Accounting in Sichuan, and his works such as *Accounting*, *Accounting*

Yang Youzhi

Outline, *Advanced Accounting*, *Advanced Statistics* and *Auditing* are considered to be authoritative works in the field of accounting in our country. He was also known as the "Grand master" of the accounting discipline in China and had trained countless professionals in his 52-year teaching career.

Also in 1946, Sichuan Kindergarten Normal College hosted by Lu Xiu, the famous preschool education expert, was opened at Jixiang Street. The site of this college was the mansion borrowed from Xiang Chuanyi, the chairman of the Sichuan Provincial Council.

Lu Xiu (**1896 ~ 1982**), female, born in Wuxi, Jiangsu Province, went to the United States for study in 1932, specializing in early childhood education, and received a master degree in preschool education from Columbia University. In 1934, she was married to Feng Hanji, the famous scholar and later the curator of the Sichuan Museum. After the nationwide outbreak of the War of Resistance Against Japanese Aggression, the couple returned to Sichuan where she devoted herself to the cause of infant education to spread the most advanced infant education ideas and methods from the West. She prepared and founded Chengdu Experimental Kindergarten at Chadianzi (and the kindergarten had the Infant Department which was very rare at that time). She also edited and published the magazine *Experiment on Infant Education*, and served as a professor in the Department of Housekeeping in West China University. Lu became the pioneer and guide of the experiment and exploration of modern infant education in the rear area of China at that time. After the founding of the P. R. C. , she continued to pay attention to infant education while serving as the deputy director of the Sichuan Women's Federation and the director of the Civil Affairs Bureau of Chengdu. Among all her deeds, what deserved our special attention is that the Home of Infants she founded on Old Road with her savings had totally fostered more than 100 infants including triplets, premature infants and frail infants. They all grew up here healthily, which made an outstanding contribution to the infant care career throughout the province and had a great impact on the whole country. In 1964, her former classmate Deng Yingchao came to the Home of Infants and was so impressed that she decided to donate her wages immediately. The Chengdu Experimental Kindergarten opened by her had undergone several changes and finally evolved into Chengdu Fourth Kindergarten located at today's Chadianzi. The former Infant Department has also evolved into today's Experimental Nursey of the Organizations Directly under Sichuan Provincial People's Government located at Xinnanmen (New South Gate). The Home of Infants she founded came to a close at the beginning of the "Cultural Revolution" in 1966.

Chengdu Experimental Kindergarten, 1940. Photo courtesy of Yang Xianfeng.

The mansion of Dai Jitao (the founding member of KMT) in Chengdu, was located in the middle of this street and the Chengdu Municipal Bureau specially set the door number of this mansion as " New No. 1 " at that time. After Dai Jitao committed suicide in Guangzhou, his corpse was carried back to Chengdu and was put into a coffin in this mansion.

Dongmen Street

The first section of the Yangxi Line, as is now known by Chengdu residents, used to be Dongmen Street. This street was the Wufu Hutong in the Manchu City in the Qing Dynasty and was renamed Dongmen Street because it was the *hutong* that passed through the east gate of the Manchu City.

There were five gates in the Manchu City in the Qing Dynasty with two on the east, among which the one on the north side was called Yingxiang Gate (inside the gate was Wufu Hutong and Changfa Hutong, and outside the gate was Yangshi Street and Wufu Street), the other on the south side was called Shoufu Gate (inside the gate was Citang Street and outside the gate was Xiyu Street). People in Chengdu usually called the two gates Big East Gate and Small East Gate. The east gate at the east entrance of Dongmen Street was the Big East Gate of the Manchu City.

Today's famous Chengdu No. 1 Orthopaedic Hospital is located at Dongmen Street. It was founded by Du Qiongshu and Guo Jun, the successors of the Dus' Orthopaedic Department. The forerunner of this hospital was the Western Urban District Orthopaedic Polyclinic located in Shizi Alley, and moved to Dongyu Street in the year of 1957. In 1959, it moved to Dongmen Street and was renamed Western Urban District Orthopaedic Hospital. Du Qiongshu himself was transferred to Sichuan People's Hospital at first and then to Sichuan Institute of Traditional Chinese Medicine.

Huaishu Street

Located between Changshun Street and Tongren Road, Huaishu Street was the former Huaishu Hutong in the Manchu City of the Qing Dynasty, which was renamed Huaishu Street. After the Reform and Opening-up, the road which started from Yangshi Street and led to the west exit of the city, was newly built with a project name "Westward Extension Line of Yangshi Street", known as Yangxi Line for short. After the completion of the new road, it was named in sections. From east to west, these sections were respectively named Dongmen Street, Huaishu Street, Yongling Road, West Fuqin Road, Shuhan Road, Shuxi Road and Xixin Avenue. This road became the main entrance of Chengdu-Guanxian Highway after the completion of the highway. As the informal project name of the Yangxi Line had long been widely spread, the formal name of Huaishu Street was replaced by the common name of the Yangxi Line and was less well known.

There used to be many old locust trees and even a forest of locust trees in Huaishu Hutong. Now only a few trees are left along with several old and tall ginkgo trees standing at the side of the busy street. Huaishu Street is the only street in the urban district of Chengdu with a few ginkgo trees on its main trunk road.

Huaishu Street, 1910. Photo by Wilson [Britain].

The private residence of Wu Junyi (1886 ~ 1961) was located at No. 34 on the west end of Huaishu Street. Wu Junyi was a famous jurist, the cousin of Wu Yu. He once served as a professor at Peking University, the dean of Chengdu University, the Secretary General and dean of Law School of Sichuan University. Xiang Zonglu, a famous scholar, had lived in the residence of Li Bingying on this street when he was in Chengdu from 1935 to 1941 (Li Bingying was also a famous scholar and served as the dean of the Chinese literature department of Sichuan University, Kwang Hua University, North Sichuan University and Sichuan Normal College).

Xiang Zonglu (**1895 ~ 1941**), born in Chongqing, was well-read when he was very young. He could recite the voluminous works such as *Selections from Zhao Ming* so that he was called " Xiang Bookcase " by people. When he studied in Tradition-Reserving Academy, he was Liao Ping's favorite disciple as well as his informal academic secretary. He had been serving as a professor at Chongqing University and Sichuan University for a long time before his death. During the War of Resistance Against Japanese Aggression,

Xiang Zonglu

he died at Fuhu Temple in Mount Emei during his tenure as the director of Chinese literature department of Sichuan University. Xiang Zonglu was a famous ancient literature scholar in Sichuan. He annotated more than ten kinds of literary and historical classics. Because he complied with the strict tradition of the previous scholars in Sichuan who were very cautious about writing books and establishing theories, he seldom published his research results in his lifetime. It was not until many years after his death that his works such as *Collation*, *the Correction of Shuo Yuan* (*Garden of Anecdotes*) , *the Epilogue of the Correction of the Book of Changes*, *the Notes and Collation on the General Structure of the Star Map in Han Dynasty* were edited and published by his disciples such as Qu Shouyuan and Wang Liqi.

In the Republican period, there were three famous literati and historians who died at an early age in Sichuan such as Liu Xianxin at the age of 36, Wu Fangji 36 and Xiang Zonglu 46.

East Mapeng Street and West Mapeng Street

East Mapeng Street and West Mapeng Street used to be two *hutongs*, the Rende Hutong and Guangde Hutong, adjacent to each other along the direction from east to west in the Manchu City. They used to be the places where the Manchu and Mongolian soldiers kept horses. A lot of bamboo and wooden horse sheds with few residents were built here. In the Republican period, the government no longer kept horses there and constructed several private houses so the street names were changed into East Mapeng Street and West Mapeng Street.

In 1912, Sichuan Foreign Language School moved to East Mapeng Street from Zhaozhongci Street and was renamed Sichuan Public Foreign Language Specialized School in 1914. In September 1919, Ba Jin, at the age of 15 and under the name of Li Yaotang, was admitted to the school together with his third elder brother, Li Yaolin. He had been studying in this school from tutoring courses to preparatory courses and then to undergraduate courses of French until the spring in the year of 1923 when he left Chengdu for France via Shanghai to study abroad. Ba Jin had been studying in his home school with a private tutor since childhood. Since he had never been to a primary school or a high school and was listed as an auditor, thus had no diploma. Despite of these, Sichuan Public Foreign Specialized Language School was the most important school that Ba Jin had attended as a teenager. It was in this school that he not only preliminarily mastered English, French and Esperanto (note: Ba Jin was one of the pioneers of the Esperanto Movement in our country), but also published his first article and his earliest batch of literary works, participated in a social struggle (a strike and petition movement against warlord Liu Cunhou) for the first time, joined a society for the first time, and edited a magazine for the first time. Therefore, Sichuan Public Foreign Specialized Language School played a very important role in Ba Jin's growth.

The former site of Sichuan Public Foreign Specialized Language School at Mapeng East Street in the 1960s.

Located on East Mapeng Street. later merged with Shude High School, Chengdu No. 1 Middle School is now called "Chengdu Shude Experimental High School". It used to be opened on the site of the former Sichuan Public Foreign Specialized Language School on which Sichuan First Normal College was also founded in 1914, and was then moved to Yandao Street in the year of 1919. Due to the fact that the forerunner of Chengdu No. 1 Middle School was the Sichuan Girls' High School founded on this site (Sichuan Boys' High School was opened at Wushitongtang Street at the same time), Chengdu No. 1 Middle School had been one of the only two girls' high schools in Chengdu for a long time since the founding of P. R. C. (another girls' high school was Chengdu No. 11 Middle School). Now both boys and girls are admitted to this school.

In the Republican period, a kind of bean paste and red tofu made by a housewife were sold in a house on the East Mapeng Street, which gained a good reputation and was known as "Madam Bean Paste".

Mapeng West Street, 2012 Photo by Yang Xianfeng

The former residence of Sun Zhen, the famous general during the War of Resistance Against Japanese Aggression, is inside the campus of today's Ximapengjie Primary School.

Jiaojia Alley

Jiaojia Alley was the Shangsheng Hutong in the Manchu City stretching from Upper Changshun Street in the east to Tongren Road in the west. It was renamed Jiaojia Alley in the Republican period because in this alley there used to be the residence of a Machu officer who changed his family name Esuli into the surname of Han as other Manchu people did in the late Qing Dynasty.

Jiaojia Alley, 1986 Photo by Zhang Xinan

When the Qing army entered the Shanhai Pass, the Manchu people all used their original Manchu surname (In Manchu language the first name is equivalent to the last name, both of which were called "Hala" and were deemed as the surname or family nor last name in Han language) such as Yehe Nara, etc. According to the customs of Manchu, Manchu men are called only by the first name rather than the last name, such as Nurhachi and Nalan Chengde. Influenced by the Han culture, some Manchu people adopted the first Chinese character of the translated name as their new family name, which was then called "substitute family names with first names". In light of this, some people even changed their Manchu family name into Han family name thoroughly. By the end of the Qing Dynasty, the majority of Manchu people had already changed their Manchu family name into Han family name, for example, Aisin

Gioro was changed into Jin (金) and Zhao (赵), Wanyan was changed into Wang (王) and Wang (汪), Guaerjia was changed into Guan (关) and Guan (管), Bur Jijite was changed into Bai (白) and Yin (尹). Therefore, the Esuli family in Chengdu changed their family name into Jiao (焦) and was called "Jiao Family" by neighbors. As the family became the best known in this alley, the Shangsheng Hutong was renamed Jiaojia Alley.

Around the year of 1940, CPC's Special Committee in Chuankang Area was once set up at 20 Jiaojia Alley. Many cultural celebrities in Chengdu such as the Tibetologist Zhang Yisun, the phonologist Li Zhi (see "Kuan Alley"), the classical literateur Qu Shouyuan and the mythologist Yuan Ke used to live in Jiaojia Street.

Zhang Yisun (**1893 ~ 1983**), born in Peng'an, served as the professor at Tsinghua University, Shandong University and Sichuan University, and used to be the director of the Institute of Liberal Arts of Sichuan University. In 1992, as a new graduate from Peking University, he wrote a well-known article *the Judgement on the Action Brought by Liang Qichao against the Composition Time of Daodejing*, which was included in the famous *Discernment of Ancient History*. It was highly praised by Liang Qichao and had a great influence on the academic circles. With this achievement, he was

Zhang Yisun

admitted to teach students in Tsinghua University. In 1928, he began to do research on Tibetology in Yuan'en Temple and Yonghe Lama Manastery, studied Tibetan language, prepared for the compilation of Tibetan-Chinese Dictionary, and published *the Glossary for the Set Theory of Tibetan and Chinese Language* and *the Tibetan-Chinese Comparative Analysis*. In 1937, he came to Chengdu to establish the Western Borderland Culture Institute on Tingshu Street (this institute once moved to Mr. Chen's Ancestral Lineage Hall at Dabei Street in Chongqing County in order to evade bombing of Japanese Army) so that he could carry on the project of Tibetan-Chinese Dictionary. It was during this period that he became one of the famous Tibetologists in our country. After the founding of the P. R. C., he was the chief editor and complied the first Tibetan-Chinese Dictionary in our country with a total number of 53,000 entries and 3.5 million words. In order to secure the compilation quality of this dictionary, he went to

Tibet at the age of 65 in 1958 and kept working there for two years under a very harsh working and living condition. The *Tibetan-Chinese Dictionary* was the Tibetan-Chinese dictionary with the highest level of compilation and the largest collection of words in our country. After its publication, it won numerous awards and was almost archived by major libraries all over the world. " *The Tibetan-Chinese Dictionary* is much more than a dictionary of Tibetan and Chinese languages. It is a comprehensive encyclopedia of Tibetan religious culture compiled by Tibetan and Han scholars together", said a British expert on Tibetan studies. Unfortunately, this dictionary was not published until the death of Zhang Yisun two years later.

Qu Shouyuan (**1913 ~ 2001**), born in Chengdu, was a famous scholar of traditional Chinese culture in Sichuan Province. He had been teaching at Sichuan Normal University for a long time and used to be the dean of the Chinese Department, the chief librarian, and the director of the Institute of Ancient Literature. He was knowledgeable and had the common features of the former scholars in Sichuan Province. On one hand, his research covered a wide range of areas and had a broad understanding of ancient cultures, not limited to one generation. The scope of both his researches and teaching could cover the period from the Qing Dynasty

Qu Shouyuan

to modern times. On the other hand, he was strict in studies and wrote books carefully. It was not until his later years that his works such as *Brief History of Chinese Literature*, *Guide to Literary Selections*, *Notes and Interpretations on the Anecdotes Said to Be written by Han Ying Using Poems as Annotations* and *Platitude on Confucian Classics Studies* were published under the urge and persuasion of all parties. The most important work written in Qu Shouyuan's later years was *the Annotations on the Complete Works of Hanyu* compiled by him.

Yuan Ke (**1916 ~ 2001**), born in Xinfan, graduated from the Chinese Language and Literature Department of West China University in 1941 and studied ancient Chinese mythology all his life. As the most famous mythologist in China, he once served as the president of the Chinese Mythology Society and was a researcher of

Sichuan Academy of Social Sciences when he was alive. His major works included *Chinese Mythology and Legend*, *Dictionary of Chinese Mythology and Legend*, *Selected Annotations on Ancient Mythology*, *the General Theory of Chinese Mythology*, and *Annotations on the Classic Book of Mountains and Rivers*, etc.

Yuan Ke

In the Republican period, at the east entrance of Jiaojia Alley there was the famous "Mr. Ma's Sweet Potato" in Chengdu. The sweet potatoes toasted in the big stove were only sold in this place at that time and were popular among ordinary people while they are appearing on every corner of all streets today. Mr. Zhou Juwu once wrote a poem:

The little path of Jiaojia Alley, slippery,
The customers wait in the rain, hungry.
Fires burns brightly in a red-mud stove,
An aroma wafts from the sweet potatoes.

After the founding of the P. R. C. , "Mr. Ma's Sweet Potato" stopped its business. According to some records, when Zhu De and Deng Xiaoping, both of whom were Sichuan natives, returned to Chengdu after the founding of the P. R. C. , they were eager to taste Mr. Ma's Sweet Potato again.

Guojielou Street

Wooden bridges are the passageways built above small streets and alleys in ancient towns of China, which are similar to today's pedestrian overpasses, but have a roof on the top and look like the gallery bridges above the river. Guojielou Street used to be the Jixian Hutong (also called Yongxing Hutong) in the Manchu City and was named after such a gallery bridge inside this Hutong, beside which there was the Guojielou Horizontal Street. There were several gallery bridges (Arcade-house also belonged to the architectural form of gallery bridges) in Chengdu before the founding of the P. R. C. but were all dismantled during the expansion of streets. And there is no one left to be seen now.

Guojielou Street, 1987 Photo by Zhang Xinan

Upper Section Street

On both sides of Lower Changshun Street in the Manchu City were some half-section alleys. There was no East Section Alley in Chengdu in the Republican period while the Western Section Alley was demolished during the reconstruction of the old city a few years ago. Upper Section Alley has long been called "Upper Section Alley" and now it is called "Upper Section Street". The name of Lower Section Alley had not been accepted by the locals because the lower part of the human body was called "lower section" in Chengdu dialect, which would be very vulgar when it was used as the street name. On the Lower Section Alley once lived a family with the last name Yao. They were the descendants of Yao Yuanzhi, the clan-grandson of Yao Nai, who was a prestigious litterateur of Tongcheng School. Also a scholar, Yao Yuanzhi was a famous calligrapher and a painter in the Qing Dynasty, and served as the left censor of the department of inspection. In Yao Yuanzhi's residence in Tongcheng, there was a Bamboo Leaf Pavilion, so Yao Yuanzhi styled himself "Mr. Bamboo Leaf Pavilion" and his masterpiece was titled *Notes Written in the Bamboo Leaf Pavilion*. Today, the Bamboo Leaf Pavilion remains in the Beijie Primary School in Tongcheng, Anhui province, which is listed as the Tongcheng's Key Cultural Relic Protection Unit. In the year of 1923, the Yao's applied to the Chengdu municipal authority on behalf of the descendants of Mr. Bamboo Leaf Pavilion, requesting the Lower Section Alley be renamed as Zhuye (Bamboo Leaf) Alley. Their request was approved by the government, and Zhuye Alley came into existence in Chengdu. The alley was located to the west of Lower Changshun Street between Sidao Street and Jiaojia Street. but it was demolished during the reconstruction of the old city.

The first Chengdu Municipal Party Committee of CPC was established in the winter of 1927 while Zhang Xiushu was the first party secretary of the committee. Its liaison office of the committee was set up in the Li Jingxuan's private residence at 8 Zhuye Alley (Li Jingxuan served as Liu Wenhui's chief of staff and had already joined CPC at that time).

As for the Upper Section Street and Half Section Alley, there are some points to be noted. First, the pronunciation and meaning of half-section (半截) in Chinese are identical to the those of half-knot (半节), so the Upper Section Streets mentioned above were miswritten as "Half Knot Streets", which should be corrected as "Upper Section Streets". Second, after the founding of the P. R. C. , Chen Yi's third brother, Chen Jirang lived at another Half Section Alley (now demolished) beside the original site of Sichuan Cinema, so the Upper Section Alley was mistaken for Chen Yi's former residence in Chengdu. Third, the Upper Section Street still exists on the east side of Lower Changshun Street between the Second East Street and the Guojielou Street. The street sign reads "Upper Section Street", a very short alley with the house number from 12 to 20. But among the eight door signs, there are three mistakes in writing such as "Upper Knot Street", "Upper Knot Alley" and "Half Knot Alley" (written in different periods), which become the most prominent errors of the Chengdu street signs.

Erdao Street, Sandao Street, and Sidao Street

On both sides of the north end of today's Changshun Street are several *hutongs* in the Manchu City. In the Republican period, the names of these *hutongs* were no longer used and were replaced by new names. Because these *hutongs* were located on the north end of the city, the first *hutong* along the direction from north to south was today's West Street. For convenience, the second (Er), third (San) and fourth (Si) *hutongs*, which had no striking features at that time, were named Erdao Street, Sandao Street and Sidao Street respectively.

Erdao Street was divided into East Erdao Street and West Erdao Street by Changshun Street. East Erdao Street used to meet Dongchenggen Street in the east. After the founding of the P. R. C., when the government rebuilt Dongchenggen Street, the slanting street in the past was changed into a straight street. Therefore, to the east of the north end of the newly constructed and straightened Dongchenggen Street, a slanting section of the old Dongchenggen Street remains. At the same time, East Erdao Street was cut off by the northern section of the straightened Dongchenggen Street, so the Erdao Street met the old Dongchenggen Street at its east end and met the newly constructed and straightened Dongchenggen Street at its west end. The section of the former East Erdao Street connecting the old Dongchenggen Street and the newly constructed Dongchenggen Street was thus named Horizontal Dongchenggen Street.

Memorial Hall of Yang Youhe located in Gucheng Town, Pidu District

Yang Youhe, the modern master of Sichuan Opera, once lived on the Second West Street.

Yang Youhe (**1913 ~ 1984**) , born in Pengzhou and was given the original name Yang Yongqing. He was admitted into the Jinlan Society to study Sichuan Opera at the age of 8 and acted as the female role with the stage name Xiao Tongfeng. He performed with other actors in many places in Sichuan Province and learned skills from them. He widely absorbed experience and made innovations with his heart. He had promoted reforms in many aspects such as scripts, singing tune, performance, costume and make-up. Yang became famous when he performed in Chongqing in 1931 and was invited by Pathé Company to make a record in Shanghai in 1938. In 1940, he performed the newly rehearsed *Opera Phoenix Pavilion* and was highly praised by Guo Moruo, Tian Han, Yang Hansheng and others. After the founding of the P. R. C. , he won the first prize in the first National Opera Watch Performance in 1952. In 1956, he went to Beijing to attend the second opera appreciation seminar, and gave a speech on the theme of "*The Basic Skills Training and Performance Requirements of the Female Role in Sichuan Opera*". It was recorded by experts sent by the Chinese Opera Academy and compiled into the book "*Performing Arts of the Female Role in Sichuan Opera*", which was prefaced by Mei Lanfang and was reprinted three times with a great influence on the whole country. After that, various local operas all over the country all invited him to give lectures or teach skills. He successively served as the academic director of the Experimental School of the Southwest China Sichuan Opera Theater, the principal of Chengdu Opera School, the vice president of Sichuan Opera Theater in Chengdu, and the honorary chairman of the Sichuan branch of the Chinese Dramatists Association. He was both martial and civil, and proficient in singing, acting, monologue and martial arts. As a master of Sichuan Opera, he had made great contributions to the development of the art of Sichuan Opera. In 1980, the Ministry of Culture of the P. R. C. , China Federation of Literary and Art Circles, the Chinese Dramatists Association and the provincial and municipal cultural departments jointly held an activity in Chengdu to commemorate Yang Youhe's stage life of 60 years.

Yang Youhe taught his disciple in the 1950s. Photo by Zhang Shuhua.

Sandao Street should have been divided into East Sandao Street and West Sandao Street by Changshun Street while the Renli Hutong on the east had already been divided into two sections at the very beginning and had the name of Upper Section Alley or East Section Alley. Therefore, the old name of Upper Section Alley was reserved instead of being changed into East Sandao Street in the Republican period. From then on, only West Sandao Street was called Sandao Street.

Sidao Street should also have been divided into East Sidao Street and West Sidao Street by Changshun Street, but the *hutong* on the east had already been divided into sections such as Jixian Hutong and Yongxing Hutong. Because there used to be a wooden bridge gallery, Yongxing Hutong was renamed Guojielou Street in the Republican period while Jixian Hutong was called Lower Section Alley. Therefore, only West Sidao Street was left, and was called Sidao Street.

On May 15th, 1918, *Wuwu Weekly* (renamed *Wuwu Daily* later) was founded at 45 Sidao Street (later moved to 46 Daozi Alley, i. e. today's Duozi Alley). The weekly newspaper's main supporters were members of the former Chinese Revolutionary League and some of the Sichuan Army generals who supported Mr. Sun Yat-sen at that time. It had representative offices and special correspondents in major cities around the country as well as nearly 10 major overseas cities with a rich source of manuscripts and a bright anti-imperialist patriotic standpoint and was popular among readers. The newspaper had a circulation of more than 30,000 copies per issue, and even issued more than 40,000 copies during the Paris Peace Conference. On September 24th, 1918, it was on the column of "*New Theory*" that this newspaper published the article *Theoretical System of Marx's Socialism* written by the famous Marxist Hajime Kawakami to make a comprehensive introduction to *the Communist Manifesto* to Sichuan people.

Affiliated Hospital of Chengdu Traditional Chinese Medicine College was established on Sidao Street at the very beginning. After it moved to West First Ring Road, Sichuan Province Research Institute of Traditional Chinese Medicine was set up on the former site of the hospital. Besides, Sichuan Province Skin Disease Prevention and Treatment Institute was also founded on this street.